6/8

THE SWEETEST LITTLE CLUB IN THE WORLD:
The U.S. Senate

THE SWEETEST LITTLE CLUB IN THE WORLD:
The U.S. Senate

by
Louis Hurst
as told to
Frances Spatz Leighton

Prentice-Hall, Inc., Englewood Cliffs, New Jersey

Many of the pictures included were taken by
Striar/City News Bureau.

The Sweetest Little Club in the World: The U.S. Senate
by Louis Hurst,
as told to Frances Spatz Leighton

Printed in the United States of America

Prentice-Hall International, Inc., London
Prentice-Hall of Australia, Pty. Ltd., Sydney
Prentice-Hall of Canada, Ltd., Toronto
Prentice-Hall of India Private Ltd., New Delhi
Prentice-Hall of Japan, Inc., Tokyo
Prentice-Hall of Southeast Asia Pte. Ltd., Singapore
Whitehall Books Limited, Wellington, New Zealand

10 9 8 7 6 5 4 3 2 1

Library of Congress Cataloging in Publication Data

Hurst, Louis.
    The sweetest little club in the world.
    Includes index.
    1. United States. Congress. Senate. 2. Legis-
lators—United States. I. Leighton, Frances Spatz,
joint author. II. Title.
HK1161.H83   328.73′071   80-13543
ISBN 0-13-879304-2

Contents

Introduction *vii*

Part I The Sweetest Little Club in the World
1. The Sweetest Little Club in the World *2*
2. Rich Man, Poor Man, Beggar Man, Thief *18*
3. Up Your Chamber *39*
4. Short Takes *54*

Part II . . . and a Cast of Thousands
5. Prima Donnas—Staffs and Stiffs *80*
6. Of Wives and Lady Loves *96*
7. Relatives, Relatives, All—All Is Relative *112*
8. A Funny Thing Happened on the Way
    to the Senate Forum *126*

Part III President, Anyone?
9. Neither Fish nor Fowl—The Vice-Presidents *136*
10. Presidents—Whatever Happened to Mr. Nice
    Guy? *153*
11. Candidates—Few Are Chosen and the Chosen
    Few *169*

Part IV Please Don't Steal the Silver
12. Party Time in the Sweetest Little
    Club in the World *188*
13. The Lunch Bunch *208*
14. Please Don't Steal the Silver *222*
15. My Kitchen Cabinet *234*
16. *You* Can Throw a Party Fit for a
    Senator or King—or Jacqueline Kennedy *247*
    Index *275*

Acknowledgment

I am grateful for the help of my friends on the Hill, who asked only that they *not* be identified—and to my helper in the typing and manuscript preparation, Dorothy Berger, who had no such qualms.

Introduction

What really goes on in the sweetest little club in the world—the U.S. Senate? What about the Senators' hideaways—what do they hide?

What was the best kept secret about Vice-President Rockefeller's life on Capitol Hill?

Which Kennedy was the greatest lover?

Which Presidential candidate wore a tattoo?

What did the Hill crowd teach Carter?

Was HHH really a boy scout type?

What is it like backstage at those famous Red Cross bandage rolling sessions the Senate wives indulge in for "sweet charity"?

And was a plot against JFK discussed at a Hill party?

The answers to these and other mysteries, *great* and small, lie in this book, which has many serious and touching moments as well as moments of hilarity. There are many surprises.

Lou Hurst does for the Senate what Fishbait Miller did for the House of Representatives. The difference is that Fishbait was a famous figure, the voluble Doorkeeper, whereas Lou Hurst is emerging from professional invisibility as the man who worked discreetly in the background as he catered private Capitol Hill parties and helped manage the whole Senate restaurant operation.

What he heard and saw during 16 action-packed years did not leave his lips until now and I was amazed at the things I learned as he secretly dictated his memoirs—as you will be!

Why did he write the book?

As Hurst told me, "If this book makes people a lot more concerned about whom they elect to public office and about what goes on that affects their pocketbooks, then maybe it was all worthwhile after all?

Frances Spatz Leighton

"There's only one way to bring about a 100% honest Congress—legalize bribery!"

Overheard on the Hill

PART I

The Sweetest Little Club in the World

1

The Sweetest Little Club in the World

I remember when I was being promoted to assistant to the manager of the U.S. Senate restaurant operation. Joe Diamond, general manager, stood by, and the chairman of the Rules Committee, Senator B. Everett Jordan, gave me a little warning.

"You will be entrusted with the greatest secrets of the world," Jordan said, studying me with a fixed stare. "You will leave what you hear behind the doors of this Club. Just put it out of your mind."

I had become rather friendly with the chairman who oversaw the restaurant operation of the Senate. "What do you mean, Senator?"

"Just disregard it," he said. "Consider it damn gossip."

"Hell, Senator," I persisted, "how can this be when I hear with my own ears a Senator being offered hundreds of thousands of dollars for his vote and a little more if he can sway a few other votes?"

He gave me a dirty look. He had no answer.

I didn't talk as long as I was working for the Senate. At least not to outsiders. And surely not to reporters—I'd have been out on my ear the next day. But I did talk freely to a few of the Senators who took me into their trust, and to them I occasionally bemoaned the ethics of some Club members, as well as the goings on in the restaurant and party catering operation—utter waste of taxpayers' money and downright thievery.

Once Senator Everett Dirksen cornered me before a party and with a few drinks in him proceeded to lecture me. "Hurst," he said, "you're too damn honest to work on the Hill. You'll never make a damn thing out of yourself among these cutthroats. Quit trying to blow the whistle. One of these days you're going to blow yourself out of a job. Reformers never make it in Washington."

I didn't blow myself out of a job, but I did end up with a breakdown, so looking back, I have to admit old Everett was right.

I look back at my Hill career, and I cannot believe that I survived. Some people complain that they must please two bosses on their job. I had bosses too numerous to mention. Bill Cochrane, Rules Committee staff director, was one of my big bosses. Every chairman of the Rules Committee—Jordan, Howard Cannon of Nevada. Restaurant subcommittee chairmen, Robert Byrd of West Virginia and James Allen of Alabama. Members of Rules like Hugh Scott of Pennsylvania, Claiborne Pell of Rhode Island, Mark Hatfield of Oregon, and Harrison Williams of New Jersey. The architects of the Capitol were my bosses—George White, J. George Stewart. The assistant architects of the Capitol. The sergeant at arms. The liaison between the Rules Committee and the Restaurant Subcommittee.

The Vice-Presidents were my bosses—Agnew, Rocky, Nixon, LBJ, Humphrey, Ford. Every Senator was my boss—one hundred strong. The wives of all the Senators, as well as a few mistresses, were my bosses, who could, if they had really ganged up, have gotten me fired in a flash. The secretaries of all the Senators were my bosses, as were the administrative assistants, most of whom could sign for their Senator and give orders in his name.

All, all, my bosses! It's a miracle that I didn't get an ulcer. However, it did play havoc with my nerves and cause me to have a short, six-day breakdown, which hospitalized me in New Hampshire.

Much was going on in New Hampshire at the time. It was November 1975, but already the country was gearing up for the next year's Presidential election. Sargent Shriver had already announced he was in the running. In Manchester, New Hampshire, there was talk of nothing else. But that isn't why I was there.

I was there because I wanted to do something of lasting value and to escape the Senate rat race. Senator Thomas J. McIntyre of that state was helping me with HUD to finance setting up a home for the elderly in New Hampshire. Various society women had expressed interest in aiding this project.

I explained that I had seen too much abuse of the elderly in nursing homes and was eager to operate one that would be a model of its kind and would be run as a charitable organization, benefitting the elderly who need help.

I was elated, of course, and I was entirely too keyed up after arriving in an exhausted condition from Washington to check out the potential site for the home.

Several hours later everything went blank, and when I woke up, I was at a local Catholic hospital, where I spent a few days as a psychiatric patient. Doctors said it was nervous exhaustion. And before I give my job all the blame, I must hasten to add a contributing factor—I had been taking 30 milligrams of Valium for several years on a doctor's prescription. I changed doctors and prescriptions.

As a result of this incident, I realized I could no longer stand the fast pace of Capitol Hill or bear the responsibility of setting up the kind of senior citizens' home I had dreamed of, and I took an early retirement, signing my retirement papers November 25, 1975.

I was offered all kinds of jobs from lobbying groups and others who had dealt with me on the Hill or seen me standing discreetly in the background at the Senators' private parties, keeping everything running smoothly. And keeping my mouth shut. "You know all the Senators and their quirks," said one lobbyist. "We need you to run parties for us. Name your price."

This did not excite me since I was used to getting offers. One had been to handle the food operation on a cruise ship that would entertain Senators and other dignitaries and let them gamble outside territorial waters.

I took a rest, and after reading the book *Fishbait*, written by my colleague on the House side of the Hill, I decided it was high time someone finished the job and wrote the inside story of the Senate. I leaned my head back and let the memories flow. . . .

I'll never forget my first encounter with Senator Talmadge. I happened to be taking care of a cocktail party, and over at one end of the bar which had been set up in a committee room, I noticed a man waiting for a drink. Suddenly he cleared his throat and spat on the floor.

I immediately asked the bartender, "Who the hell can this be who has the right to spit on the floor?"

The bartender said, "Not so loud. That's Senator Talmadge from Georgia. When you've been here a little longer, you'll learn to think nothing of it. You'll develop a little blindness."

"I have all the blindness I need right now," I said, "but not the kind you're talking about."

I had casually known William Colmer in Hattiesburg, Mississippi—the same Bill Colmer who had given the famous House of Representatives doorkeeper, "Fishbait" Miller, his first Capitol Hill job and who had become a Congressman from my home state. I had worked in restaurants in the private sector and at the Pentagon and at Walter Reed Hospital. But nothing prepared me for the chaos and confusion and lawlessness of working for the Senate of the United States—the sweetest little club in the world.

I got used to seeing Herman Talmadge. I knew him when he could walk and when he couldn't walk. When he couldn't walk, he was holding up the wall.

I would see him at 6:30 in the morning when I was coming in, and many a morning he didn't seem to know which end was up. He would be trying to find his office. When he let me, I would help him. At such times, he obviously hadn't been home.

When he wasn't letting me help him, he would light into me, cussing me out: "You bastard, get out of my way." Since he was a member of the Club, I simply ignored it and went on my way. Sometimes, even later in the day, he would still be angry and sullen if he saw me using the elevators marked "Senators Only," as I frequently did when running from one Senate eating or party place to another.

He would growl, "You're not allowed on this elevator," and I would quickly get off and wait for a public elevator rather than make a scene.

If the Senator knew his wife was coming in that morning, preparatory to some luncheon they were hosting, he would be an entirely different man—gruffly friendly and grateful. He was anxious to get straightened out before her arrival.

One day, however, when she was hostess at a private luncheon at which Herman was host, he hadn't succeeded and still appeared to be under the weather. Betty Talmadge had arranged an open-bar service luncheon. I was standing right there at the bar, which had been set up in a hearing room, and saw Betty Talmadge stiffen as her husband came through the door and headed for a drink.

Instead of letting him take the drink, Betty took him by the arm and pulled him along with her to a chair. Like a schoolteacher with an unruly student, Mrs. Talmadge sat the Senator down and said, "You sit there and don't dare move. I'll get you some coffee. You hear me? Don't move."

She and I rushed and got a waitress to serve the coffee, and the Senator sat sullenly drinking it while his wife hovered near. Suddenly he leaned back to take a better look at her and grumbled, "What's eating you?"

"You're in no condition to meet people from Georgia," she said briskly. "What if a reporter gets ahold of this and it appears in the papers?" The Senator sipped a little more as he thought this over.

Mrs. Talmadge continued to scold her husband: "This is all you get to drink until the guests get here."

"What in the hell are you worried about?" the Senator demanded suddenly. "I'm not worried about who's coming or where they're from. They don't like my condition? Let them get the hell out of here. I'm paying for this damn lunch."

I made out the bills for special functions, but there was no way of knowing who really paid for parties. The bill would be sent to the sponsoring Senator or his wife, and sometimes he would be reimbursed by an organization or company.

Unless it had been arranged for a special-interest group to pick up the check—with the permission of the Senator—we didn't know who was paying.

Some Senators would tell me a name and address and say, "The bill goes to these people." It could be any kind of organization. In the case of Talmadge's office, I have seen members of his staff, at some luncheons or dinners, collecting money at the door as the guests came through. I had no way of knowing what was being charged, nor was it my business.

Sometimes a Senator—usually a new one to Capitol Hill—would tell me to put a table at the door and have someone take the money. I would have to explain, "I can arrange for the table, but my food personnel and I are not permitted to take money, tickets, or anything of monetary value. We deal only with the Senator's office, and how it is handled from there is up to the individual Senator."

Some Senators could not believe this fine point in the Club rules, and I would have to refer them to the Rules Committee, which would reiterate that we could not take money or tickets, nor could we collect cash at an open bar set up for the party.

This was their Club, and they could do as they damn well pleased, including charging whatever they wanted per drink at a party under their sponsorship. They could get drunk and disorderly without fear of anyone like me telling them their drinks were being cut off or that they had better take their business elsewhere.

Whatever happened, I had to bite my tongue and remember that this was their Club. Some people would give their eyeteeth to be invited to one of the Senator-sponsored parties. And it was only their eyeteeth, safely anchored in their mouths, that were absolutely safe at some of the parties.

I remember once when Elizabeth Taylor was not yet married to John Warner, and she arrived at a party in a fabulous fur—some woman said it was sable. At any rate, someone took her wrap and gave it to a *policeman* to be responsible for it. We had had our lesson.

Once a mink stole disappeared while parked with other wraps in the hallway outside Room 1318 of the Dirksen Building. The poor woman who owned it had talked to me on the phone the next day and was almost in hysterics. It had cost $2,500. Fortunately, she had had it insured, but we never came up with anything resembling a clue, and naturally the Capitol police do not enter private homes to search. But it would have been interesting to know just where that coat traveled that night. We weren't going to let that happen with Liz Taylor's sable.

The sweetest little club in the world, known as the Senate, made its own rules, and the Club broke its rules. It was the rule that drinking could be done at private parties held in committee rooms or hideaways, but drinking in the Senate restaurants was positively forbidden. By rule and by law.

The law was enacted to assure the public that their elected lawmakers were not passing legislation while in a befuddled state or writing laws influenced in any way by the presence of John Barleycorn.

Senator Carl Hayden would come into the Senate restaurant in the early morning, after a toot the night before, and ask for "my buttermilk." This was the signal for a certain waiter to go get something from private stock—a double shot of bourbon, which was served to the Senator in an iced-tea glass of buttermilk.

No wonder Hayden needed a hair of the dog. At our parties on the Hill, he'd fix his own drink. He would ask for a glass with two ice cubes in it. Then he would reach over for a bottle of bourbon, and fill the glass up himself, all the way to the brim. Then he'd sit and sip for a half-hour, and walk over to the bar and ask for another glass and two more ice cubes.

Senator Magnuson would come in anytime, even 7 or 8 A.M., call for a seltzer water, and mix it with scotch—Chivas Regal. This stock was left over from parties. One of the waiters kept some for emergencies such as this.

It was, as I've said, illegal to sell liquor or serve it in the Senate restaurants, but these were the lawmakers themselves, and the Club could do no wrong. I personally never served anything to their wives in the restaurants, nor did I put a charge on the overhung Club members who were drinking the leftover squeezings from parties past.

The public would be surprised to know how many Club members put faith in liquor as their healer. Hayden used to say, "There's nothing keeping me alive, Hurst, but liquor and women."

Another such believer was Russell Long. He used tomato juice and bourbon in equal proportions—five ounces of each. That was before he rearranged his life, remarried, and went on the wagon.

Senator Lee Metcalf had a little technique of his own. He would come in and order a plain glass of seltzer water. Then he would pour out part of the seltzer, and bring out his flask of vodka, pouring some in. Since vodka has no odor, many on the Hill turned to it for daytime salvation.

Many's the time Metcalf would show up around eight in the morning, before we were even open. And if his head felt bad enough, he might repeat the performance later in the day.

I would close my eyes to what was going on. "You can't fight City Hall," as the chairman of the Rules Committee, Senator B. Everett Jordan, would tell me. "They need it to function."

Though this was in the manner of first aid and stimulated the goodwill of our bosses, I still avoided being the one who delivered the liquor. Strangely enough, it disturbed me to be breaking the law.

Some key staff members got the same freebie, the morning after. Some of them were like acting Senators, and demanded and got equal treatment. If they had blown the whistle, who knows what would have happened!

The way one waiter operated was by keeping a file cabinet with a combination lock to store his liquor. And it was stocked with nothing but the best—or at least the most expensive. He stocked Cutty Sark. He stocked Wild Turkey and Old Grand Dad. He stocked Chivas Regal—at about $28 a half-gallon.

When I complained to the powers within the Rules Committee, they said, "Forget it." It didn't occur to them to worry because I knew too much, too, and even more than the waiter knew.

More than once a waiter was generous in serving Senators' wives drinks, only to have the Senator chew him out for getting his wife tight.

Senator Hollings and his wife, Peatsy, were frequent drinkers at parties, but were trying to keep each other from drinking.

Carrie Lee Nelson, the wife of Senator Gaylord Nelson of Wisconsin, used to be noted around the Hill for the outrageous things she would say after having a bourbon too many. On one occasion her loose tongue so shocked her that she gave up drinking altogether, except for a little wine. It happened when, at a party, she found herself telling Senator Javits not once, but twice, that he bored her.

He had not believed his ears the first time and had said, "What?"

"Senator, you bore me!" she had repeated, adding that he ought to listen when she talked.

Now and then Senator Everett Dirksen got good and mad at a generous waiter for helping Mrs. Dirksen get her whiskey sours and martinis. She drank doubles, which took effect quickly. Those were times the Senator's silken voice turned very sour. Though he was a heavy drinker himself, he did not want his wife drinking.

When Joy Baker, the wife of Presidential candidate Senator Howard Baker, was revealed to have a drinking problem, I felt very sorry for her. As Dirksen's daughter, she had grown up in a household where heavy drinking was the norm.

When I went to work on the Hill, I was surprised to learn that the Kennedy women were hearty drinkers. Joan drank both bourbon and Scotch. Ethel would drink anything served. Eunice also drank, but I forget her favorite.

I remember that when Joan would come to a party with Ted or a little in advance of him, she had to have a few drinks to get herself organized—it was her cure for shyness. At that time it was kept fairly secret. But later Joan became emancipated and sought help for her drinking problem.

Mrs. Mike Mansfield, wife of the majority leader, also needed a few drinks to get started, and so did Mrs. B. Everett Jordan, wife of the Rules Committee chairman. Other wives also "never dropped a drip," as we used to say. Some of them took their hard liquor in coffee or orange juice—most preferred theirs on the rocks.

When these ladies came into the dining room, I knew there could be trouble. If they asked me to fix them a drink, I would refuse, pointing out that drinks could not be served in the Senate rooms as a matter of law. They learned to get around me, knowing there was sure to be a waiter who would oblige. He would bring them their drinks from his private stock and be handsomely rewarded.

I will not pretend to be a paragon of virtue but I never slipped anyone a drink in the dining room.

I saw Mamie Eisenhower drink her share. Again, it was on the rocks. The Secret Service knew. The FBI knew. Everyone knew! They talked about it with us. It was the biggest joke on the Hill— pretending she didn't. It was only at private parties that I saw her drinking—at the kind of parties where the President would drop by, but the press was never present, because it was strictly off limits.

It was the same way at the times Vice-President and Pat Nixon attended this type of private gathering. As far as I could see, the two families were never invited to the same private Hill parties.

At these private parties—neither Mamie nor Pat stood on ceremony—each lady stepped right up to the bar and ordered. All-in-the-family kind of stuff. After all, the Senator's wife, the usual party hostess, was often an equally serious drinker.

At the White House, when Mamie became First Lady, there was a strict rule imposed by the President that all glasses were to be removed from the area of the First Lady if there was a photographer around.

Betty Ford's drinking problem did not begin at the White House or after leaving the White House. I remember her when her husband was in the House of Representatives. The Fords would attend parties on the Hill, because he was the leader of the loyal opposition. You could not avoid noticing the quantity of liquor she drank—she drank it straight, on the rocks.

When Senator Hayden used to do this, I thought nothing about it, since he was a man. So, I didn't think of him in the same terms as I did a delicate woman, especially the wife of the Minority Leader of the House.

We used ten-ounce tumblers for bar service, unless wine was ordered, or we were asked specifically for a stemmed glass—an all-purpose cocktail glass. Betty was served the ten-ounce tumbler—with only a few ice cubes and the rest liquor.

We were never allowed to write on a bill the word "liquor" or designate the alcoholic beverage, such as bourbon or scotch. We were only permitted to indicate the drink as "special beverage," a term that covered everything from alcohol to lemonade. According to the rules, flowers could be called flowers, but liquor had to be indicated in code.

Robert Kennedy was the drinker among the three brothers. Jack Kennedy, the President, liked wine and champagne and an occasional martini. But Robert liked everything—bourbon, Scotch, gin, vodka.

To my knowledge, Senator Edward Kennedy just drinks Bristol cream. He orders this most expensive of sherries by the case for his office. I have known Ted Kennedy for years and seen him at many parties. I have never seen him drink anything but Bristol cream.

I've known a lot of good, steady drinkers on the Hill. But some have been greater and more spectacular than the rest. Among the heavy drinkers of the past—some now reformed—I would list, without quibbling about the exact rank, Warren Magnuson, Russell Long, Herman Talmadge, Lee Metcalf, and LBJ, who was in a class by himself. I've always respected the drinking capacity of Texas politicians. Long before gasohol, they proved that the state's oil resources and alcohol do mix.

Of course every now and then a member of the Club goes out

and fights John Barleycorn—while everybody applauds, though not necessarily following suit.

I really liked what former Congressman Otis Pike of New York wrote when Richard Bolling of Missouri joined the ranks of public fighters of the old demon, "I know that, even drunk, Dick Bolling would contribute more to the nation than ten average Congressmen sober."

I was happy to see the change in Senator Long after he married Caroline, a staffer who had worked for Senator Sam Ervin. I never saw him take another drink. His appearance changed, and his clothes became immaculate. His attitude was entirely different, too, and he was no longer boisterous or loud.

After I left the Hill, I was happy to hear that Herman Talmadge had also done an about-face, going to the same drying-out place that Betty Ford and Billy Carter did, and no longer drinking.

But I digress. To return to this roll of honor, I would include Norris Cotton, the New Hampshire senior Senator for umpteen years. Then there was Edmund Muskie of Waterville, Maine, who was unlike his teetotaling Maine counterpart, Margaret Chase Smith. And George Smathers of Florida, who tried to teach his friend Jack Kennedy the finer points of drinking, but failed. JFK thought girls were much more interesting than bottles. And finally, the grand master of them all, Everett Dirksen of Illinois, who owed much to the bottle for his famed deep-throat voice.

I hate to say it, but I grew up absorbing politics with my mother's milk. And mother had learned politics at her mother's knee—Southern politics of the Big Daddy kind.

My house was the meeting place for some of the biggest names in Southern politics—Huey Long, Theodore Bilbo, "Pat" Harrison, Paul Johnson—all of whom were at one time or another governors and United States Senators.

Huey Long would come from his home base of Louisiana to visit with his buddy, Theodore Bilbo. And both of these scalawags would end up at my house, bringing along other buddies. The reason they were at my house was that my daddy was the sheriff of Hattiesburg, and he was part of their clique. He scouted around and found out all sorts of things they wanted to know, and helped decide who was a good man for a job—or at least their kind of man.

My grandmother harbored a certain contempt for Huey Long, because he'd been a peddler of patent medicine and had sold two concoctions with different names though both came from the bark of the same tree. He claimed one came from the bark high up and the other lower down—which did not impress Grandma.

Though they came to see Father, they really enjoyed their encounters with Grandmother, Julie Belle, who lived with us and would not let them get away with any inflated ideas of their importance. Dad would complain they came more to see Julie Belle than him.

Julie Belle dipped snuff, while Huey Long chewed tobacco, so they would sit together spitting into the same old empty coffee can. If he ran out of *tobaccy,* he would dip into grandmother's snuff. He used to tease Julie Belle about her wooden leg. She really did have one, having lost her leg to cancer of the bone. It didn't slow her down.

Huey would say he was going to feel her wooden knee, and Grandmother would say, "You do, and I'll take my damn crutch to you." Huey would throw back his head and laugh until he shook all over. He loved to laugh.

I would sit on the other side of the room, pretending to do schoolwork, so I could listen to all this banter going on. I'd hear Bilbo bragging about how he ran Mississippi.

As my father poured the bootleg whiskey, eventually draining dry the fancy keg on its rolling wheels, Bilbo and Long would put their elbows on our kitchen table, as they argued over who had more control over the people in their respective states.

"I own the people," Bilbo would say.

Later, I was no longer the little boy pretending to do his homework but had come to Washington and was in the office of the chief of staff of the Army as a purchasing supply clerk. The Pentagon was brand new, and I was one of the first to be called to work there.

The kitchen table is gone and so are most of the cast of characters, but Grandmother's kitchen lives on in my memories of Deep South politics and bootleg liquor poured royally by the county sheriff from a five-gallon cedarwood keg—naturally kept replenished by frequent confiscations from local stills.

Theodore G. Bilbo. I must admit he was the man who most

influenced my life. Grandma called him "Rascal" most of the time, "Teddy" the rest. My dad called him Teddy too. Only in Mississippi was he that. In Washington he was Theodore or Bilbo.

Only Virginia Zimmerman, his secretary, who came from Mississippi, called him Teddy or affectionately "Theo." Her father was Governor Zimmerman, who had put Bilbo into politics in the early days, I was told.

Bilbo originally was a sheriff, which was why he and Dad struck it off so well. Bilbo cultivated Dad, because he knew that in the South the sheriff was the man who had his finger on the pulse of the public and knew where everything was, including the good bootleg whiskey. The sheriff knew who the working man was going to vote for. And he could influence the farmers and the lumbermen.

Eventually, my daddy had to make a decision, and he rose above the politics of the South. He was being pressured to join the Ku Klux Klan, in order to hold his status in the group and assure backing for his job as sheriff. Instead, Father packed us all up and took us to Washington, D. C., where he had lined up a job through his political connections—engineer at the Department of Commerce. Good old Teddy Bilbo had arranged it all.

There were things Father would do for his friends and things he would not, and he drew the line at becoming a Ku Klux Klansman.

Teddy Bilbo was a governor when I first knew him. He was quite embarrassed by his troubles with his wife, who he claimed stole all the silver from the governor's White House in Jackson, and moved it to their pecan-and-cotton plantation.

The state demanded that she return the silver. Bilbo didn't want this silly scandal hanging over his head, because he wanted to be elected to the U. S. Senate. He, too, tried to get his wife to let go of the silver, and she countered by divorcing him.

But the state got its silver, and Bilbo got his Senate seat.

It certainly did not hurt my career to have a close tie with a governor who became a Senator. Anytime I had a problem or needed something, I turned to Senator Bilbo, even though I was just a teenager. Seeing Bilbo, Daddy, and their gang operate, I'd learned early to work through channels. Having gone through any number of little favors, I immediately turned to my powerful family friend, when I finished high school and realized I would need a scholarship or an opportunity to work my way through college.

Bilbo had already helped me earn a good salary as a senior in high school. Since I was the eldest of nine children, it was imperative that I earn my own way. Bilbo had arranged for me to work evenings and weekends at the Union Station post office on Capitol Hill.

This time he assigned his secretary, Virginia, to see that I was "taken care of, because he's one of my boys." Virginia Zimmerman was not just a secretary. She was a part of Bilbo's every waking hour. He had gotten himself a small efficiency apartment in the 200 block of Massachusetts Avenue, N.E., on Capitol Hill.

He didn't need more. He spent all his time with Virginia at her lovely large apartment across town on 16th Street, N.W. There were five rooms and a live-in maid. Bilbo took all his meals at his secretary's glamorous apartment, only going home to his own to sleep.

Virginia knew Southern politics from the ground up, as I did. She knew everyone in Mississippi of importance to Bilbo. And besides she was beautiful. When Bilbo came to Washington in 1934, he persuaded his lovely blonde friend to come as his private secretary. Having no wife to look after him, he would have been lost without her.

Bilbo and Virginia trusted me, and I would drop in and enjoy the luxurious apartment whenever I had a craving for the better things in life. Even in high school, I had visual problems which had never been diagnosed.

In spite of what others say of Bilbo, I will never cease to be grateful for what he and Virginia did for me. They arranged for me to attend Millsaps College in Mississippi and to study braille at the nearby Mississippi Institute for the Blind, in case I should suddenly lose the rest of my sight.

All of this education was free of charge. And as if this weren't enough, he twisted the arm of a friend of his who had a restaurant in Jackson to let me work whatever hours I could spare from my studies. I received room-and-board, and $7 a week, which in the '30s was a bonanza.

I learned to cook, to jolly the customers and make them want to come back, and I even learned to wait tables. I did not realize that my whole career would be in food, and for this, too, I thank Teddy Bilbo, wherever the good Lord has placed him.

At the end of one year, I knew that my health could not take this strenuous routine, and reluctantly I gave up college and returned to Washington. The year was 1938.

Bilbo and Virginia had sent me little notes of encouragement, but when he saw I was back, Bilbo patted me on the shoulder and said, "It's all right, son, you'll have plenty of other opportunities."

I did. But it was many years before I was able to return to school. Then it was to study food scientifically, and I went to Johns Hopkins School of Hygiene. I had a dream of getting an institutional-management degree and feeding the multitudes inexpensively and nutritiously.

By now it was 1951, and my colorful benefactor was dead, having died in office in August of 1947. His last act on my behalf was to get me into Walter Reed's food department, but the job did not come through until after his death. At the hospital, I was a dietetic supervisor, and I knew for sure that food was my game.

Virginia remained my friend. For a time she worked for Senator James Eastland. But her heart was not in it. She still mourned for "Theo."

When her son, who was a full-fledged colonel in the Army, asked her to come to Philadelphia and keep house for him, she was ready to leave Washington and her happy and sad memories. We corresponded regularly until she died in 1963, having lived to see her son become a lieutenant general.

When I had visited them in Philadelphia, we all sat reminiscing about how Bilbo had changed all our lives. And we laughed as I reminded Virginia of what Senator Bilbo would say to me: "Remember son, virtue is its own reward—and a damn poor one."

I suppose I should mention what I was doing during the war—World War II. I worked my way up in the Pentagon to supervisor of transportation, which meant the handling of interdepartmental office moving in the War Department.

Secretary of War Stimson liked my work, and had me transferred to help him in wartime procurement, especially of cameras used in intelligence. I had G-2 Military Intelligence clearance to go into his office.

It was at about this time that I became engaged to a young college professor at George Washington University. She taught during the week. But weekends we would meet at tea dances in downtown Washington, and become dancing fools, staying on our feet continuously from 2 to 5 P.M., except when we sat down to drink two pitchers of beer—39¢, no cover charge.

But dancing was not my fiancée's only special interest. Because of her, I spent considerable time at the Franciscan Monastery near Catholic University, and ended up changing from Baptist to Catholic. I took my instructions at St. Matthew's Cathedral, which is now the Cathedral of Washington.

She and I married secretly at St. Matthew's Cathedral in a small informal wedding, which later ended in an annulment, because I could not overcome the power of her aunt's wealth and influence.

The aunt was in the social register, as well as being on the board of directors of various companies, and deeply involved in banking and mining. I had once gone with her to have tea at the home of Mrs. Calvin Coolidge, when Mrs. Coolidge lived in Washington as a widow.

The gist of her aunt's displeasure was that her niece, who had earned a Ph.D. in education, had married a man who not only did not have a bachelor's degree but worked at a job because he *had to.*

"I am cutting off your rent, your charge accounts, and I am dismissing your maid," she said. "You will also please return my convertible. I'm sure your young man can take you by taxi to that one-room palace you saved him from."

It was true, she had taken me away from a light housekeeping room, with a bath shared with five girls. The two women faced each other, and I could see the approach of doom.

At first we did keep in touch, but it was too painful, and we drifted apart. Eventually, I read in the newspapers that the aunt had died and my onetime wife had inherited all her money and holdings.

So she took her place in society while I went on to learn the inner workings of the Senate.

2

Rich Man,
Poor Man,
Beggar Man,
Thief

Money, money, money. Who's got the money?

Almost everybody. Senators are like a bunch of gossips when it comes to pointing the finger and talking about the big-money boys. Even the richest pretend to be poor and point the finger at someone else—"He's the one with the money. Not me."

Who is the richest? It's hard to say who has the most hidden wealth—and numbered Swiss bank accounts are whispered about—but the most conspicuously wealthy Senator is H. John Heinz III, heir to the great food fortune.

The handsome young Senator from Pittsburgh—only thirty-eight when he came to the Senate in 1977—is rumored to be worth about the same number of millions as he has "Varieties," give or take a pickle or two. Among the Senators who are so adept at calculating other people's money, the estimate is that Heinz has to be worth between $35 and $57 million.

In the same league is another food magnate, John Danforth, another Republican, only two years older than Heinz. Danforth, who came to the Senate at the same time, is part of the family which owns Ralston Purina.

Nobody knows, really, who has salted away the most, but Senators argue now and then as they speculate whether these two could put their hands on the most money in a showdown, or whether it's really someone like Herman Talmadge—and they kid that they'd like to go to a yard sale and buy one of his old coats that his wife claimed was full of $100 bills—or Russell Long, Lloyd Bentsen, Lowell Weicker, or Ted Kennedy. Not to be left out in the cold are Richard Stone, Barry Goldwater, and that cutup from California, Sam Hayakawa.

Senator Charles Percy reputedly put $16 million in trust when he came to Capitol Hill. He was a self-made man, working his way up from college-kid office helper during summer vacation to chairman of the board and chief executive officer of Bell & Howell.

And John Warner is no pauper. His land holdings in the hunt country of Middleburg, Virginia, are the envy of his gossipy colleagues as well as his luck in wives. Elizabeth Taylor Warner and he swim in a heated pool in a converted barn that is so beautiful it could be on the cover of *House and Garden*. Warner has a landing pad for helicopters, which he and Liz prefer. In fact, many of their friends arrive by helicopter.

Many members of the Club or their aides charter, own or lease airplanes—Goldwater, for one. For others earthbound in cars, gas was available at discounted prices at the gas pumps in the underground Senate parking garage—until the press got wind of it and there was hell to pay.

Colleagues have a tinge of envy, and I have heard them wonder what it would be like to be Ted Kennedy and afford to be a dollar-a-year President, as he would probably be. I did not see it, but those who did say that he keeps a framed copy of the first check he ever received from his father, as a kid in the 1930s.

The United States gets its money's worth in the Kennedys and always has. John did not accept his Presidential salary. Robert plowed much of his into helping migrant workers and other poor. Ted is one of the most effective men on Capitol Hill. He is much in earnest in helping people who are sick, elderly, or mentally retarded. The whole family pitches in. If you have a Kennedy on your side, you have the family.

I'm afraid it's also true that if you offend one member of the family, you have the whole clan on your head.

The same kind of loyalty is felt in Ted Kennedy's office. Ted is a very loyal person. He's loyal to all around him, and few leave his staff. Strangely enough, Ted has never had a problem with his staff, even though everyone, without question, is overworked.

Those who come into his office for the first time stand amazed. It is like a beehive. People talk in shorthand. Whereas most Senators have one receptionist to handle drop-in callers and phone calls, Kennedy has receptionists falling over each other. There is so much mail that the Senate had to provide a separate room outside his office to handle this flood.

He's everyone's image of a good son, and so even if they don't live in Massachusetts, they write asking for help and telling him about some injustice, or just seeking some information that they know he'll be nice enough to look up. Someone always does. He has one of the largest staffs in the Senate, though some are paid by the Kennedy Foundation and not the United States taxpayer.

As I said, the United States gets its money's worth in the Kennedys.

I sometimes ponder how it can be that the Kennedys are the most conspicuous family in the nation, and yet there are so many unsolved mysteries about them. John Kennedy's death, after countless investigations by police, FBI, amateur sleuths, and a full Congressional committee, still seems to have as many holes as a sieve. Bobby Kennedy's death is still a mystery to many of us. And what happened at Chappaquiddick has puzzling aspects.

It's amazing how eager women are to marry Congressmen, no matter how old the gentlemen might be. I used to laugh when I read in the society columns how Senator Theodore Green of Rhode Island, "the most eligible bachelor in Washington," had attended a party the night before. For Christ's sake, the Senator they were talking about was over ninety! Besides, I don't believe Senator Green ever spent an extra cent to make a woman happy. There was a story that he had painted his house in Rhode Island only in the front because no one could see the rest. I don't know if this is true, but I could believe it.

The Senate saw instances of his high respect for even the smallest of coins. He refused to spend money for transportation unless it was absolutely necessary and would take a trolley instead of a taxi. It was not that he was hurting for money. He was one of the richest men of the Senate, even without his salary.

But the best example of the Senator Green approach to the

buck was that he knew a place where you could buy men's socks by the package at cut rate because they were seconds. He would buy a package of argyles, not the least concerned that the socks were not even in matching pairs.

But coming back to Senator Green as the most eligible bachelor, he would attend several parties in an evening—he was invited to everything—and thus be well fed by the time he got home.

Once a hostess caught him peering at a little list he had drawn from his vest pocket. "Are you checking to see where you're going next, Senator?" his hostess asked.

It is not known whether Senator Green realized he was being addressed by the hostess or not. "No," he said bluntly. "I'm checking to see where I am now."

The most eligible bachelor in Washington can afford to be insulting.

I was always amused to see how Senators tried to save money, doing anything from getting a staff member to shop for them and "forgetting" to pay, to clipping coupons from the newspaper for bargains at the supermarket—one of John Sparkman's tricks.

Senators get so many perks and gifts, it's hard for the average admirer to find a gift that will give him a charge. When Senator Charles Percy came to his sixtieth birthday, his staff got together to figure it out. The winning idea came from Nadine Jacobsen, and what was it? A balloon ride over the Blue Ridge Mountains of Virginia, taking off from Bristol, Virginia.

The general public has no idea how many gifts come pouring into the office of almost every legislator on Capitol Hill. A few accept no gifts or nothing over the value of $15. Senator Paul Douglas of Illinois had the wisest rule: "Accept nothing you can't eat within three days."

Gifts from foreign governments must be reported. Only three members of the House and one lone Senator—Ted Kennedy—bothered to list what they had received in 1978. Kennedy's foreign gifts were a painting of Tolstoi given to him by Brezhnev and valued at $150 and a balalaika from a Russian farm group, valued at $250.

Money, money, money, there is no end to money and valuable gifts and perks—the name that the Hill calls perquisites, which are defined in Webster's New World Dictionary this way: "something additional to regular profit or pay, resulting from one's position or employment, especially something customary or expected, as a tip or gratuity. Something to which a person is entitled by virtue of status, position . . . prerogative; right: as the Frank is a *perquisite* of congressmen."

Besides their $57,000 salary, when I retired at the end of 1975, Senators were entitled to free mailing privileges, free health care, insurance for a proper burial, retirement pay (no matter how much money they earned in other careers after leaving Congress), free furniture and redecorating for their offices, discount buying of supplies and household items for themselves and their homes, free travel at home and abroad.

Also, the perk of being permitted to pick up an extra $25,000 for making speeches to outside groups—a favorite way lobbyists and industry groups arrange to reward powerful Senators for their support—$2,500 to $5,000 a talk.

I thought of that when I read that students were boycotting a lecture of Alex Haley, author of *Roots,* because they would be charged $2 per person to attend it. I've never seen students up in arms and picketing because a legislator is receiving $5,000 for a speech he is making. The difference is that sometimes the fee is hidden from the naked eye, paid by some corporation and ultimately charged off in the high cost of the product or goods. They do not realize they are dipping into their pockets just as much as they would have dipped for that $2 to hear Alex Haley.

When Senator Robert Byrd, Majority Leader, cut a record to share his fiddling with the nation, some of his colleagues were jealous to learn that his royalty earnings from it would not come under the $25,000 limit on outside earnings. Fiddling was ruled to be not in the same class with speaking. Fiddling was in a class of its own!

The Hill crowd can always find a way around any effort to take away their perks. When it was ruled that any unused office allowance would have to be turned back to the government at the end of a term, some quickly got the clever idea of using up all leftover funds by buying postage stamps—proving you *can* take it with you.

Once a Club member, always a Club member. Ex-Senator Jack Richard Miller of Iowa was given a high position in the U. S. Court of Customs and Patent Appeals in 1973 after he was defeated for reelection to the Senate. However, I would still see him regularly back at the Club, buying his favorite smelly little cigars at the usual 40 percent discount, just as if he were still on his way to the floor.

Incidentally, employees of the Senate do not get wholesale prices. Only members of the Sweetest Little Club in the World get them and continue to get them for the rest of their lives.

Anything a member of the Club touches turns to money and value skyrockets. When ex-President Jerry Ford sold the inexpensive house he had bought in Alexandria as a minority leader of the House of Representatives, he got $137,000.

Not bad, but ex-President Richard Nixon did a lot better. He sold his San Clemente home for $1.2 million, and much of its inflated price may have come from improvements put in by an open-hearted Uncle Sam as well as the magic of big-name tenancy.

Everyone wants to live in a house once occupied by a President. Who wants to live in a house once occupied by a Vice-President? Almost everyone, if his name is Nelson Rockefeller, whose home in Washington, D.C., went on sale for $8 million. Unfortunately, only Sargent Shriver and his wife, Eunice Kennedy, of the Kennedy clan could come up with cash.

Senators get to feeling that membership in their special Club entitles them to view the whole world as their oyster—or at least all of Washington, D.C. One of the best laughs I got was when a bunch of Senators went to the National Press Club to participate in a chili cookoff and prove which state produced the best chili. Among the spirited competitors was Senator Barry Goldwater.

Goldwater bent an elbow with the press boys for a while—after losing—and finally left. Another senatorial contestant, however, seemed to feel his loss more strongly and stayed on and on. The next morning the story that made the rounds of the Hill was that the Senator had left the National Press Club and tried to flag down a mail truck to take him home.

It was natural for him to feel it was the prerogative of the Senate Club. I've seen all kinds of unauthorized vehicles commandeered around the Hill by some important House or Senate member who is throwing his weight around. Usually the driver simply does what the member wants and explains it to his boss later.

Whatever members want, members get. As a sort of slush fund, there's always about $20 million or so lying around. The Senate Contingency Fund runs about $40 to $50 million a year. The Senate passes it every year, without specifying what it's going to be used for. They have to pass it. How else could they ride around in pool cars? The Senate post office has a fleet of such cars at the beck and call of the sergeant of arms. The post office doesn't get to use these cars. They're for the Senators, their wives, children, girlfriends, key staff members, and others whom the Senators deem worthy. At a moment's notice, a Senator can call for and get a free ride.

I found out about this in 1959, when I was a purchasing manager with an office in the Dirksen Building. The post office was on the same floor, so I saw everything going on there. I was also very friendly with Dave Jennings, the postmaster and a nephew of the now deceased Senator Olin Johnston of South Carolina. Jennings still spends a lot of time on the Hill as a union lobbyist and a labor representative.

There were always forty or so new cars around, Mercurys, big ones. They usually used them because they were less conspicuous than Lincolns or Caddies. I always said to Dave, "I'd sure like to know if some of these Senators hell-bent on economy, like Proxmire and his wife, use these limousines." Dave would never tell me.

I would see chief clerks of committees, Senators, key staffers, Senators with their wives, getting into the pool cars behind the drivers. The chauffeur would not wear a cap for these nonofficial rides. Neither would the riders enter these cars outside the Capitol Building where their constituents or reporters could see them. They would always get in, either in the basement of the Dirksen Building or the driveway leading into the Russell Building courtyard. It's conveniently out of sight, and I've never seen a reporter around, not even for the many summer parties I've set up there.

The Staff Club used the courtyard a lot. A certain large and powerful organization also gave a party out there. They rented the kind of tent that is used for garden parties on private estates. We had 1,200 to 1,400 guests seated under the tent. It turned out to be a clear night, and the $2,000 for the tent rental was wasted. Tables and chairs were rented for an additional price. The cover charge was in the neighborhood of $12 per person and included all the liquor one could drink. We lost money on the deal. The actual cost per person was over a dollar more than we took in. There went the deficit.

My superior, Joe Diamond, handled that affair. Later, he came to me, crying because he hadn't charged enough. When I had originally seen the menu, I had cautioned him to allow for three drinks per person, making the cost per head $19.25. That would have allowed us to make a small profit. As it was, we lost about $1,500 on this one event.

Besides, a few rascals had used the event to raise money. There's a law stating you cannot raise campaign funds or funds of any kind on public property, since this belongs to the taxpayers.

We found out that the party-giving organization had pulled a fast one. Without telling Diamond about it, they simply had charged $25 per head and quietly pocketed $13 per person, letting us hold the bag for the deficit. Later, they told him the money was needed to pay off various debts. Once the restaurant signs a contract stipulating the price, it is impossible to change that price. Had we made waves, the committee would have written to the Rules Committee, complaining. And we well knew that complaints, especially by Senators and political friends of Senators, must be avoided at all costs.

Incidentally, it *is* permissible to sell tickets *off* government property and hold the party in the committee rooms or restaurants off-hours. But things get lax, and I've seen small fund-raising parties at which $500 to $2,500 was collected from each of a small select group of guests. If the name of the Senator sponsoring it is big enough, we pretended we didn't see what else was going on besides our service of food.

Any time food is served outside the restaurants, there is automatically a 20 percent surcharge—except in the Capitol itself. Not that it makes sense but the members of the Sweetest Little Club in the World simply decided they just wouldn't pay it in the Capitol building. They would pay it in the Dirksen Senate Office Building. They would pay it in the Russell Senate Office Building. But they would not pay it under the Capitol dome.

So that was the rule. But every Senator is king, or at least a prince or princess, and can spit on the rule. It was not a matter of wealth, it was a matter of emotion.

Take Senator Ted Kennedy, who was not a poor man. I had more arguments with him over that 20 percent than almost anyone. When he had food brought to his office or any room outside the restaurants, he would see that 20 percent, and it was like a red flag.

He would have his secretary, Angelique Lee, call me and say he wanted his bill straightened out. The message delivered was that he sure as hell wasn't paying any 20 percent.

I would take it to Joe Diamond, the manager, and he would instruct Louise Hoke, the bookkeeper, "Take it off. Take the damn charge off. The Senators make the rules; the Senators break the rules."

I would be with him as he delivered his instructions, and I would say, "There is no rule on Capitol Hill. No organization, no rules except hit or miss."

Life was hell.

Muskie was the same way. It got so bad he wouldn't even speak to me, he was so mad about the 20 percent. So was Birch Bayh. So was Mondale. And John Tunney of California. Ted Kennedy took him under his wing—Tunney and Kennedy were fast friends, and Kennedy told him how to operate in the Club.

The Kennedys, except for Robert, preferred gifts to tipping. Robert Kennedy was very generous with his tipping, and he always sent the people directly involved in service to him Christmas gifts of money, $25 or $50 or even $100. It made him very popular.

Ted Kennedy then followed in the tradition of his generous brother, Bobby, sending Christmas gifts to every waiter and waitress who had served him during the year. I would get $100 and a Christmas card from him, which carried the Senate's seal. I knew him well enough so that he signed the card "Ted." But I never presumed to call him by his first name in front of anyone.

As a matter of policy, I never called any of the Senators by their first names during business hours on the Hill. After hours or when they came to my home as guests, that was a different matter.

Several Senators, Senator Strom Thurmond among them, were so tight, it was said they squeaked when they walked. They left no tips to speak of and could be counted on to outsit their luncheon "guests" rather than pick up the tab. If worse came to worst, they could remember a sudden emergency and ask to be excused. Some were famous for their fast footwork.

During my time on the Hill, Harry Byrd, Jr., did not entertain and did not allow his accounts to be used by anyone. Sometimes a person seeking to throw a party would say, "I'm a friend of Harry, Jr."

But we had been told by his office that we could not charge anything to Byrd and that he would pay cash as he went. We would say, "You'll have to go to his office and bring me an authorization." We would give the annoyed person a form to take along—a special-function authorization. I can't remember anybody coming back with that form approved.

Even his own staff didn't use the party rooms. The staffs in some offices signed their own approvals, but in those cases the Senator had authorized them to speak for him and make arrangements for him. But Byrd had not done this, in fact, quite the opposite.

It was hard to believe this man was so rich—he had inherited vast wealth and was earning a great deal of money every year as the apple king of the world. I also was told he controlled radio, TV stations, and newspapers in Virginia, and was on the board of ABC. And has an interest in coal mines in Virginia.

Hard to believe. He ate mostly in the carry-out, the only place you could get a grilled cheese for 15¢ and milk shake for 25¢ after the price had doubled in any restaurant off the Hill.

He would stand in line, looking very humble. And if I recognized him and tried to let him ahead of the line, he would say, "No, thank you, I'll wait my turn."

After Harry, Jr., succeeded his father, J. S. Kimmitt, Senator Mansfield's administrative assistant, was sitting there having a cup of coffee in the cafeteria when he suddenly beckoned me over. I thought something was wrong with the coffee but he said, "Look, don't you realize that's Senator Harry Byrd, Jr., standing in that carry-out line. You'd better take care of him."

I told him Byrd just didn't like anything that drew attention to himself, but he insisted it was terrible that a member of the Club should be standing in line. He didn't like to see a Senator eating in a carry-out. Neither did we, but we had discovered Harry, Jr., liked it that way.

Still, pushed by Kimmitt, I went over to the Senator and offered to get what he wanted so he wouldn't have to stand in line. "No, indeed," he said. "I'll wait my turn." He was not smiling, and I realized he did not appreciate the fact that I was drawing attention to him. I quickly withdrew to the cafeteria and Kimmitt.

I said, "You see what I mean? The man doesn't want to be bothered."

Kimmitt shook his head and said, "You never know what these characters are going to do next."

Byrd would order grilled-cheese sandwiches and a milk shake, vanilla—not even double thick, the way I liked mine. That was it. He would take this lunch into the cafeteria and sit among the tourists; he wouldn't even take it into the staff cafeteria. Among the tourists, no one would recognize him. If he had gotten the same sandwich and milk shake in the private Senate restaurant, it would have cost considerably more—45¢ for the cheese sandwich and 35¢ for the milk shake. Tip at least 25¢. But I have never seen or heard of his eating in the private dining room, even at the Capitol. He would, if he was really hungry, go in the cafeteria line in the tourists' cafeteria.

One of his favorite things was the Senate bean soup, 15¢. As I write, the price is now a big 35¢.

If I have given the impression that some wealthy Senators were close with the buck, I should apologize for not having added in the next breath, "But their wives made them look like pikers in maneuvering to save pennies."

The Tuesdays on which the wives of Senators came to do their charitable duty and roll bandages for the Red Cross were a nightmare. Fuss and feud and complain without end!

They deserved high marks, however, for imagination. For a time they had a laborer from the superintendent's office act as free waiter. But someone had to put together and deliver the complicated $15 or $20 order, and that fell to a poor bus girl. I've heard her come back and say, "Would you believe it? They got together and gave me this dollar." And she held it high in disbelief as we chuckled. We felt sorry for her but what could you do?

But they still had to pay the 20 percent service charge for

bringing food over from the Senate restaurants to their meeting room, and they were up in arms about it.

Many brought their own food from home in a brown bag to avoid the problem. Others brought a sandwich and ordered only the meagerest of items from the restaurant. At that time, salad was 25¢, pie was 15¢, coffee or tea 10¢, and bread and butter 5¢. There was no charge for the homemade salad dressing we sent over if Mrs. Talmadge had brought some of her famous ham and the ladies had brought only their bread.

If a lady got salad, coffee, pie, and bread and butter, the 20 percent service charge on this magnificent bill of 55¢ would be only a dime. That didn't even cover the cost of the linen's rental for the room, which was $1 per tablecloth and 5¢ per napkin.

Still the ladies were refusing to pay the 20 percent service charge, and it was like pulling teeth to get that last dime.

They complained to their husbands. They complained to me. Finally, Caroline Long, the wife of Senator Russell Long, and Antoinette Hatfield, wife of Senator Mark Hatfield, complained so much to the chairman of the Rules Committee, that Jordan finally said to me, "To hell with it, Hurst, don't charge them."

I said, "Look, Senator, I don't know what they're complaining about. Even on a three-dollar meal, the surcharge is only sixty cents. We're not getting enough to take care of the linen, the cleaning of the room, the breakage, the loss of items to souvenir hunters."

"What's your point?" Jordan asked.

"My point is, Senator, there is no damn wonder you guys have a deficit. Can't operate this way."

Jordan broke in: "To hell with it, Hurst. You worry too much about the taxpayers. Everybody's going to survive."

And you know, he was right. Even though the ladies never had to pay another 20 percent service charge again.

It was a joke around our shop that Lady Bird Johnson tipped more generously than her husband, the Majority Leader and later Vice-President. Everyone was much happier to see her arrive than to see Lyndon.

They were also happy to see the dear friend of the Johnsons who had turned over her home to them when Johnson became Vice-President, the one and only Perle Mesta—"Hostess with the Mostes'."

Good old Perle was always picking up the check when she and Lady Bird met for lunch on the Hill. Once, the Vice-President, Perle, and Lady Bird had dinner in the Senate restaurant, and Mesta still grabbed the check and tipped very generously—over 20 percent.

Lady Bird tipped in the same generous way when she ate alone, and she was never too busy to inquire about families of the restaurant staff.

In contrast, Pat Nixon never did show this extreme interest. Lady Bird, I remember, would stop at Marie German's door—she was office clerk for the restaurant—and inquire about all her people back home. Marie was not even from Texas. She was from Maine.

My impression of Pat Nixon was that she was distracted and nervous but holding onto herself to keep from showing it. Her aloof air gave her the nickname of "Marie Antoinette" around the Hill. The word was that Pat Nixon had changed the most after her husband's elevation to Vice-President, and that as a Senator's wife she had been very warm and friendly.

Senators didn't have to spend their own money to look generous. There were all too many outsiders anxious to entertain at their own expense.

Senator Peter Dominick of Colorado had a very rich constituent. This guy not only owned a gold and a silver mine, but a breeding farm as well. We gave a big luncheon for all the Senators, sponsored by Dominick and paid for by the wealthy mine and breeding-farm owner. Money didn't matter.

Steak for everyone. But not ordinary steaks. The constituent furnished them himself from his breeding farm. The Senate restaurant usually served six-ounce steaks for luncheon. But at this luncheon we served 250 twelve-ounce, New York sirloins.

The rest of this sit-down luncheon was equally luxurious. He didn't even look at our regular menu, only a special order would be good enough. "I'll fix the menu myself," he insisted. And he did.

The baked apple dumplings with cheese sauce, served hot, got so many raves, and so many people asked how they were made, that I thought I'd let you in on the secret.

BAKED APPLE DUMPLINGS
With Cheese Sauce

Peel and core apples; fill center with brown sugar, cinnamon, and butter. Wrap apple in pie dough, bake in 375- or 400-degree oven for about an hour. Serve hot with cheese sauce.

Cheese Sauce: To a large can of condensed milk, add 2 cups grated fresh sharp cheddar cheese. Combine in saucepan over low flame, about 15 minutes, stirring constantly until it melts and mixture thickens. Pour over the dumpling, and serve hot.

Of course, there were many other goodies on the luncheon menu, from shrimp cocktail to an unlimited quantity of quality booze. This constituent was so well satisfied with the luncheon, saying the food and service had been great, he insisted on giving me a $100 tip. I was pleased to accept it. But even more satisfying to my soul was the chance to work for a man who didn't haggle about prices and who appreciated good food, well prepared and served.

I always made the same effort to please and to do the best I could within budgetary restrictions, whether the customer was generous or penny pinching. I was really delighted that this constituent was so satisfied. But that wasn't the end of it.

Arriving home one night, some months later, I was advised that there was a package for me, sent air express, waiting at National Airport. Since I hadn't ordered anything, I felt there must be some mistake. But I went anyway, thinking that one of my bosses might have neglected to tell me that he wanted me to pick up a package for him.

But much to my amazement, I discovered that it was indeed for me. On a lined piece of note paper, torn out of a tablet, was a simple note from the tycoon, saying he hoped I would enjoy some real steaks. He had quietly sent me an unexpected gift of a hundred filet-mignon steaks, twelve ounces each. I never saw the man again, but I never forgot him either.

I don't want to give the impression that Senators and Congressmen cannot be generous too.

The public does not know what kind things are done by Senators and Congressmen every day of the year, without reimbursement. The legislators pay for it from one office account or another—or even sometimes from their own pockets.

I know one case in which Congressman Herb Harris of Virginia got involved personally when a constituent could not find a long-lost brother. A family dispute had caused the brother to split six years earlier. Now the missing man's mother had died.

Harris, acting as a detective, found out that the man was getting Army retirement checks. Though the Congressman could not give the family the man's location, because of the Privacy Act, he personally sent a wire to the missing man telling him about the death of his mother and giving the telephone number of his sister, who had long since forgiven him and was waiting to talk to him.

It took Harris only fifteen hours to locate the man and bring about an emotional family reunion.

It's nice to be a member of the Club and have all the perks, such as being waited on hand and foot and traveling to far-off lands. All that free travel gave the Hill wits something to work on.

Once when it was announced that a group of Senators were going on a work session to emerging nations to study how American loans were being used, someone quipped that the United States gave money to such unstable nations that their whole governments are run by Kelly girls.

One of the dangers a member of the Club runs into in being an honored guest in foreign countries is having to smile while ingesting strange foods. Animal eyeballs are a delicacy, as are dog meat and monkey flesh.

When Vice-President Mondale visited China, word came back that the only time he showed a momentary sign of weakness was at a banquet when he was faced with digging into a specially prepared chicken complete with head and claws—a la stuffed pig. Only the feathers were missing—fortunately.

I remember when, during the student rebellion in the '60s, a bomb went off in the men's rest room on the Senate side of the Capitol and the main Senate restaurant was partially destroyed. It was just lucky no one was in there. However, a very historic stained-glass window in the restaurant showing General George Washington on a horse, consulting with General LaFayette, was partially destroyed.

It's repaired now, for the assistant architect of the Capitol, Mario Campiolo, personally gathered up every precious bit and piece of this irreplaceable work of art and carefully supervised the fitting-together of the puzzle.

Every time you turn around, there's a new scandal in the Club. Someone is accused. Someone is pointing a finger. It doesn't mean he's guilty. It just means someone is pointing a finger.

Daniel Minchew, former AA to Senator Talmadge, blew the whistle on his former boss and pointed to a whole list of alleged financial irregularities.

What was the outcome? At this writing, Minchew has been sentenced to a small jail term. Talmadge has gotten by with a "small hand slapping," as it is called by the Club members—a reprimand by his peers.

Minchew had been the chief accuser of his boss, who was charged with filing about $43,000 worth of false office-expense claims, and being overreimbursed in campaign costs. Minchew testified he had set up a secret $39,000 bank account for his boss from diverted campaign gifts—illegally obtained Senate funds.

Mrs. Talmadge also got into the act, testifying that the Senator was in the habit of stashing $100 bills in an old overcoat kept in a closet, and she brought seventy-seven of them with her as proof. The Senator had previously claimed that his "pocket money" had come from little gifts of $5, $10, and $20 from kindly constituents.

The Senator and his lawyers claimed that neither his ex-wife, Betty, nor his former chief aide was to be believed, and maintained he was the victim of poor bookkeeping. Furthermore, he claimed Minchew had diverted some of the money to his own use.

Eventually, Minchew pleaded guilty on one count, and the Senator, after making restitution of monies wrongfully received, had to stand before the Senate and hear himself *denounced* for financial misconduct, unbefitting a Senator.

Instead of being desolate, Talmadge called the action "a personal victory." It could have been worse—he could have been censured. And the Ethics Committee did not recommend that the Senator be stripped of his seniority or committee chairmanship.

As a matter of fact, very soon after the denouncement, both lobbyists and fellow Senators threw a $1,000-a-plate fund raiser to help "poor" Talmadge run for his fifth term. His fellow Senators were not required to come up with $1,000 for their tickets but their presence was like money in the bank in saying that Talmadge had not lost his clout.

In fact, Senator Henry Jackson, who had been one of the chief denouncers, stood there proclaiming that "as far as my personal relations are concerned" he had "always found him a person of integrity and honor" while Senator Russell Long went him one better to acclaim Talmadge for his "great common sense." Anyone who works on the Hill for any length of time is not surprised at such turns of events.

I know it's hard for the average individual to understand how things are handled in the Club. I think the best lesson in Hill *inner politics* comes from the report of the Senate's Select Committee on Ethics, which examined the case of Senator Thomas Dodd of Connecticut as precedence, at the time it was taking up the case of Senator Talmadge.

I'm not going to add a word, I'm just going to let the report tell the story:

Public hearings were held from March 13 to 17, 1967.

Conclusion: From testimony received at the hearings, the Committee concluded that from the period of 1961 through 1965 seven fund-raising events were held for Senator Dodd, and the receipts from these events totaled not less than $203,983. The Committee also found that during Senator Dodd's senatorial campaign for re-election in 1964 political committees supporting his re-election collected $246,290. From the receipts of the fund-raising events and campaign contributions, the Committee found that Senator Dodd had authorized the payment of $116,083 for his personal use. The Committee also pointed out that after the 1964 campaign, Senator

Dodd accepted $8,000 in cash from funds of the International Latex Corporation. They found that from the period 1961 through 1965 Senator Dodd requested and accepted reimbursements from both the Senate and private organizations for the same travel. The Senator was also found to have accepted the loan of three automobiles in succession from a constituent and these automobiles were used for personal transportation for a period of twenty-one months between 1964 and 1965.

Based upon these findings the Committee recommended the censure of Senator Dodd on the grounds that for a period of five years he exercised the influence and power of his office as a United States Senator (a) to obtain, and use for his personal benefit, funds from the public through political testimonials and a political campaign, and (b) to request and accept reimbursements for expenses from both the Senate and private organizations for the same travel.

Decision of the Senate: On June 12, 1967, floor debate began on S. Res. 112, which had been reported from the Committee on April 27th, to censure Senator Dodd "for his conduct, which is contrary to accepted morals, derogates from public trust expected of a Senator, and tends to bring the Senate into dishonor and disrepute." A substitute for S. Res. 112 was offered by Senator Russell B. Long that would have admonished Senator Dodd not to engage in any conduct that might be construed as unethical and urging the Committee to draw up a code of conduct for Senators. This amendment was rejected by a roll call vote of 2–94. Senator Tower then offered an amendment to substitute the words "reprimand" for "censure," "accepted standards of conduct" for "accepted morals," and to delete the reference to bringing "the Senate into dishonor." This amendment was defeated 9–87. Senator Tower also introduced an amendment that would have substituted only "accepted standards of conduct" for "accepted morals," and this was defeated by a roll call vote of 18–78.

The most significant amendment, and the only one that was accepted, was offered by Senator Allen Ellender of Louisiana. Senator Ellender's amendment deleted from the resolution the charge that censured Senator Dodd for using his office "to request and accept reimbursements for expenses from both the Senate and private organizations for the same travel." This amendment was passed by a roll call vote of 51–45.

On June 23, 1967, the Senate by a roll call vote of 92 yeas to 5 nays censured Senator Dodd "for having engaged in a course of conduct over a period of five years from 1961 to 1965 of exercising the influence and power of his office as a United States Senator, as shown by the conclusions in the investigation by the Select Committee on Standards and Conduct, to obtain, and use for his personal benefit, funds from the public through political testimonials and a political campaign." The resolution further stated that his conduct was ". . . contrary to accepted morals, derogates from the public trust expected of a Senator, and tends to bring the Senate into dishonor and disrepute."

There was so much money changing hands around Capitol Hill that it was sometimes embarrassing. Money would be so carelessly handled that sometimes I and others on the restaurant staff would inadvertently get involved.

I remember once it was an obvious bribe of $400 in a plain envelope meant for a Senator—his name was on it—that got into my hands. When the "bag man" finally caught up with me, he had a very good explanation of what the money was for—"The Senator wants to pay some of his bills and I'm taking care of it for him."

I didn't change expression nor did I believe it for a minute as I handed over the envelope.

Once it was $3,000 stuffed into a plain brown envelope, and another time it was a check for $6,000, which a lobbyist was delivering to a Senator but, probably through nervousness, left under a plate of food.

On these occasions, not a penny was given as a reward. Oh, well.

Sometimes those whose votes are bought don't stay bought. I was told of one fairly recent case in which certain Panamanian interests slipped money through sources to a particular Senator to get his help for their cause of getting the United States to turn over the Panama Canal to the Panamanians. Then some American business interests sought his help, and he accepted their contribution, too. I was told the Senator stayed bought the second time and voted against the treaty and for the United States to maintain control.

As I proofread this book, the newspapers are suddenly full of a new Hill scandal in which seven Congressmen and one Senator—Harrison "Pete" Williams of New Jersey—face potential bribery charges.

In what was quickly dubbed the FBI Sting and Operation

ABSCAM, government agents, posing as filthy rich Arab sheikhs and businessmen, allegedly offered bribes to the legislators in return for special favors and influence, and videotaped their reactions.

One Congressman, who was photographed stuffing $25,000 into his pockets, held a press conference to protest that things weren't as they seemed—he wasn't *accepting* a bribe, he was just gathering evidence and had been on to the phonies all the time.

In the case of Senator Williams, arrangements were allegedly discussed under which the Senator would receive titanium mining stock in exchange for his help in getting government contracts.

I was not too surprised to see that, though some Club members deplored "the greed of some legislators," the greatest outcry was against the FBI for tempting them.

I'm always amused when ethics committees and such attempt time and again to stop corruption. When they got a law passed that individuals could contribute no more than $1,000 to a candidate, it was no time at all before smart lobbyists had figured out that a neat "solution" would be to form Political Action Committees so that trade organizations, industrialists, and big businessmen could contribute all they want to a candidate. Eventually, a limit of $10,000 was set.

At this writing there is no limit on the total amount of money that any single candidate may receive from all the contributing PACs, but there is a move afoot to limit the total to $70,000.

I don't know what the new tricks will be, but they'll be there. I have overheard stock deals in which a Senator was being offered the chance to buy a block of stock for an outrageously low rate. Once a stock that was listed at about $50 was being practically given away for $1 a share. I saw the Senator hand over $50 for fifty shares and heard him laugh that it was a pretty good buy.

In another case, an aide to a Senator got three hundred shares of AT&T for $100—33⅓¢ a share—from someone who just happened to be involved in getting the government to take over railroad deficits. As the aide commented, it was a perfectly legal transaction, and if someone was willing to get rid of the stock to get some quick money, why should he be foolish and not buy.

On the Hill, one can justify almost anything.

In one case, I saw a Senator's aide get five hundred shares of what I understood to be Swiss bank stock. I was told the stock was worth about $25,000 and that taxes would not have to be paid on it until the stock was brought back to the United States.

I went home dumbfounded that day. I had not been aware of this more sophisticated maneuvering before. My impression was that the aide was not the one the stock was really intended for but his boss and several other Senators.

I learned on the Hill that it's not only what a Senator gets that's important but what his aides get or appear to be getting. And it's not only the aides but the Senator's family—his wife and children. Sometimes a foxy wife had taken advantage of the situation, I would hear the Senator bemoan, and had sold the stock and gotten the money. And the Senator had to keep quiet.

Is it any wonder that a favorite story around the Hill is the one about a lobbyist who drives a special-order, personalized $100,000 Rolls-Royce to the home of a Senator and says, "Senator, my organization wants you to have this."

The Senator becomes indignant and responds with irritation that any group should even think that he would accept anything that could be misconstrued as a bribe on upcoming legislation.

The lobbyist quickly backs off, apologizing and saying, "You are absolutely right, Senator. It would be deplorable that such an interpretation could be made. And it could. But now, sir, what would you think if I were to tell you that we would like to *sell* you this car for fifty dollars?"

The Senator quickly replies, "Well, John, that's a different story. In that case, you can put me down for two."

3

Up Your Chamber

I remember when I had to stay on the job for three days straight during a filibuster on civil rights. I started work on a Tuesday at 6:30 A.M., stayed all day, stayed Tuesday night, Wednesday, Wednesday night, and finally left Thursday, about 3:00 P.M., a total wreck.

As long as the Senate was in session, I had to make sure there was adequate food for everyone. I killed time by sitting in the gallery and listening to Senator Robert Byrd read a book of poems aloud to keep the bill from passing. LBJ was the champion of the underdog in this case, pushing to get the vote through, and Byrd was pushing just as hard to keep that from happening.

The general public doesn't realize that most legislating is not done in that great forum, the Senate chamber. That's just for window dressing. The real legislating is done at cocktail parties, at small meetings of a few men with power deciding how they are going to instruct their Club member followers, and behind closed committee doors.

A filibuster results when an angry group rebels because they haven't been able to strike a deal. They are the minority holding up the works for the majority by not letting anyone but themselves talk on the floor of the Senate. But the talking they are doing is not for persuasion. Heavens no. They are reading aloud from things like poetry books.

That old pro, Senator Carter Glass of Virginia, said it all when he commented that in twenty-eight years of legislating, which included serving as president pro tempore of the Senate, he never knew a speech to change a vote.

History gives Lyndon Johnson credit for the milestone civil-rights legislation. I give Lyndon Johnson credit for something else—the temper of *Jaws* and a *Star Wars* sense of power.

I used to listen in inadvertently on a lot that was going on, and I remember that to get on the Democratic steering committee, Olin Johnston of South Carolina had to promise LBJ and Bob Kerr that he would vote for a natural-gas bill they backed.

When you saw the three men together, which was often, you knew they were planning something, though now and then I would hear one of them add, "It's what the country needs." They were way ahead of Charlie Wilson of General Motors in being sure that what was good for them was good for the nation.

What was good for Capitol Hill was also good for Olin Johnston's family. He had a nephew who was postmaster general of the Senate, another who was Senate doorman, and still another headed the duplicating section which then made photostats of documents. Xerox machines were yet to come.

Olin Johnston was quite a character—always drooling tobacco juice from a cud in his mouth. His clothes were a mess, though expensive. Olin paid his dues in the Club by giving many parties in the committee room after hours. He was a good heavy tipper and naturally got the best service around the Hill.

Ralph Yarborough of Texas was Lyndon Johnson's whipping boy. Any time Lyndon needed someone to blame, it was said on the Hill, he blamed ole Ralph. It was said that LBJ was determined to keep Yarborough in the Senate for this purpose, when LBJ became President.

Even I, on the sidelines, could clearly see that Yarborough was strictly a yes man to LBJ. And that wasn't all I could see. It was evident that Yarborough needed his own whipping boy to make up for the abuse he took from Johnson—and some of his whipping boys were the cigarette machines that couldn't fight back.

Many's the time Yarborough, in a foul temper, would turn a cigarette machine upside down if it didn't produce, and slam the money out of it. Capitol police merely asked him politely if he would please not do it.

For a Senator is king of the Clubhouse. As just one more proof, some Senators had a special arrangement with police buddies to stand guard outside their hideaway doors when they were entertaining sweeties. LBJ, for one, had his door guarded at times by some policemen who were beholden to him, as did Kerr and Olin Johnston.

I remember back in the days when Bobby Baker was a hot shot on Capitol Hill, giving Democrats their instructions from Lyndon Johnson, their leader, and hobnobbing with such men as Bob Kerr and Olin Johnston.

Bobby Baker spent a lot of time with the LBJ gang at the wild Quorum Club. It was in the Carroll Arms Hotel, just across the street from the Dirksen Senate Office Building, which was originally called the New Senate Office Building, but the hotel is now an office building. The club dissolved and had nothing to do with a new club with the same name.

Olin Johnston, George Smathers, Bobby Baker, and Lyndon Johnson would get together at the Club and get half tanked up. Then they would start playing the piano and singing at the top of their voices, always including LBJ's favorite, "Yellow Rose of Texas."

There was not only singing, but also girls on laps, a little striptease, and a little shouting of "Take it off, take it off."

I know how it went. I saw a little of it myself.

But one man didn't even have to see it to get incensed. He was a Senator who heard the noise from across the street. His office was in a corner of the Dirksen Building, and he claimed he couldn't think with all that racket when the window was open.

He got so enraged at the use of taxpayers' money to pay for the time Senators were spending in this den of iniquity, that he got up on the floor of the Senate to raise hell about it. He ranted and raved and told exactly what he had heard. He deplored the behavior of certain Senators. He said the public had the right to know.

Before the day was over, Marie German, who worked for me, called excitedly to tell me all that had been said on the floor of the Senate, urging me to be sure to read it all in the *Congressional Record* the next morning.

The next morning I looked and looked, but not a word was in

the *Congressional Record,* which purports to reveal every golden word spoken on the floor of the House and Senate. What had happened?

Eventually, I found out. Kerr and Lyndon Johnson had talked to the angry Senator and had gotten him to have his whole speech stricken before the *Record* got to the printers.

The Club protects its image.

It's dangerous to tell all the wheeling and dealing that goes on on Capitol Hill. Lobbyists fall over each other in their race to get into an office to influence a Senator or his aide. But once a Senator has given his word that something will be done, he can be a formidable enemy even to a President, until the Senator fulfills his promise.

Since Senator Bob Kerr was a powerhouse in his time, it is fair to use him as an illustration in point and suffice it to say, nothing much has changed up there.

Senator Kerr had given his word that a certain man would be named judge in his home state of Oklahoma. Unfortunately, Bobby Kennedy, who was Attorney General, didn't like the man. Kerr did not beg, cajole, or plead. He simply held up a bill that President Kennedy was interested in. It took quite a while but eventually JFK stirred himself to investigate what was holding it up.

It was like opening a Pandora's box. The President suddenly found out that Kerr was furious at brother Bobby for holding up the judgeship and making him look bad in his home state. As one Senator commented to me, "If a Senator seems not to have the power even to get a judge appointed, tough titty on getting reelected."

Jack Kennedy personally called his brother at Justice and said, "Bobby, the man had better be nominated." In no time, he was, and Kerr quickly pushed through the bill the President wanted.

There was always a power play going on.

The Senators had an expression they used when someone was

trying to put on the dog for them and couldn't afford it. They'd say, "He's trying to blow gas higher than his hole."

The credit for originating this great philosophical comment goes to Lyndon Johnson, when he was majority leader.

Maybe things will change a hundred years from now, but the Senate is still pretty well seniority-ridden. I like what Senator Carl Levin of Michigan said on the subject. "I learned about seniority when Hill veteran Senator Tsongas sent me to the end of the line in the men's room."

When there are surprise weekend Senate sessions at which there must be a live quorum, the sergeant at arms uses military planes at Andrews Air Force Base to go get Senators from their homes or wherever they may be. Not only have I seen them fly to Massachusetts to get a Kennedy—Bob or Ted—to Rhode Island for Pell, and New York for Javits, but immediately after the vote, to fly them back.

I can hardly wait to see what happens when the new marble palace, the Senator Hart Office Building, is completed. Those with the greatest seniority will have to move there to show their clout. But this won't mean it's the best building.

The same thing happened when the Senator Dirksen Office Building first opened. There was a mad dash among the old boys with seniority. To get in. Then to get out!

Most Senators with seniority prefer the older Russell Senate Office Building, because of its marble fireplaces and high ceilings. They moved back out of the new Dirksen Office Building, saying it was a nightmare—ill-planned and ill-conceived. The Senators found their offices stark, without charm, and staffers complained they had to work on top of each other in small, cramped rooms.

Most people who testify in hearing rooms, or sit there as observers, do not realize that when the solemn proceedings are over, the joint may soon be jumping. Yes, it's true! Committee hearing rooms are also used for special functions. The words "partying" or "party" are never used. They are called "special functions" to give them dignity.

Whatever you want to call them, there are twenty-eight such rooms available for after-hour use in the Dirksen Building and another eight rooms in the Russell Building.

Besides these committee rooms, there are dozens of hideaways where Senators can hold smaller parties of their own. Everyone of importance has at least one hideaway. After a Senator has served one term, he becomes eligible for a private hideaway. It's the equivalent to a young executive in private industry finally getting his key to the executive wash room.

One day Senator Fulbright was entertaining at luncheon for a black African leader, who insisted he wanted a white waiter. This presented an emergency, and I was called to round up a white waiter. As it was explained to me, the African was annoyed that people of his race were doing menial work, and he wanted to see a white person doing it.

And so it happened that one white man hovered behind the black African leader, handling nothing but his needs, while our regular black waiters served everyone else in the room.

My real indoctrination into the *Alice in Wonderland* world of the Senate restaurants came in 1965, when I was elevated from my first job at the Hill. I had come in 1959 as purchasing manager and quality-control man, but with the illness of Joseph Diamond, the general manager of the whole Senate restaurant operations, I was made assistant general manager.

During a meeting with the chairman of the Rules Committee, Senator B. Everett Jordan, I asked if there was a specific set of policies to use as a guideline in operating the Senate restaurants. Senator Jordan laughed and said, "The only policy is—it depends on who you deal with, and who you are, and what day it happens." Meaning that every Senator, including his entourage, is the boss.

I blurted out, "Do you realize that there are two hundred and twenty-seven regular jobs involved here, plus a vast number of part timers, who are called in frequently for special service parties, and are hired from the outside? With the amazing variety and quantity of food operations we are overseeing, you tell me there are no guidelines? Do you mean to tell me that with the size of the organization you are dealing with, that there is no set policy—no rules or regulations?"

Senator Jordan just laughed. "There never has been any policy written. This is a very private Club, where the members are in charge. It might be a good idea to give me some suggestions as to what you think policy should be. I doubt whether the Club members will take kindly to it, however. Frankly, I don't think this damn bunch will follow any policy."

To me it seemed like a tragicomedy. Here, we were expected to serve over two million meals a year—that was in 1965—and running almost a half-million deficit. It appeared to me to be more a tragedy than a comedy.

It was hard to imagine. There were, in the Capitol only, for the Senate alone, a kitchen, a public dining room, a press dining room, the Senators' private dining room, the Senators' Inner Sanctum dining rooms, where only men are allowed. In addition there were the family dining room, two private dining rooms used for private parties (S-120 and S-138) for the Senators or their constituents—for private parties sponsored by the Senators and breakfasts.

Prayer breakfasts were always held in S-138, known as the Vandenberg Room. S-120 had no special name—it was larger than S-138, which would accommodate approximately thirty people at a sit-down affair and about seventy-five stand-ups. S-120 could hold fifty sit-downs and about 100 to 120 stand-ups.

This was only the beginning. There was more, much, much more. We were responsible for service to S-207, the Senate reception room, and EF-100, which is the Presidential reception room.

The Senate reception room (207) would hold 110 seated, 150 for a stand-up buffet. This room was the special province of the Senate sergeant at arms. It was really his turf. Even a Senator himself had to get the sergeant at arms' permission to use this room. It was a magnificent room, paneled in mahogany with inlaid hardwood floors and marble fireplace. This was the room traditionally used for the inaugural luncheon after the ceremony on the east steps of the Capitol. The very first meal the new President eats is in this room.

The sergeant at arms controlled this room, not the restaurant management. A Senator's office would call me and say they had made arrangements with the sergeant at arms. And the Senate restaurant personnel would be obligated to see that everything was satisfactory.

EF-100, the Presidential reception room, was under the control of the architect of the Capitol. Anyone who wanted to use it had to get permission from the architect's secretary. It too had elegant paneling and a beautiful conference table. But this oblong room was smaller than 207, and could only seat fifteen to twenty at the most. That is too small for Capitol Hill, and so it was very rarely used. Only for something very private! Senatorial candidates for President would use this for small lunches, to influence a Senate leader.

When Senator Jackson was getting ready to run, he would have two or three luncheons a day for people advising him, backing him financially. All kinds of people were wined and dined by him here—economic advisers, specialists from different states to help in the primaries or advise on defense policies or foreign relations. He would have one luncheon going on here, and at the same time, two others in two different rooms. Senator Muskie also used this room, but did not do the double-up trick.

Once Senator Jackson's trick backfired, and he had to give a speech to one group and did not get to the other group in time. It was very embarrassing and did not win friends and influence votes and contributions.

Our food operation in the Capitol also covered the snack bar in the basement. At that time, a sit-down or carry-out meal in the snack bar allowed a choice of sandwiches, hot dogs, desserts, soup, hamburgers, hot fish sandwiches. The prices were the same as the cafeteria. When hamburgers, which were quarter pounders, went from 25¢ to 30¢, Senator Margaret Chase Smith rose up to fight it. She had General Lewis, her AA, complain to me that we were robbing the Senate employees.

At that time we charged 10¢ for soup, 10¢ for coffee or a coke. Milk was 15¢. These prices were well under those charged by McDonald's, and well under any outside carry-out I had ever heard of, and cheaper than eating in a government cafeteria run by GSI—Government Services. Yet, General Lewis was able to look us in the face and complain in horror that we were overcharging.

Later on, a reorganization was ordered by Senator Robert Byrd, and the General Accounting Office was to make an audit of our restaurants. The restaurant staff was instructed to submit recommendations on prices to be charged depending on the market. We would show the cost of preparing various meals and submit a suggested price to the Rules Committee and the architect's office. They would turn our recommendations down and advise the restaurant staff, "Just maintain the same quality and the same prices." In effect, the restaurant—really the taxpayers—would subsidize the diner.

There went the deficit.

It was like a Gilbert and Sullivan opera, the way the budget for the Senate restaurant operation was handled. It's just too bad we couldn't put those budgetary blues to music. It was almost as if the powers that be *insisted* on losing money.

Let me tell you just one little happening.

At formal dinners, of course, we always put condiments such as catsup into cut-glass cruets. For everyday use, however, we simply put the Heinz bottles on the tables with the label showing.

The Heinz people were so delighted when they learned of this that they wanted to give us a rebate on the purchases in appreciation of the good public relations for their image. General manager Diamond accepted the rebate a few times, not for his own pocket but for cutting the restaurant's deficit.

Then the Rules Committee learned of this, and they were *not* delighted. They were, in fact, so horrified that they issued a new rule that all labels must be taken off bottles of condiments so that trade names would not appear in the papers. Poor Diamond had been proud of his saving of money and had made the mistake of bragging about it to Hugh Alexander, who was chief counsel of the Rules Committee and liaison to the Senate restaurants.

Customers would tell me, angrily, they would rather brown-bag it than stand in our lines. It didn't take an efficiency expert to know there was something wrong with the way the cafeterias were organized. People, with trays of food getting cold, would have to stand in line to pay, stuck behind a Senator who might be trying to make up his mind which cigar to choose.

In trying to please everyone, the cashiers were delaying customers endlessly, while they sold Alka Seltzer for hangovers, and any number of things that had nothing to do with food. Each cashier had a two-drawer file cabinet to root around in. I would watch them sell Alka Seltzer like it was going out of style, the morning after a party—which was about every morning.

It took me five years of constant pressure to get the Rules Committee to allow me to set up a cigar stand to sell Alka Seltzer, newspapers, combs, and even ladies' hose and hairnets that were so in demand. I would smile as secretaries came to work and then rushed to finish their morning grooming. Obviously they hadn't been home.

On the subject of Senate restaurant help, there was mass confusion—and why not? One waiter was a complete alcoholic. But at least he had experience. Another had no knowledge at all about the restaurant business but had struck the fancy of a powerful Senator who had insisted he get a top job.

With such men around—and there were others—business became a Mad Hatter's game, with our waiters talking in circles, with great dignity, getting things mixed up, promising Senators everything and delivering nothing.

It was even funnier because we were serving one hundred men, each of whom—with a handful of exceptions—thought he was a king. As one proof they thought they were kings—and still do—no woman, even if she holds the rank of Senator, has ever set foot within the restaurants called the Inner Sanctum—one for the Democrats and one for the Republicans.

These are still an all-male refuge, where male members of the Club can go without fear of being overheard by females.

To return to the after-hours life on the Hill, the cost of renting a committee room for a party varies greatly. There is no set fee, and I have often thought there should be. Instead, the cost of the room is 20 percent of the room service—in other words, 20 percent of the evaluation of the food eaten in these rooms and supplied by our Senate catering service.

If there were only a few people, who could be served $50 worth of food, we could only charge $10 for the use of the room. The same room with a big party that involved $2,000 worth of food brought the cost of the room up to $400. Sometimes we had to open a committee room for a gathering that only served tea or coffee and cookies at $10 total, and the group only had to pay $2 for all the service.

I really headed for trouble when I tried to keep our food operation from losing money on a Magnuson-sponsored party.

Maggie, as everyone on the Hill called Warren G. Magnuson of Seattle, Washington, ordered a huge luncheon to be served to three hundred guests. He wanted New York cut sirloin steaks. He wanted everything from soup to nuts, including shrimp cocktails and hot apple pie with sharp cheese.

Since we always prepare 10 percent more than ordered to be on the safe side, we were ready to serve 325 luncheons in the committee room of the Dirksen Building.

The room was beautiful. The flowers the Senator had ordered were in place, and so was the booze at the bars. I thought that the price we had given for the dinners was eminently fair at $5.25 per person, not counting the booze. We would just break even.

As the guests started arriving, I grew green around the gills. Where was everyone?

When only about fifty guests showed up, everyone sat down to eat, and I learned that they had known about the cancellations, but had not bothered to notify us. Well, that was their problem, not mine. I had fulfilled the contract.

I sent the guest check to Maggie's office to be signed, since the Senator was the sponsor of the party. The Senator's office sent it to the Commerce Committee, of which Maggie was chairman. They had handled the arrangements. Suddenly everything hit the fan.

A committee clerk called and said he had no intention of having the people who were there pick up the check for anyone except themselves, and the exact count was sixty-eight.

I told him I had been guaranteed three hundred meals and had even prepared twenty-five extra, "for which you were not charged." I told him all the food had been wasted, and that any cancellation had to be made the day before the party.

He said that was my problem, and all he was going to pay for was sixty-eight dinners. He said that if I gave him any trouble, he was going to take the matter up with Magnuson himself.

I called the general manager. "Look," I said. "You're going to have trouble with Magnuson's office. One of your buddies on the Commerce Committee is raising hell with me. Will you get him the hell off my back, and I hope I never have to talk with him again!"

He replied, "What are you bothering me for? It's your problem."

"Not anymore," I said. "I guess he thinks he can get away with this with you, so I'm calling to alert you to expect a call. I hope to heaven you don't let him get away with it."

The general manager said worriedly, "Will you read me the order?"

I said, "Sure." I read him the special-function order, which showed him that everything was as I had stated. "They could have called and changed the count the day before," I added. "This is totally unreasonable."

Diamond said, "I'll take over. Who do these people think they are dealing with?"

I waited that afternoon, and didn't hear a word. Finally, I called the manager at home and asked if he'd talked to the man. He told me nervously, "Oh, yes, you can forget about it. I got it all straightened out."

The next morning I went in a little ahead of my usual seven o'clock and examined the guest check which I had sent over. It had been cancelled, and with it was a new check written out for sixty-eight meals.

I studied the figures carefully. My original bill, counting the alcohol, the setting up of the bar, the flowers, the use of the room had been $2,940. The new bill was for $846.40.

Deficit—$2,093.60. I did some more figuring. The extra twenty-five meals at $5.25 added $131.25. I didn't bother adding them together. It was just too sickening.

PR people from all over the country, many representing lobbyists' groups, would call me after they got the clearance from a Senator to hold a party in a particular room. I would discuss the menu with them, and when an organization is trying to please a group of Senators, price is no object.

It is certainly true that more politicking is done after hours in the parties in the committee rooms than takes place in daytime. Or in the Senator's office. With a few drinks in him, the average Senator becomes a much better listener. Also he has gotten rid of his watch dogs, his staffers.

Some staffers, however, are part of the Senator's wheeling and dealing. A staffer can be much more easily approached and asked about the Senator's desires. The staffer becomes the go-between.

Sometimes I would know the importance of the organization to the Senator by the room he sponsored for it. The best and most elegant committee rooms were often booked two years in advance, to be sure an important event had the proper setting.

When I retired in 1975, we already had 112 reservations for 1976, and some of them had been made in 1973.

Even service-oriented organizations, like the Randolph Hearst Foundation, would have to book a large room over a year in advance. They would bring in a group of bright young scholarship students, and entertain them for a week, even feeding them three times a day in the committee room. I recall meeting Patty Hearst at two of these times, when she came with her parents, Randolph and Catherine Hearst.

We had many a problem. Diabetics. We tried to keep a selection of things always ready for them—sweets without high calories, fresh fruit, fruit juices. Nearly every day we had someone passing out and had to make a call to the nurse. Some had tags, so we'd know if it was diabetes or what. We were not allowed to touch the patient. The nurse would take care of it. She gave shots or sugar to those with diabetes.

Then, of course, there were numerous Senators with cholesterol and blood-pressure problems—patients not supposed to have animal fats. For their sake, the restaurant used only vegetable oil.

Once a tourist fell and hit her head. She was elderly, and the doctor said she had passed out for lack of food. She tried to say it was the restaurant's fault. I had to resist an impulse to tell her that our service was not quite that bad.

Another tourist slipped on water on the floor of the cafeteria. She sued and tried to get back the whole cost of her Washington trip, including hotel and all expenses for two weeks. Her lawyer claimed it had ruined her vacation. The restaurant simply furnished the doctor, and her Medicaid furnished the hospital. The woman learned you cannot sue the government without the government's permission.

We had complaint after complaint of people spilling things on their clothes and wanting us to take care of their dry-cleaning bill. As a rule, we didn't argue, but took care of it through petty cash. Especially if it was the wife or child of a Senator.

Even Senator John L. McClellan of Arkansas grumbled that we ought to pay for the cleaning of his suits, because his cottage cheese (every day) would not stay on his spoon. We didn't tell him it was because his hand was getting too shaky.

All we said was, "Give us the bill, Senator, after you have the suit cleaned. We'll take care of it." And he did. About every six months, he would remember and complain. We didn't argue.

But there went the deficit.

I remember when Senator Harold Hughes of Iowa announced he was not going to run, but was going to lobby for religious organizations, give his life to religion. He said, there was no way he could remain in Congress and be true to his God at the same time—there was no way a man could remain in the Senate without having his morals and standards corrupted.

Senator Hughes's drinking problem had started prior to his coming to the Senate. In the Senate, he was a teetotaler. He had begun drinking while working as a long-distance trucker, and that's when he drank. He called himself a drunkard at that time of his life.

He became thoroughly disgusted with everything the drinking way of life stood for. I never met a man who was more honest, sincere, and dedicated than he. How unfortunate the U.S. Senate doesn't have his services anymore! I recall one conversation I had with him when he had reached the nadir of disappointment, and was telling me that he was tired of being part of a closed or hidden ruling body.

I said, "In other words, Senator, are you saying we are becoming a secret government?" He answered that we were, and that he didn't approve of the closed-door hearings, which kept the people from knowing what elected officials were saying about legislation that would affect all of them.

"When elected, I was a very proud man," Hughes said. "I felt I could fight for what I considered right. But I found it was a waste of time." He deplored the underhanded voting methods on the Hill, the trading of votes, and the ease with which it was hidden from the press.

James Abourezk of South Dakota was a maverick, and he decided that one term in the Senate was enough for him. In fact, more than enough.

He was bitter when he sat in the empty Senate dining room one day, telling me why he did not choose to run in 1978 when his term ended. He was not a Club member, he told me, nor did he want to be.

"The whole indoctrination of the Senate," he told me, "was to be a good Club member and give up the ability to think and vote one's own convictions. The leadership of the Senate doesn't want it. You're expected to give up your integrity."

I remember being impressed that, angry as he was, he didn't use a single cuss word. The strongest statement he made was "I refuse to wear a muzzle just to make some of the old boys happy."

But it was not just battling the leadership that made Abourezk different. It was also his failure to join in the entertainment around the Hill or to become one of the gang in any way.

One of his sons joined an Indian protest movement and went to live on an Indian reservation. The news broke that this son was living on food stamps. Instead of being humble and embarrassed, Abourezk said that his son had a right to live on food stamps if he wanted to. It all made me wonder what the story would have been had a Kennedy son gone to live on an Indian reservation and drawn food stamps. The kid would have been a hero!

4

Short Takes

The Kennedy brothers were the most watched and envied members of the Club for their boyish good looks and determination to have a good time, no matter what anyone thought. Robert Kennedy enjoyed nude swimming parties both at private homes and at the White House. I knew a girl who was in charge of keeping all the children away from the pool area of one such private party that Bobby attended. We would hear all about it the next morning.

His wife, Ethel, did not try to cultivate many of the Senate wives, and I would hear wives griping that Ethel was entertaining a lot of movie stars and not inviting them.

However, the Kennedy brothers were not much for giving parties on the Hill. They gave their parties in their homes, instead of the public rooms of the Capitol. I don't remember any of them using our facilities much except Jackie, when she gave a luncheon now and then for Senate ladies.

Not all of the pool parties involved skinny dipping. The daytime pool parties were perfectly proper—at least to start with. I did hear a theory advanced by some Hill staffers that the reason some people were thrown in fully clothed was to encourage them and give them the excuse to jump out of their wet clothing.

After one of Bobby Kennedy's famous pool parties, on a Saturday afternoon, a Congressman was so proud of having been thrown into the pool with his clothes on that he rushed to his office with his wet clothes still sticking to him, so his girl Friday-sweetie could see him and be impressed. If the theory was right, he missed the whole point!

One thing the Kennedy brothers had in common was an unconcern about clothes. At the beginning of the day, Ted Kennedy usually looked like the end of the day. His clothes always seemed to need pressing. He never seemed to notice when one side of his collar was over his coat and his tie was listing to one side. As a reporter once commented to me, "He looks like one of us—sloppy."

But compared to Bobby Kennedy, the youngest Kennedy looked like a prince. Bobby really looked like a pauper—his shirt collar sprung open, his tie haphazardly tied, in or out of his coat or maybe just loose around his neck, his shoes unpolished.

Staffers seeing him would say, "I guess he got thrown into his swimming pool *before* breakfast today."

I don't remember ever seeing Senator Ted Kennedy without some sort of protection around him, from his own staff. But as talk of his possible candidacy heated up in September of 1979—more than a year before election day—Ted became the first "noncandidate" in history to have four Secret Service men assigned to him for around-the-clock vigilance.

When he and Carter met, as at the opening of the John F. Kennedy Library, it was hard to know which was the President, judging by all the Secret Service activity. The cost of Ted's Secret Service men, in this initial period, did not come out of the $16 million authorized for protecting Presidential candidates in 1980—the same sum as in the 1976 election—but from other Treasury funds.

Of the whole clan, I must confess Jackie Kennedy was my favorite, even as far back as her husband's days in the Senate. She was not only very pretty—perhaps the most beautiful, or close to it, and the youngest of the Senate wives—but in those days, the most unpretentious. Jackie would hear the ladies complaining to me about this and that and make a face.

From what I heard, she herself was supposed to be difficult to please. However, my personal experience with her was very pleasant. She liked the way I did things. Far from giving me any trouble, she would murmur in my ear, "I'm sure you're glad to get rid of us." Then she would announce aloud what a successful luncheon it had been.

If Jack and Jackie Kennedy were entertaining only three or four, they would eat in the Capitol Senators' private dining room. JFK was one of the few Senators I recall always being very gracious—pleased with the food and service, and paying promptly without a big fuss. His office, I remember, even paid by the event, instead of maintaining a charge account.

I recall one occasion vividly. Jackie Kennedy, as First Lady, was returning to the Hill as the guest of honor at a luncheon given for her by a Senator's wife. This was a very special occasion, not the regular Senate ladies' luncheon. Only women were to be there. It was a hen party to welcome back one of their own.

The Secret Service men had already combed the room and looked under every table and flowerpot in G-219, when the First Lady suddenly arrived early, accompanied by two Secret Service agents.

Jackie spied me, came over, as if she had just seen me yesterday, and shook hands with me. "Please join me," she requested. And in a relaxed manner, sat down, took off her shoes, noting, "Oh, that feels good." The party hadn't started yet, and her feet hurt.

I believe she was wearing black leather pumps. It was hard to believe that this woman, who treated everyone as if he was her equal and who was so informal, was the wife of the President and a member of the international jet set. All the time, she chatted away in an easy manner, calling me Lou, as usual, and asking me what was new in the Club.

In a companionable way, she asked about this and that Senator or his wife. But as soon as the first guests arrived, she played her expected role as First Lady. In a stiff, formal manner, she stood up to receive the guests. About ninety women filed down the receiving line, and she greeted them with warmth but formality. From time to time she would glance over at me, with a look that seemed to say, "Oh! I wish I were sitting down again."

Later, she teased me, saying that I would have to serve her in the Inner Sanctum. When I reminded her that no woman had ever been served there, she threatened to run for Senate, so I'd have to serve her there. Ironically, after her husband's assassination, she was asked to run for the Senate or Vice-Presidency. She refused, saying, "No thanks," to both.

Staffers around the Hill used to say, "Save me from Texas politicians." I agreed with them. The Texas politicians I have seen were generally power mad, wanting to play the Godfather of politics.

From all accounts, they are great at telling everyone else what to do. As for women, they liked theirs *mean and lean* and their drinks heavy, strong, and plentiful. And it's true, they liked everything big.

John Tower, though small, fit the bill. He could be very noisy and curse like a sailor. He had one of the biggest tempers on the Hill—Texas size—and often was on the verge of a fist fight at Hill parties.

Still, the women liked him for his toughness, and he liked them tough, too.

Lloyd Bentsen was a different kind of Texas fox, sly and cunning in gathering the ladies around him. He liked small get-togethers, and liked to dine and wine in his office or out of his office.

One of his favorite dining partners was said to be a very important gal—an assistant to a Cabinet officer. Staffers who saw her said she was one of the best-looking women to make herself at home on Capitol Hill and my waiters reported money was no object when Bentsen was dining with her.

Texas, of course, did not have a patent on sports. Take a staid state like Maryland. It produced a swinger named Brewster, who never did get the hang of keeping a low profile. Senator Daniel Brewster, nicknamed "Sonny," was a hell of a nice guy, but he did tend to be a bit conspicuous—and even made the news after he was defeated for reelection by being arrested and fined for driving "impaired" by alcohol. At the Hill he was more kindly treated.

Once, I recall, a close friend of mine found Sonny staggering around the Senate parking lot and got him safely to the office of the

Capitol Hill police so they could quietly see him home or phone someone to come get him.

As a Senator he kept things lively, getting a divorce from his wife to marry his college sweetheart. But it didn't last long, and he divorced and married again after his defeat.

The happy ending is that he now lectures on the dangers of alcoholism, was appointed to the Maryland governor's advisory council on alcoholism, and doesn't permit that ole demon rum in his house. "I nearly died of alcoholism," he is not ashamed to confess and admits that alcohol "impaired" his effectiveness in Congress.

Then there was the dude of Florida.

I remember George Smathers well, a very personable man, a good dresser, sharp, not conservative, a bit on the flashy side. Smathers was handsome, tall, in the LBJ tradition. They were friends.

Even before he cultivated Johnson's friendship, Smathers was best friends with John F. Kennedy, when Kennedy was a Senator. As a matter of fact, Smathers was friends with all the Kennedys, Robert and Edward, too.

George Smathers was strictly a ladies' man. All the women knew him, and he knew them. For he was a partygoer, a social climber. While he had very small personal resources, that didn't hold him back. For who needs money with friends like LBJ, Kerr, and the Kennedys? Smathers had it made.

I never saw him attend a Hill party with his wife. He would always leave with a pretty girl, sometimes with several. They were going on to a nightclub, they said.

Girls just swooned over George Smathers, much as they did over Jack Kennedy. Smathers was another "eligible married man," as the saying on the Hill went. He was eligible for a good time.

Stories went around the Hill that Smathers was a guest at Bobby Baker's house. There were actually two places you would frequently find Smathers and Bob Baker together—either in Baker's house in the South West section or the old Quorum Club, whose members were fun-loving legislators, lobbyists, and key Hill staffers.

I went there more than once. It had an intimate bar, very dimly lighted, soft music at all times, a speakeasy atmosphere. This was the headquarters for the B-girls of Capitol Hill, who would sit around the bar, waiting for one or another Senator, like a Venus's-flytrap, waiting for flies. These beauties did not hide their lovely flesh behind an abundance of clothes. They offered cleavage when cleavage was still a dirty word. And they liked wraparound skirts.

Once I counted, and saw Smathers surrounded by twelve pretty Hill staffers and bar girls, all fighting for his attention. He had his arm around one, was listening to another who was talking away. Suddenly, one of the girls pulled him down, and he ended up sitting on her lap, high stool and all. Everybody applauded.

I certainly wouldn't want to give the impression that all Senators played around with their own or someone else's female aides. Many maintained a friendly relationship that was simply that. Senator John McClellan of Arkansas would sometimes bring along one or two of his female aides at lunchtime and tease them mercilessly. But that was as far as it went. He was a very straitlaced man, and never was there a breath of scandal about him.

But where McClellan was a rare Senator was that he still seemed to be very much in love with his wife, Norma, after many years of marriage. Now that was unusual.

Not only was the Senator loyal to one woman. He also was loyal to one dessert. Every employee in the restaurant knew that, when Senator John McClellan ordered dessert, he meant apple pie with cheese, and he wanted *hot* apple pie.

Once the Senator sent back his pie, claiming it was not hot. The chef put the pie back under the broiler. While it was getting hot, the plate was getting hotter. The waitress took it and set the dessert dish on a dinner plate to serve it, warning McClellan, "The chef says the dish is very hot, and you'll get burned if you touch it. Be careful, Senator."

McClellan ignored her and grabbed the plate, pulling his hand back instantly, yelling, "Jesus Christ!"

Since the Senator was such an unemotional man—a bit on the dour side, you could never get a rise out of him—his outcry was the talk of the restaurant.

It was the only time. He was never heard to express any strong emotion again. But the story lives on!

When Milton Young of North Dakota announced that he was retiring at the end of his term in 1980, he was retiring with an unblemished record. He had served continuously in public office since 1924 and was never defeated for reelection. The Republican dean of the Senate, Young served longer consecutively than any other Republican in the history of the Upper Chamber.

His list of laurels seems endless—longest period of time any Senator served in leadership position in the twentieth century, for example. And in 1968 he received the highest percentage of votes of any Republican Senator who had an opponent in the election. He carried every county in the state.

But it's the man himself and his life-style that fascinated me even more, because Milton Young was a happy man. No playboy he, he even took his own wife to lunch regularly. Theirs was a his-and-hers Senatorial team. Patricia, who was one of the nicest people I knew, was the Senator's secretary before marrying him.

To be part of her husband's life, Pat continued to work for her husband—but without pay. One of the most touching scenes I will remember is watching Pat help her husband walk after poor health made him feeble. She would get him to the very door of the Senate chamber, but then someone else would take over because a wife is not permitted to enter, even to help her husband gallantly to his seat.

Mike Mansfield, the old college professor from Missoula, Montana, didn't dally, but he was among the top tipplers on the Hill.

His own party members said he would go down as the worst Majority Leader of the Senate. What was wrong? He didn't have finesse. The Senators were always griping that Mike was too blunt and also lazy and lackadaisical. He didn't put push behind legislation. Lyndon got him in there, but he sure wasn't much help to Lyndon. All he had going for him was loyalty to LBJ—Lyndon had him eating out of his hand. He would not have been leader without Lyndon. And Mansfield didn't have anything moneywise.

Nor was he one of the well-dressed men of the Hill. He would only get really dressed up when some foreign dignitary was coming. He alone dared to leave his jacket in the office and come into the restaurant wearing old pants and a checkered shirt.

But Mansfield was a good man as Club members go, and an honest man, and Carter did recognize this in making him ambassador to Japan.

As Jimmy Carter would be in later years, he, too was a former governor of Georgia, yet there never was a more modest man: "Richard Brevard Russell, Jr., Democrat of Winder, Ga." That was the single line he permitted about himself in the biographical section of the Congressional Directory.

He took the place of Carl Hayden as president pro tempore, and, it was said, was better at the job. For Russell didn't rub people the wrong way and was a much smarter politician. Hayden had been a pushover for other politicians and lobbyists. But Russell stood fast to his convictions and had deep concern for the welfare of the country.

Russell was easy to please. He liked his booze and his women. However, he did not attend parties, but took his ladies to lunch. Just a variety of girls, blonde, brunette, redhead, he didn't discriminate. He just wanted them shapely and jolly, and was especially fond of those who laughed and talked a lot.

When Russell died, Sam Nunn came to Washington, November 7, 1972, to fill Russell's unexpired term. Nunn made a good appearance, but was a stickler for work and did no entertaining while I was there.

Russell had been a bachelor, involved with many women. Herman Talmadge from the same state, on the other hand, was obsessed with one woman—his wife. I never thought they would get a divorce. She seemed to be underfoot all the time, or hovering around him.

She acted like the boss. I would get orders from her and orders from him. I once asked him how to handle it. Talmadge said, "Hell, just give her whatever she wants."

Betty Talmadge entertained a lot. She was a queen bee and made everyone know she was. She was a take-charge gal. I would stand there entranced as she made her grand entrance into a party. As my dad would say, "She was a lot of woman."

Robert Byrd and Harry Byrd were better known as "the fiddler and the apple king." How strange that both Virginias—east and West—happened to have a Byrd in the Senate, and such birds at that.

Harry Byrd, Jr., has the whole state of Virginia on a string—newspapers, TV and radio stations, land holdings. He's the "apple king of the nation." Since Harry inherited much of his wealth and prestige on the Hill from his father, the famed Senator with the same name, many Senators maintain that he does not deserve as much credit for his position as his West Virginia colleague.

Robert C. Byrd of Sophia, West Virginia, came up the hard way from abject poverty to Majority Leader of the Senate. Colleagues say Harry Byrd may have his state on a string, but Robert has the whole Senate on a string. And though Harry Byrd may be one of the richest men in the Club, Robert Byrd is rich too, except that his riches lie in power.

By Hill money standards, Robert is a relatively poor man. So how did he make it to the top leadership?

He made it to the top by giving slavish service in the early days after being elected to the Senate in 1958. Such power doesn't happen overnight. He used to do anything any other Senator wanted done, short of shining his shoes. But now *he* cracks the whip.

Even so, he's not nearly as tough as Lyndon Johnson, who kept Democratic Senators as serfs or captives by sheer domination when he was majority leader.

The difference between LBJ and Robert B. was that Robert could relax but Lyndon never could. Secure in his Hill position, Majority Leader Byrd allowed himself the luxury of turning to a hobby and making up for all the fun he had missed through the years.

Suddenly, he became a showman. Invite him anywhere, he'd take along his fiddle and entertain the crowd. He played at small private parties around the Hill and before the Washington press corps at a huge banquet given by the Washington Press Club—sawing away at "Amazing Grace," Carter's favorite.

Then suddenly he was on TV—even appearing on Grand Ole Opry. Then the Hill crowd heard he was cutting a record.

At the Capitol, some said he had finally flipped his wig because he started appearing in the halls and on the subway with his fiddle and playing it as he went. When he didn't have the fiddle, he would be carrying a transistor radio turned on high.

In fact, one gal in his office, who had been his ardent supporter, finally left his staff, telling some of us that she was becoming embarrassed because of everyone laughing at him behind his back when he "fiddled around in public, especially on the Senate subway where all his colleagues and tourists ride."

For once, I defended a Senator's behavior, giving my opinion that playing a little music was a lot more wholesome than getting falling down drunk and having to be led back to one's office.

I have always been a Robert Byrd fan, for the simple reason that one cannot help but stand in awe of his record for achievement and public service—first man to be selected as West Virginian of the Year twice; chosen by the Gallagher Presidents Reports in 1974 as one of the five "Best Public Servants of Achievement"; chosen in 1978 by the *U. S. News and World Report* as "the fourth most influential man in the United States."

I found Robert Byrd inspiring in another way—his love of family. He was interested in everyone's family. He especially cared about the family of everyone who worked for him, and I remember once when he took a bunch of West Virginia kids to the cafeteria. He seemed to be personally interested in their attitudes toward life and their goals—and they were just grammar-school kids.

In the restaurants, Robert Byrd was not the best tipper, but since he was not overly blessed with worldly goods, like the rest of the Club, we didn't fault him. I would hear Democratic Senators talking about the leader. I remember one said, "The best thing you can say about him is he isn't like LBJ." They were talking about how LBJ would tell them "how it's going to be and when and where and be absolutely unmovable." In contrast, they said, they felt free to stop in and ask Byrd to make an exception in their case or do them some favor.

Robert Byrd had an uncanny way of knowing how to please

people and of doing nice things. For example, if someone had a bedraggled tie, he would pretend to like it and say, "Let's trade." The other person would end up with a custom-made tie, and he would end up with a friend for life.

Senator John Warner, the Hill crowd crowed, became the first Senator to be elected on his wife's publicity. I've known Warner for years and liked him, and I knew Elizabeth Taylor slightly, before she met him.

I did not ask Liz for her favorite chicken recipe, but got it from a friend of the Warners, Sylvia Stewart of Alexandria, who helped John with his campaign for Senator from Virginia.

The favorite part of the chicken for Elizabeth is the wings. But here is the recipe for the whole hen, as Elizabeth gave it to Sylvia. Even the title is Elizabeth's:

ELIZABETH TAYLOR WARNER ROAST CHICKEN

Prepare a 3-pound roasting chicken for the oven, save the giblets, cleaning and dusting with salt and pepper. Then fill with a good grade of prepared stuffing combined with 2 beaten eggs, ½ cup milk, and the proportion you like of chopped celery, chopped onion.

Roast the chicken at 450 degrees for an hour and turn down to 300 degrees, until very tender.

Meanwhile, prepare the gravy, boiling the giblets until tender and then chopping them up fine. Take the stock in which they have been boiled and mix with flour to thicken. Season with onion salt, thyme, basil, salt and pepper, and soy sauce, to taste.

Now you can eat with your favorite star. But if, as in her case, the wings are your downfall, just buy a package of wings, sold separately at the grocery store, and roast them along with your whole chicken.

Clinton Anderson of New Mexico, a former insurance man, had been Secretary of Agriculture under Truman, who had picked him out of the whole Congress as the image of the super farmer. The Hill crowd found it amusing that Truman should have chosen a champagne-loving man for his image of a farmer. In fact, they pointed out, nothing about Clint reminded one of a farmer.

He didn't dress like a farmer—he loved good clothes. He didn't eat like a farmer—he preferred gourmet food. The Hill crowd decided Truman must have picked Anderson because he liked his dry sense of humor.

Evidently, Anderson agreed with his Hill colleagues that he wasn't the farmer type because he resigned from his Cabinet post in May of 1948, after less than three years, to run, successfully, for the Senate.

Senator James Buckley of New York was a stinker. Even his conservative colleagues on the Hill complained to me that he was stuffy and acted holier-than-thou, while availing himself of the party circuit.

What really burned the Senators up was that he did not reciprocate. He did practically no entertaining but showed up to have a few drinks at everyone else's party. This did not add to his popularity. I was not surprised when he turned out to be a flash in the pan—losing after one term—though he may try again.

But while he was there, following his election in 1970, he made my life a little harder as well. In the restaurants, Buckley was hard to please. His food wasn't hot enough, or the service wasn't fast enough. I had to bite my tongue to keep from telling him that the service might be a little faster if he tipped a little better. He was very cautious with a tip.

Delaware's William Roth, Jr., was the most obstinate man I ever met. I remember the time he decided to take some guests into the Dirksen Building elevator. This particular elevator was the one Senate restaurant staff used for transporting carts with hot food to Senators who were eating in their offices or hideaways.

Senator Roth had made up his mind that staff could not use the elevator until he and his friends were through with it. We mentioned that other Senators' lunches were getting cold, while the food was standing by. He said, "Positively no. You'll have to wait."

And wait we did. We just stood by and said nothing. We had done all we could—advised Roth that other Senators' lunches were getting cold. But he couldn't have cared less. And since he was a member of the Sweetest Little Club in the World, he was king.

Roughshod Roth was far from the most popular man with the restaurant staff, for he was very hard to please, tipped very little, and maintained a haughty air, speaking to none of us.

William Scott of Virginia was one of the worst-dressed Senators ever to serve in the Senate, according to the *Washington Star*. (Bets were taken on when he'd last had his suit cleaned.) And one of the most traveled Senators. On the Hill they called him "King of the Junketeers." Every part of the globe. Born 1915. One termer, 1972 to 1978. Used it well to educate self.

Senator Alan Bible of Nevada was said to have been the most complicated man of his time on the Hill, next to Senator Robert Kerr, who had so many deals going that his closest aides hardly knew what he was up to.

Bible lived at the Capitol Hill Hotel, which is now the police headquarters for the Hill. He and Senator George Aiken of Vermont both lived there, but the two men were poles apart. Aiken was a blue nose, and very straitlaced, whereas Bible prided himself on posing as one of the "bad boys" of the Hill.

I would hear him shouting in the hall, perhaps for laughs, that he was going to legalize prostitution. It was legal in Nevada and why not give this blessing to everyone? With a few drinks he didn't care whether he was proclaiming this to a member of the Club or a constituent. He was also interested in doing something to help nudist colonies gain acceptance—or so he said.

Bible was a heavy drinker who could hold his liquor, but you would know how many he had by how loud his voice became. The

Hill crowd kidded that Bible was doing his bit for the antipollution program by being a bad example—I never saw him without a cigarette in his hand.

The great irony about Bible was his name.

Richard Schweiker of Pennsylvania was a poor dresser, no good as a mixer. Yet he was Ronald Reagan's Vice-Presidential choice in 1976. Reagan's downfall was in the belief Schweiker could do him some good because he came from one of the largest Eastern states. That was a mistake. Schweiker was not that powerful or that much of a politician. Like Senator Dole, he was not strong enough.

When Schweiker first came to the Hill, he was considered to be a hippie, since he wore his hair long and over his shirt collar. He saw he was off base and cut it to Hill standards.

The Senator received the Anti-Defamation League award of the B'nai B'rith in 1971. He belongs to the American Legion, Navy League, and Sons of the American Revolution. He was on the Senate Select Committee on Nutrition and Human Needs, which Reagan might reason would influence parents because he was concerned with their children and their welfare. McGovern was on that too—chairman, in fact—and it didn't help him, either.

Schweiker had the hippie vote. His attitude suited them, but it wasn't enough. Reagan and he were a good team on that score— Reagan conservative and he liberal. But on the Hill it was said that Schweiker was too liberal to be a Republican and that having him hanging from Reagan's kite had helped bring it down prematurely.

The thing that I remember most about Roman Hruska was that he was proud of sharing the religion of Thomas Jefferson, who was a Unitarian. And also the religion of Justice Harold Burton of Ohio. Hruska hailed from Nebraska.

You will notice that I like to avoid mentioning whether a Senator is a Republican or Democrat. To me it doesn't matter much. I have learned that a man on the Hill is more under the influence of the state and region he comes from and the Hill colleagues who get hold of him than he is under the influence of a political party.

That reminds me of the story about the aging Senator who was asked what medicine he was taking to keep himself so peppy and interested in all the goings on on the Hill.

"Don't need medicine," he said. "I'm under the influence of money."

I have my own list of ten favorite Senators—living and dead. They just happen to be the ones I like, but not for great legislation or any particular good deeds aimed at me. In my book, they're tops.

1. Mark Hatfield of Oregon.
2. Gale McGee of Wyoming.
3. Clifford Hansen of Wyoming.
4. Hugh Scott of Pennsylvania.
5. John Kennedy of Massachusetts.
6. Hubert Humphrey of Minnesota.
7. Jennings Randolph of West Virginia.
8. B. Everett Jordan of North Carolina.
9. John McClellan of Arkansas.
10. Frank Carlson of Kansas.

If I had to give a reason for liking these men, it would have to be for their attitude toward people and life, corny though it may seem. Take John Fitzgerald Kennedy. He had an eagerness to help underprivileged and aged and mentally retarded people. He had grace. I never thought there would be a guy living like Kennedy, who, with his resources and wealth, still so loved humanity.

Sure, he played around and loved a lot of women. But he also loved humanity.

Frank Carlson was equally nice to everyone. In all the years I knew him, I never heard him complain about anything—except Richard Nixon, a painful subject to him. The Senator retired in

1969, after serving eighteen years, just at the time Nixon entered the White House.

After his retirement, Frank Carlson remained an adviser to the Republican Party, even coming back to help Nixon during the Watergate scandal. But Nixon's tricks dismayed, shocked, and outraged the Senator so much that advising the President was extremely distasteful to him. It almost killed him, he told me.

The last time I saw Carlson on Capitol Hill, Nixon was still hanging on to his office. Over a cup of coffee, Carlson told me that he was fed up. He told me he had retired to get away from Washington and Hill activities. He hated to say no, when the Republicans asked for his help. But he couldn't tolerate Nixon's shady activities. He was so disillusioned, this time he would just have to refuse to get involved.

And he did just that, staying at his snug cattle ranch at Concordia, Kansas.

John Williams of Delaware was the man who said, "No Senator should be allowed to run for reelection after he reaches sixty-five." He introduced a bill to that effect. But it got nowhere. I could have told him in advance that no Senator is going to vote himself out of the Sweetest Little Club in the World.

Williams was the Senator who was given full recognition for having exposed the Bobby Baker–Lyndon Johnson–Robert Kerr connection. Kerr had demanded $400,000 for his vote in defeating a measure. Bobby Baker attested to it, when the Bobby Baker influence-peddling scandal broke. According to Bobby, Kerr was furious that the payoff was whittled down to only $100,000, and even that was $400 short.

At the time Humphrey was scared, too, at the Bobby Baker mess. So was Dirksen. Williams wanted to expose the whole bunch. HHH was afraid the scandal would reflect on him, as Vice-President, with his Lyndon Johnson connection. Dirksen, as Senate minority leader, had been playing ball with Johnson.

I really respected and liked Senator Williams a great deal. He was a man who felt a Senator should always be above reproach. In all the time I knew him, he was always a gentleman and a fair man.

A real conservative Republican, Williams once told me that the government has just about twice as many people as it needed. "And that," he asserted, "spelled inefficiency." He really hated the cocktail circuit. Felt it was a bad influence on government. He himself was a nondrinker, and I never saw him attend a party.

Lee Metcalf of Montana had the record for the shortest session in history as president pro tem. Three seconds. When he presided, he took three seconds to recess the Senate. His bio in the Record was also short—5½ lines. They called him the Gray Ghost because you never heard about him.

Around the Hill, Lawton Chiles of Florida was looked at as one of the relatively poor members of the Club. Instead of making his mark in a show of affluence, he made his mark in a show of hard work. He received the Special Gavel Award for being the only Senator to preside over the U.S. Senate for 100 hours during 1971.

Samuel Ichiye Hayakawa took Tunney's California Senate seat, much to the delight of the Hill crowd. Everything about Hayakawa tickled their fancy, his tam-o'-shanter, his dancing. He's a very friendly man, a new breed, the type who just naturally inspires good-humored, amusing stories from those around him. Some of the stories were even true—such as that he took disco dancing lessons, and at seventy-three, goes discoing with young beauties at least once a week.

Adlai E. Stevenson III of Illinois was a pleasant, easy-to-please guy, a good tipper, who never complained. As one of the younger Senators, he was a sociable man, who attended all the Hill parties. However, he himself, did not entertain on the Hill, and as far as I remember, did not even use his charge.

Senator Stevenson always appeared well-groomed, and had the reputation of being an egghead like his father.

Hugh Scott of Pennsylvania was another Senate member of the egghead variety. For some reason I got along well with the eggheads on the Hill, better than with the rest of the Senators. I guess the eggheads were smart enough not to let my lack of fancy degrees stand in the way.

With Senator Scott, I shared an interest in antique furnishings and art. In 1966 he wrote a book called *The Golden Age of Chinese Art*, which is a joy to read and leaf through.

I saw Hugh Scott as one of the great men of the Hill, very hard-working and an authority on many phases of politics. He was also an excellent speaker who could organize his thoughts very rapidly.

Scott started writing books back in 1949 when he was a once-defeated candidate for reelection to the House, who had tried again and made it. The name of that first book was *How to Go into Politics*.

In 1968, after he had been chairman of the Republican National Committee and had become a Senator, he took another plunge into the writing game with a second book, *How to Run for Public Office and Win.*

The following year, 1969, he became minority leader of the Senate, retaining the post until he retired at the end of his term in January 1977. Scott replaced Dirksen as the top member of his party in the Senate.

I am happy to say that my discussions about art were not all one way. He was very interested in a tapestry which I have in my living room and which had been given to Marie Antoinette by a Marks family of Austria. One of the family had presented it to her at the French court. It depicts a woman pushing a child in a swing.

I had the tapestry photographed for the Senator, and he was knowledgeable about the unusual weaving around the border, which had a special significance for him.

Also, he was one of the few men who made me feel more than an employee of the Club, by inviting me to his annual Christmas as a guest and not as the caterer. I appreciated it.

Hugh Scott was one of those rare men on the Hill, beloved by all his staff. They looked at him as a friendly professor who taught them politics while enriching their lives in many ways. He had, I believe, the largest staff of interns on the Hill—even more than Ted Kennedy. Everyone wanted to "study" with this authority on politics.

Illinois' Chuck Percy, a personable man with a quick smile, enjoys listening to and telling a rough joke. A slim, well-dressed man, who makes an excellent appearance, Percy was the youngest man to be elected to the board of directors of Bell & Howell—at the age of twenty-three.

Although he is one of the more wealthy men in the Senate, he had a lot of tragedy in his life. His first wife, Jeanne, died following a short illness, leaving him with three small children. One of his daughters, Valerie, was murdered in her bed. Percy offered a $50,000 reward for information leading to resolution of the crime. Nothing came of it. Her death remains a mystery.

Percy is not the only Senator to sustain tragedy.

Joseph R. Biden of Delaware, a nice guy, entered the Senate as quite a sensation. His wife, Neilia, had been killed en route to join him in Washington. Their two sons were not hurt, thank God. His only daughter, Naomi, born in 1971, had died earlier.

Truth is truth, and I must report there are so many man-hungry women on the Hill, that even as the Senator grieved, he was already becoming a target for the desperate huntresses.

Joe was not a drinker, not in the cocktail circuit, and not encouraging or seeking female company, but they waylaid him in the dining rooms and in the halls, and on the subway cars that shuttle between Senate office buildings and the Capitol—waiting to ride with him.

For a time Biden caused as much commotion in the halls and the subway as Ted Kennedy. Hill wits said he was rivaling Kennedy as "most eligible." Then, they'd add that the only difference was that Ted Kennedy was married.

It was a relief to everyone except the frustrated females left behind when Joe Biden finally picked a bride, Jill Tracy.

Senator Jesse Helms of North Carolina was a nondrinker and a religious man. He did no Hill entertaining—was a family man. Helms was in the broadcasting business, radio stations. Mary Tucker, who had worked for Margaret Chase Smith, was a caseworker for Senator Helms, and she would talk to me by the hour about how great a man Helms was.

Seldom was a Senator so appreciated by the members of his staff, and he reciprocated their goodwill by holding a big party for them at his home in Arlington.

Helms had an unusual career in that he came up from the ranks of Hill staffers. He was AA to Senator Willis Smith and later to Senator Alton Lennon, both of North Carolina. Also rather unusual is the fact that Helms was once city editor of the *Raleigh Times*.

Just to show the kind of thing Helms was interested in, he was a member of the board of directors of Camp Willow Run, a religious youth camp at Littleton, North Carolina, and deacon and Sunday School teacher at the Hayes Barton Baptist Church at Raleigh.

Around the Hill, Helms was called a lovable egghead, to set him apart from the eggheads who were not as likeable as he.

Senator Daniel Ken Inouye of Hawaii had lost an arm during combat in World War II. However, he neither demanded nor wanted any special treatment. I would see him do things with his one arm that seemed impossible. He had excellent control of all his muscles and was so adept that he was able to light his cigarettes with one hand.

He did everything for himself, and the lack of one arm was inconspicuous. Inouye wanted to be treated just like anyone else, and did not want anyone to rush forward and try to help him. If we wanted to do anything to make his dining easier, we had to do it before he arrived at the table—very discreetly.

He was a charming man with an excellent personality, pleasant, easy to get along with, a good mixer. A good dresser, who would take a social drink and manage it well, he was an asset at parties. Inouye was a devoted family man and not a skirt chaser, making him a member of a minority on the Hill.

While he did very little entertaining, he did sponsor a party for the placing of the statue from Hawaii in the Capitol's Statuary Hall—King Kamehameha. It was a rather large party, and about 250 people attended. I recall that his wife, Margaret, didn't come to this party, and that, surprisingly, Hawaiian food was not served but a buffet supper, a huge steamship round of beef and spiced shrimp.

I am glad that I knew Wallace Bennett who was elected to the Senate in 1950 from Utah and reelected in 1956, 1962, and again in 1968. The Senator was a devout Mormon, and renewed my faith in the human race.

In fact, his life was an example for others. If it is possible to say a man exuded niceness, I would say it about him. He and his wife, Frances, were almost inseparable. They truly enjoyed each other's company, and she spent a lot of time on the Hill, especially as Bennett grew more feeble.

I remember when they celebrated their fiftieth wedding anniversary. They talked to me about a party, but decided it would be too expensive. What they wanted would have cost about $250, but the Senator was saving his money for his retirement. It ended up with the couple handling their own party in the Senator's office with my unofficial help.

Those who want to know the thinking of my friend Bennett can read the book he authored, *Why I Am a Mormon.*

George Murphy of California is the guy who drove Senator Margaret Chase Smith frantic, and no doubt he enjoyed it. At least, he never made any obvious attempt to placate her. The teetotaling lady legislator grumbled about the time Murphy spent in cocktail lounges. She complained that when it came time for important business, he was nowhere to be found. Then like the cavalry, he'd suddenly arrive just in time for the vote and get a big Hollywood hero's welcome from those Senators who needed his support.

George Murphy loved to be surrounded by beautiful women. I would see him with gorgeous women, young, elegant, expensively dressed, chic, Hollywood-type girls, who definitely did not work on the Hill. He would escort them into the Senators' private dining room.

The Senator hung out at the Sheraton Park. He had the reputation of being a drinker, but he sure didn't show it. He held it well. He didn't attend many parties on the Hill. That way he kept the gossip down or tried to. He got mad when the press caught him with a girl, and I once heard him exclaim, "That goddamn press. They never tell the truth." Someone retorted, "Maybe he doesn't either."

At the Senate restaurant, he was a generous tipper and easy to please.

Senator Margaret Chase Smith had the shortest biography in the whole Congressional Directory. After her name, there was the single word "Republican." Nothing about Maine. Nothing about the fact that she was the widow of Senator Clyde Harold Smith. Nothing about the fact that she had been a schoolteacher in Skowhegan or a business manager of a country newspaper. Some said her biography showed her modesty. But others claimed she simply didn't want anyone to know anything about her.

I'm afraid to say I did not have too good a relationship with the lady Senator. It was my misfortune to be the recipient of her complaints. Since military and veterans' problems were of special interest to her, she felt she was an authority on what was going on at the Pentagon.

She would catch me in the hall or at the door, and complain about the restaurant deficit. She would ask why the Senate Restaurant could not operate without a deficit if the Pentagon charged lower prices and could. She jawboned me so often about the sterling quality of the Pentagon restaurant management, as compared to the Senate restaurant management, that I finally got my dander up and went there to investigate.

I learned actually more than I wanted to know—that the Pentagon was covering up its deficit just the way we were. They told me there was no way they could prepare the food at the prices set by their board.

I took notes, and I was ready for my next go-around. The next time Margaret Smith caught me, I pulled out the paper and showed her the figures that I had gotten from their catering service. I also showed her many Pentagon prices that were higher than ours.

Most important of all, I explained that an outside firm controlled prices and labor costs at the Pentagon. This meant an outsider decided the grade or quality of the meats purchased. The Senate, I told her, was not ready to relinquish this control.

At this writing, it still isn't.

I remember how, in the 1960's, the Senate hired Horwath & Horwath, restaurant efficiency experts, to make a study and recommend what could be done to make the Senate restaurants more efficient. They charged around $100,000, and nothing came of it. Even Marriott turned down the offer to run our restaurants, when they heard our requirements, saying they could not make a profit.

Most chains will not promise to use all American foods. They use a considerable amount of imported beef and meats of all kinds as well as seafoods to get them a lot cheaper. Nor will they promise to use only top-quality foods.

The basic rule we lived by was that everything must be American—domestic and top of its line. Caviar was the only thing we got from overseas—and that not too often.

But to return to life with Margaret Chase Smith, another of her frequent complaints to me concerned odors of food in her Russell Building office. Her office was above the Russell restaurant, true enough, but three flights up. No one else complained, even those who really had reason to. You don't tell Senators to try moving to the other side of the building, and so I bit my tongue when I was tempted to come up with the perfect solution.

It wasn't just food odors that bothered the good Senator. It was also smoke. If she was in an elevator, she would not allow anyone to enter who was smoking—and this in the days before Califano and his edicts. And if an elevator stopped for her, and someone like Jim

Eastland was there—puffing on his big cigar—she would not get on.

When there was a private party in one of the committee rooms, Senator Smith would frequently call me or Senator Jordan, to complain that people were walking around in the hall with drinks in their hands. Over and over we explained that while drinks were not permitted in the Senate dining rooms, they could be served in private rooms to those who were providing their own liquor. Of course it was true that we frequently arranged the purchasing of the liquor for the group holding the event, but that was beside the point.

But I was not Senator Smith's favorite target. That honor as I started to tell, went to Senator George Murphy, the ex-movie star, of Hollywood. Whatever he did irritated her. He wore a white carnation every day. And that drove Margaret Chase Smith wild. She said he had copied it from her—and I wouldn't be surprised if he had. He delighted in tormenting her, and before he arrived with his carnation, the rosebud on her lapel was the highlight of the Senate. She never voted without it.

Murphy and Smith would make remarks in private that would get back to each other. But the time came when Senator Smith emerged victorious. Murphy had given her the perfect opening. He had failed to arrive for an important vote, and she was furious. The sergeant at arms had to retrieve him from the men's bar at the Shoreham Hotel.

After he arrived in the Chamber, Senator Smith got up and gave a speech about having been kept waiting three hours—she was that steamed up.

The lady Senator responded with bitterness when she failed in her reelection bid in 1972. She immediately told her staff she was going to let them all go except for one person who would take care of the mail—Mary Tucker. Of course General William Lewis, Jr., her AA, would still be there too. He was totally dedicated to her and worked harder than anyone else on the Hill. His every move was in her behalf, and she ate with him, left at the end of the day with him, and the two were near constant companions.

But this is the story of Mary Tucker. The term would have been up in January. But one day, over the Christmas holidays, she went to attend a funeral in New York. When she returned, she found that Senator Smith had fired her.

Mary frequently rode into work with me, and so I shared her distress when she told me that the short-tempered Senator had fired her for being gone just one day. Though she only lost two weeks' work, what worried her greatly was the black mark on her record, after she had worked on the Hill for some twenty years. It would certainly not help her get a new job.

I assured Mary that she would certainly be in demand. And sure enough, she got a job with Senator Jesse Helms of North Carolina.

At the end, only Senator Smith and Lewis manned the office. Actually, because of the Election Day Massacre, constituents had to cool their heels and wait for the new man, William Dodd Hathaway, a Democrat, to take office before they received help with their problems.

Part II

...and a
Cast of Thousands

5

Prima Donnas-
Staffs and
Stiffs

When I went to Capitol Hill in 1959, there were about 4,000 Senate employees. When I left in 1975, the Senate population had grown to 18,000, not including Senators themselves, or interns who work for free, or near to it, just for the experience.

One Senator for example, Hugh Scott of Pennsylvania, at one time had eighty-four interns under his sponsorship in his office.

Senator William Proxmire looked at the exploding Hill population with a mixture of anger and contempt. He bestowed his Golden Fleece award in August 1979 on the Congress of the United States for fleecing the taxpayers by hiring so many additional staffers. Calling it an example of ridiculous government spending, Proxmire pointed out that in the last ten years, the House of Representatives had increased its employees by 60 percent. But the Senate had gone hog-wild and increased its staff by a "fat, whopping 100 percent."

The cost of the Senate staff, however, has not increased a mere 100 percent, he said, but rose 270 percent—from $150 million of ten years ago to $550 million a year today.

The thorny Proxmire said, "Senators and staff are now stumbling over themselves. Additional staff generates additional work, much of it unneeded at a time when Congress has difficulty coping with its regular routine and oversight functions."

The Senator adds that then new buildings are needed to house the additional staff, and that means more restaurants, more garages, more committee rooms, again the need for more staffers to handle these facilities.

The Hart Senate Office Building under construction at this writing is a perfect example. It will require hundreds of additional staffers when it is completed several years hence.

I'm glad I won't be there.

As far as I was concerned, all Hill staffdom was divided into three parts—prima donnas, stiffs, and regular guys and gals. The latter, though in the minority, made life bearable.

I still shudder now when I look back and see so clearly how I was forever rising to the bait when some staffer gave me a hard time. It was a case of the pecking order—some Senators gave their people a hard time, and these staffers in turn got rid of their hostility on the restaurant staff.

I remember, for example, that I had a really violent complaint from Ethel Low, who was Senator Robert Byrd's administrative assistant, regarding the prices of food in the cafeteria. She used as her yardstick for comparison Swiss steak, which was priced at 85¢ for a six-ounce portion. She said that the House restaurant she had visited had only charged 65¢ for the same size portion.

Immediately, I went to my office and called the manager of the Longworth Cafeteria—a person whom I had taken under my wing at the request of a friend and gotten a job.

I found out from her that the House restaurant was selling a five-ounce portion of Swiss steak for 95¢, instead of the 85¢ we were charging for a larger portion.

I asked Miss Lowe if I could come to see her, stopped by in Senator Byrd's office, and informed her I had found out the Longworth restaurant was selling the steak for *more* money than our restaurant, not *less*. I added that I didn't appreciate her bringing me untruths.

She flipped, and reported me to the Rules Committee, charging that I was impudent, unbearable to deal with, and a very poor manager.

Hugh Alexander, a Rules Committee staffer, sent for me and advised me that I'd opened my mouth just once too often at the wrong time. "Never," he said, "*never* contact a key staff member of a Senator's office to contradict his or her notion of truth."

I answered, "I did it. And I stand by it. Do you want to fire me?"

"Get the hell out of here," he replied, "and get back to work. No. You'd better stop and have a cup of coffee. It might help you to feel better. Try to get used to this place, and quit being so righteous. Remember, you're in politics, and this is *the* Club."

Daniel Minchew became almost a household word as the result of Senator Herman Talmadge's problems with the Ethics Committee and the FBI investigators.

I remember Minchew very well. I got to know him because he was very active on the Senator's behalf. He was a nice guy, but he was always crying the blues: "You know, the Senator doesn't have any money." I got sick of hearing that, especially as I thought of what they were doing to the deficit.

I told Diamond and Chairman Jordan, "Hell, how are we going to cover the breakage of china, the cleaning up, and the use of our kitchen staff to prepare this food free? That's not going to happen while I'm here."

Senator Jordan and Diamond would soothe me by saying, "Well, hold on. Minchew said Senator Talmadge is interested in helping this group. They can't afford a party, but the Senator wants to make them feel good."

The way the Senator—or Minchew, I never did find out which—helped outside groups feel good was by letting them bring in their own food to hold a party. They would let us prepare it, and then they would serve as their own waiters. We would be paid nothing for the use of the room or the preparation of the food.

By kicking up a storm I finally worked out a compromise with Diamond and Jordan. We would charge the Talmadge gang a flat fee for labor and use of china and linen and the use of the room, plus the cleaning up. It was a mere $1.50 a head.

This meant that for a party of fifty people we would only receive $75. That didn't even pay for the clean-up help and the linen bill. But it did keep me from feeling too much of a chump.

As a matter of fact, the clean-up bill for fifty people was $124. So our loss was $49—unless you added what it cost us to have our kitchen staff prepare the food.

But then, I got hot under the collar again as Talmadge's office pulled a fast one, and I discovered that we were being reimbursed for a party of fifty people, whereas 250 guests had been served.

I went storming into Senator Jordan's office. Jordan laughed and said, "Hurst, we're not going to get rid of that deficit anyway. I've been around here all these years, and there's always been a deficit. The only difference is now they call it a deficit, and they used to call it 'horse hire' to cover it up."

The difference in aides to Senators is amazing. Some are like tigers, and some are timid as mice. I'll never forget the man who gave up too soon. He was the administrative assistant to Henry Bellmon, when the Senator came to Washington from Oklahoma in January of 1970. In fact, the Senator had brought him from Oklahoma, because he was a good man.

But the AA was a man of little faith. He sat in the dining room and sadly said, "The Senator will never run again so I'm quitting." I tried to tell him not to pay attention to any discouraging remarks a Senator makes in midterm, because once they get established in Washington and get to liking the Club atmosphere of the Senate, wild horses could not drag them away.

But the AA could not believe this and kept saying there was no way his Senator would run for another term. Soon after he stopped in to tell me he was quitting. He did quit, and the Senator kept running and is still in the Senate as of this writing.

Some Hill aides rise to the top. Lyndon Baines Johnson did it, going from Congressional aide to President of the United States. And even before that, LBJ had been a lowly messenger and elevator operator. And John Connally, the governor of Texas, who aspired to the Presidency, got his start on Capitol Hill as LBJ's secretary.

The man to watch now is Senator Gary Hart, whom I used to know as Senator McGovern's campaign manager. He has something of LBJ's fire and political ESP.

Hart may be one of the key figures in solving the energy crisis. Even before others were hitting the panic button, Hart was in the fray, advocating synthetic and every kind of fuel combination, and claiming there was positively no reason why a crisis could not be averted.

Some Hill aides rise to the top financially.

There are many husband-and-wife teams on the Hill. This does not mean they always work for the same legislator, but that they ride to work together in the morning, going to their individual Hill jobs. But in one particular case I am thinking of, they did work for the same Senator.

They were a good team in learning from the Senator, as well, following his lead in every way. By the time they retired, they were living like kings, taking cruises, and returning to their spacious palace of a home. They had invested in the stocks he had recommended, and they are still going strong, raking in about $200,000 in dividends and interest as well as their combined retirement pay.

At least they enjoyed life, even while they were around the Senate, hobnobbing with their beneficent godfather. They lived high and enjoyed every minute, sharing their good fortune by taking friends to lunch or dinner and ordering only the best.

But another couple, who worked on the Hill, seemed very pathetic. They lived in a rooming house. And I felt sorry for them and commented on what a pity it was they couldn't earn a decent living between them. Someone laughed and said, "Don't feel sorry for them. They can put their hands on a half-million dollars in cash any minute they need it. They're investing and saving every penny toward retirement."

I no longer felt sorry for them when I saw them dining out on hot dogs from the carry-out shop. But once habits are formed, they're hard to break. This couple is retired now, too, and they still live the way they did on Capitol Hill. They did buy a house, but it was a small cramped one in a neighborhood not appropriate to their considerable wealth.

I have noticed that a Senator frequently picks aides who are quite like himself. A teetotaling Senator is apt to make sure a staff assistant doesn't drink before he hires him. A Senator who drinks likes to have an aide who can help him put away a bottle after the secretaries have left for the day, and things have grown more quiet. Senator Lyndon Johnson was a great one for gathering a few favorite staffers around him at the end of the day to open a bottle and listen to praise for how well he had handled various difficult situations that day.

Though they would start out with praise of the boss, with enough drinks, aides would eventually tell Lyndon where he'd gone wrong and what they would have done had they been majority leader.

I'll never forget the night a staffer—not Lyndon Johnson's—was caught by Capitol Hill police peeing into a sink. He had gotten so drunk going from party to party after hours in the committee rooms that he no longer knew what he was doing.

The only reason the Hill police caught him was because they had been told to watch him so he wouldn't hurt himself before he got out of the building. This kind of escort service is standard procedure for the members of the Sweetest Little Club in the World AND all their entourage, from trusted adviser to court jester.

The Capitol police are separate and apart from the District of Columbia police department. They are there to help the Senators and not to moralize. They can arrest a man and turn him over to the District police, but this seldom happens. The Hill handles its problems in its own way.

In the case of the staffer whose weak kidneys matched his weak judgment, he was not arrested. A report was made for the use of the sergeant at arms, but nothing came of it, outside of its making the rounds of the gossips on the Hill.

After all, they said, the guy was a decent sort when sober.

That was about the same thing as what happened when a girl started to dance nude on the table at a Senate staffers' party. Nothing. I had to call the Capitol police to get her wiggling person down off the table, but the incident never hit the paper.

The Senate is its own little world.

The Hill staffers will throw a party on any pretext. At one, a curvy staffer put on a tutu, hung a toy piano around her neck, and danced around playing it while singing "Happy Birthday" to her Congressional boss.

It sure got rid of the boredom around the office.

I got a big charge when one female staffer commented to me that chivalry on Capitol Hill was a Senator slowing down to twenty-five miles an hour so a girlfriend-for-the-night could jump out when the Senator got to her place.

Every Senator is king in his own office. He decides how much he wants to pay each staffer, and he decides what titles to give his staff members. He may decide it looks bad for him to have a public-relations man, and he may assign some secretary to add public-relations work to her burden.

Each king also decides who in his office may sign for him in the dining room. A Senator is told when he arrives in Washington, "You have two food accounts—a private account for you and your family and any authorized staffer, and a miscellaneous account. The miscellaneous account is for constituents or other outsiders whom you authorize to hold a party or a special function in a private room."

The problem was that no two Senators handled their accounts in the same way. Some Senators—such as Harry Byrd, Jr., of Virginia—did not permit anyone to use a special function room under his authorization or sponsorship. Some Senators permitted a secretary to authorize use of a room, and sign for it. Or an administrative aide might have the privilege of acting for the Senator.

Some Senators let everyone in their office sign for them. This could cause a peck of trouble. Senator Birch Bayh, for example, when he first came to the Senate had one of the most disorganized offices. He had not designated who could sign his name. So they all did, both for parties and luncheons in the dining room. It took two years before Bayh suddenly woke up to the fact that his restaurant account had grown to enormous proportions—something like $5,000.

Twelve or fifteen people had been using his name, signing for their lunches. What brought it to a head was the General Accounting Office going to the Rules Committee and insisting that the bill be disposed of by the end of the fiscal year. This was in April, which gave him until the end of June to settle up.

Senator Jordan himself told Bayh the bad news in private. The good-natured Senator was good natured no longer. Bayh had known nothing about it and said that he had never seen the bill.

Jordan explained that since Bayh had never designated who could sign for him, it had been assumed everyone could. In one fell swoop, the Senator fired several staffers and gave instructions that only two persons would be authorized to sign for him from then on—his wife Marvella and his administrative assistant.

As a result of this incident, the Rules Committee issued a new rule that any staffer who signs for a Senator must sign his own name under it.

Next to Birch Bayh, Senator Walter "Fritz" Mondale had the most disorganized office operation. But at least he kept his account current and never had a financial snafu. His snafus were in lost files, chaos, and general confusion. And when one secretary left, it was not that she had been fired, but that she had gotten disgusted with Mondale because he would not take her suggestions on how to get organized.

A happy office was that of Senator Cooper. Senator John Sherman Cooper of Kentucky did more entertaining than Huddleston or any other Senator from the Kentucky or West Virginia coal mining areas—Jennings Randolph or Robert C. Byrd.

Cooper was one of the wealthiest men on the Hill, maintaining a beautiful seventeenth-century historic Georgetown house, and traveling with the jet set. Still, I found him very easy to please.

Once a year, Cooper would have a tremendous party for the whole Senate, which he later enlarged to include the whole House. The crowd would spill over into the lovely outdoor gardens. When he left to become ambassador to the Court of St. James, his Hill staff gave him a great party, which I catered.

I remember that a few blacks were on his staff, and some of his white staffers told me that Cooper was the most liberal man of the coal-mining states. They said that Kentucky and West Virginia were more biased against Negroes than almost any state in the union because of the job competition in the mines. Cooper, they said, was the only Senator from Kentucky or West Virginia who had blacks on his staff.

I could see the great outpouring of love toward their boss when his staff clustered around him and presented him with an attaché case to remember them by in London.

In some Hill offices, staffs cater to the king, but in others, the kings cater to the staffers.

One Senator was the type of man who called certain young men on his staff "darling." He had several male staffers on whom he danced attendance.

Senator Frank Lausche had a very different and clever way of keeping his staff happy. He would order a spiced-shrimp feast to be brought to his office. Since the staff couldn't afford such delicacies ordinarily, they were most impressed and appreciative. Of course, some didn't like shrimp, but Lausche loved all seafoods and thought that everyone else must.

Lausche would also call on his past experience as judge of the Municipal Court of Cleveland in the '30s and mayor of the city in the early '40s, to give the staff pep talks. So persuasive was the Ohioan that his staff was one of the most considerate in cutting down on long lunch hours and coffee breaks.

"We're just trying to keep the boss happy," one of the secretaries said to me, as she hurried back to the office instead of sitting down and having a leisurely snack. "He's so good to us, I'm trying to show him how fast I can get this job done." So she took her coffee and sweet roll and ran.

Some staffers make their bosses look good, while others tend to be overprotective.

When Senator Charles Harting Percy was elected in 1966 and made arrangements for his swearing-in reception, the following January, I didn't know who was the tightwad, the Senator or his aide—and I didn't dare ask.

The aide was the Senator's girl Friday, who came to Capitol Hill a little later than she should have to plan his swearing-in party. That put us on the wrong foot from the first. Democrats had ruled Capitol Hill so long that there was scarcely any room at the inn for a new Republican.

The lady expected two hundred guests. The only room I could give her that would hold enough people from the great state of Illinois was the motion-picture theater in the Dirksen Building. There are seats for four hundred people to watch a movie if one is a member of the Club. Naturally, Percy's girl Friday was less than pleased to hear of this odd accommodation. But I explained that the foyer was an excellent place to set up as a bar for serving drinks.

As soon as she heard drinks, her guard was up. How much was all this going to cost, she wanted to know, giving me a song-and-dance about how the Senator was so hard up, they had to save money.

I told her I had just read that he was worth $16 million. And she said, "Newspapers don't print the truth."

After I carefully explained all the wonderful things I could concoct for this great occasion in the Senator's career, her order was two one-pound cans of mixed nuts and some potato chips.

I said, "You should at least have cheese and crackers."

She said, "That won't be necessary."

I said, "You know this party is being held in January. The custom is to serve your guests something hot. The people who elected him to office are spending their own money to come hundreds of miles."

We stood glaring at each other. It was ridiculous, and she could see that I was horrified. She said, "We can't afford it. The Senator has expenses too."

I said, "Well, think about cheese and crackers, at least. Some people don't like potato chips."

I was getting nowhere. So I asked, "What about the bars?" She said, "Well, with two hundred people, I guess we'll need two bars."

"Fine," I said. "Now about the bartenders. . . ."

She quickly broke in. "No, no. I don't need bartenders. I'm going to use some of the Senator's staff. After all, they don't cost us anything."

I really was getting concerned for the Senator and for the guests who were coming so far. Nor was I too impressed with her attitude toward the office staff. I said, "Quite frankly, if you don't mind my suggesting it, if I were you, I would just serve drinks in the office, and not even serve nuts and potato chips. The money you save on that, you can use to serve hot coffee, so people can warm up after traveling so far in those chartered buses. After all, not every one can afford to have a private plane to bring him to Washington."

I couldn't resist that little dig to show the difference between the way the common man was coming to Washington to celebrate Percy's election, and how Percy himself was arriving. I didn't begrudge him the special privilege of rank he had earned through the years, starting with being a whiz kid, but I was trying to make him look good. She said she'd take the theater.

I asked how much liquor the party would need. She said, "None from you. We'll bring our own. We don't need your help. I'll manage."

And so the Senator was toasted into office in a practically free room, which had cost him nothing but the price of two pounds of mixed nuts and some potato chips.

And there went the deficit.

I eventually decided that it was not Senator Percy who was being chintzy but only his staffer, who was trying to see how much money she could save. In the restaurants, the Senator was generous with waiters, and he even was generous with me, giving me $25 cash Christmas presents.

I was told by other staff members in Percy's office that this aide was in charge of the Senator's finances, even giving him his weekly allowance. Every time that I would get a call from her, I would cringe, knowing that she was not helping Percy put his best "foot" forward among his peers. For example, the way she handled the Senator's turn to serve lunch to the exclusive little group of Republican liberals who ate together once a week. They called themselves the Wednesday Club; President Nixon hated them and was always attacking them when he was in office. The Senators would take turns serving lunch in their own offices and discussing their policies on various bills without being overheard. To assure secrecy in what they were saying, the rule was that we would bring them their food and leave. Anything further that had to be done they would do themselves.

When Percy's turn came, his budget demon would order cold cuts so that the Senators could make their own sandwiches. She would not order the meat by the pound, as others who wanted sandwiches did, but rather by the slice. So many slices per person.

I could not believe my ears when she ordered sliced tomatoes—"1½ slices per person."

In contrast, Senator Robert Taft, Jr., in the same league financially as Percy, would have his staffer call and ask me for suggestions of what the Senators might enjoy. Knowing the likes and dislikes of the various men, we would end up with something like beef burgundy served over rice, salad bowl, rolls, butter, and hot apple tarts with cheese topping, served from the chafing dish.

The tarts would cost 50¢ apiece, but Taft would never fail to have them or another lovely dessert.

When it was the turn of Senator Clifford P. Case of New Jersey, he would frequently serve seafood Newburg, followed by petits fours of German chocolate.

Feeling sorry for the group when it was Percy's turn, I once tried suggesting to his girl Friday that she at least let me include potato salad to go with the sandwiches. "It's very popular with the Senators in the dining room," I assured her, "and you can serve sixteen people out of a gallon for a cost of three-fifty."

She looked at me without speaking so I thought she was seriously considering it. "As an alternative," I added, encouragingly, "I can give you German potato salad, which is hot and even more popular with the Senators. It's the same price and is generously laced with bacon.

She cut me off, saying, "I think we made it clear, we don't want any frills." The whole luncheon Percy served for twelve to fourteen Senators, including two cups of coffee apiece, no dessert, added up to $25.50, plus 20 percent room service.

Then, the staffer discovered that, if she called Joe Diamond instead of my office in the Dirksen Building, she could get the service charge taken off. Not content with getting the deduction, she called the Rules Committee to complain about me, saying that I was charging 20 percent more than my superior. And what were they going to do about me?

As a result, the general manager and I both got called on the carpet, and Chairman Jordan laid the general manager out for not charging for service, and ordered that Miss-Know-It-All not get special prices, no matter how she complained.

We had rubber stamps made up, which we were supposed to use on every catering bill. They gave the date of the resolution which made the 20 percent charge mandatory. Needless to say, we gave those stamps a good workout.

When I saw her, I said, "Oh, my goodness, I didn't realize you were still with the Senator."

"Why?" she asked.

I said, "I haven't been called into Jordan's office recently."

She replied, "What do you mean?"

I said, "Well, we're still using that rubber stamp for the 20 percent."

Later I heard that the lady had complained that I was always trying to belittle her in the presence of her friends.

When Senators are accused of wrongdoing, nine times out of ten, a staffer is involved in some way. There have been cases where staffers used the name of the Senator to cover their illegal deals. Sometimes the electorate never could believe the Senator was not somehow guilty, too, even though only the staffer went to prison.

Sometimes it has been the Senator who was guilty of using the aide as a scapegoat, and I'm afraid that is the more usual case. And now and then, a Senator and his aide will be thicker than thieves, and work out a crooked deal together, hiding the funds under some company name or in some numbered Swiss bank account.

One hears many things on the Hill. A case which gets my sympathy is that of Senator Hiram Fong of Hawaii, and his aide. Both were friends of mine, and I was truly sorry when the aide was sentenced to eighteen months on a conspiracy and perjury conviction. Fong was so upset, he almost collapsed. He told me he was through with Congress—he was not going to run again.

Even while the aide was still in jail, he would come to see me and others on a weekend pass. The aide was such a charming man that it was unbelievable that this thing had happened to him. But instead of being bitter or remorseful, he simply kidded around, telling me about how members of the Club got special treatment even in jail. He said he had his own TV in a private room, and played cards every night. "What else can a guy ask for?" he joked.

When I tried to ask my friend what he planned to do after he came out, he said, "I haven't thought about it. I have nothing to worry about. I have plenty of money in the bank."

I had understood when he came to the Hill that he was already a very wealthy man and did not need the job with the Senator. He was also a sportsman who went in for yachting, and he had cut a fine figure in Washington as a ladies' man.

I have learned in Washington that simply having money does not keep a person from being greedy—and politicians, as well as those who serve politicians, are no exception.

I will never forget Senator Fong saying to me sadly, "This affair has destroyed my incentive." Finding corruption in someone so

close to him had shattered his desire to continue working in a body
that was always subject to such temptation, he said.

Senator Joseph Montoya was a singularly handsome man.
Women naturally gravitated to him, and he had a good eye for
picking the cream of the crop. He was extremely well-dressed, a
good drinker, a good party man, a good tipper in the restaurants.

He was known as a good sport except when angry, and Montoya had a reputation for a fiery temper. Senator Bible was a
frequent sparring partner. Montoya's colleagues complained to me
that he always wanted his way on legislation. It was Montoya's way
or not at all. He would not compromise with his compatriots, and
everyone knew that compromise was the name of the game in the
Club.

Once I was privy to an instance where Montoya's temper was
well justified. A member of his staff permitted an outsider to use
his account to hold a large party and ran up a considerable debt
before the Senator realized what was going on. As a matter of fact,
the outsider charged more than the cost of the party, pocketing the
difference. The outsider went to prison for embezzlement. As an
object lesson, Montoya fired several of his staff and started a whole
new regime. Montoya was a very wealthy man, and it wasn't the
money that had him furious, he explained. It was the principle of
the thing.

Sometimes there doesn't even seem to be a principle. Senator
Joseph Tydings was chairman of the District Committee. He came
in one morning and fired one of my friends, a staffer on the
committee, without advance notice. He didn't have to give any, or
any reason for firing. That was his prerogative.

On the Hill, Tydings was known as an ill-tempered man and
one who hated to spend money, though the story was that he was
worth $20 million and raised racehorses as a hobby.

It's hard for outsiders to believe the things a staffer may be called on to do when Congressional members are involved. One staffer of an organization that dealt with Hill people testified that when her boss was allegedly getting ready to deliver bribe money to certain Congressmen, she had to don white gloves and personally wipe each bill clean of fingerprints and deposit the money in a fingerprint-free white envelope. Another Congressional aide testified that he had personnally delivered hand-cleaned bills to Congressmen.

I'm not going to pass on the legalities of the case, I'm merely pointing out the sometimes weird duties of staffers—as attested to in court. Everyone on the Hill hears about or lives similar cases.

Of course some will say staffers can refuse to do these things. And they can also look for new jobs. It's hard to explain that there is something thrilling and exciting about being associated in any way with the Club members of the Hill, that it's hard not to get sucked into the way of life of that particular Club member.

There is no end to the services Capitol Hill staffers perform. Daniel Minchew, Senator Herman Talmadge's former top aide testified in court about a variety of small services he rendered the Senator—such things as finding the Spanish melons Talmadge enjoyed eating and checking the tires of Talmadge's car. At another office, aides spent their vacation working on a farm so they would understand agricultural problems and be more valuable to their boss—slopping pigs and all.

Congressman Otto Passman stubbed his toe with another staffer—Shirley Davis, who claimed she had been bounced from her job as his AA, because she was a woman. Davis claimed the firing had "outraged, humiliated and practically destroyed her," and cited a letter of dismissal in which the legislator had said she had done a good job but that he felt he needed a man in the job instead of a woman.

The case went all the way to the Supreme Court, which set a precedent—ruling in a 5–4 decision that money damages could be won by Congressional employees if they could prove they were victims of discrimination.

Shirley and the Congressman made an out-of-court settlement, and the lady AA came out smiling.

The greatest triumph for a female staffer on the Hill, of course, is to marry the boss. Many Senators have married their staffers—Hollings and Thurmond—both from South Carolina, and Aiken of Vermont, to name but a few.

But sometimes it doesn't happen that way. When the wife of Senator Carl Curtis of Nebraska died, after a long illness, almost everyone expected the Senator to marry his administrative assistant, who had been with him for over twenty years.

They guessed wrong. The Senator came back to the Hill after a vacation as a newlywed. He had married the nurse who had taken care of him at a veteran's hospital after World War II.

6

Of Wives
and
Lady Loves

Who was the greatest lover on Capitol Hill?

It was not, as the public generally thinks, Jack Kennedy, with his parade of sweeties on the Hill and his skinny dipping with girls at the White House pool, attested to by Traphes Bryant, his dog keeper and electrician.

Jack may have had a parade of girlfriends, like ships that pass in the night, but it was Senator Robert Kennedy, who, the Hill experts agreed, was more than a macho man, and knew how to make a woman happy and hold her deepest affection—not for just the moment but on the long haul.

The word on the Hill was that it was Robert Kennedy whom Marilyn Monroe really loved and was trying to call on the night she took her own life. It was the hopelessness of knowing he could never be hers that had driven her to desperation, it is said.

True, Jack dated movie stars, too, like Gene Tierney, whom he almost married, and Jack did marry the most glamorous girl in the Western World.

On the Hill, there was much talk about the closeness of Jacqueline Kennedy and Robert. After Jack Kennedy's assassination, his widow used to hang around Robert's office. She and Robert would come alone into the dining room, rather than have food sent to his office. This was remarked upon, because Robert preferred to have his lunch sent to his office. The Hill gang decided the couple was coming into the dining room to show they had nothing to hide.

The Hill had been shocked that Jackie was not seen crying publicly when her husband died. When Robert died, she did cry buckets of tears in public.

I often think of the death of Jack Kennedy, and wonder what really happened. A New Orleans lawman worked very hard on the case and supposedly put together a lot of startling and mind-boggling material, but few paid attention.

What about Ted Kennedy and his highly publicized encounters with beautiful women—usually blondes? Is he the great lover his brother Robert was? Definitely not, is the consensus on Capitol Hill. Teddy is more like his brother Jack, accepting the adoration and love of women but not wanting to get emotionally involved and not really working at stirring their deepest feelings.

When Margaret Trudeau of Canada hinted at a liaison with Senator Edward Kennedy, the Hill insiders laughed and explained that, though Margaret had pursued him, Teddy had had the good sense to stay clear of a swinger who was too much in the public eye.

Oh, yes, they'd gotten together for a brief encounter, all right. But Teddy had found her an aggressive female, and Ted liked to be the aggressor himself. He liked the thrill of the chase, not the experience of being chased. He had that every day of his life on Capitol Hill. It was said that a slightly shy but elegant creature, who seemed a little afraid of him, excited him much, much more. Shy, they said, was hardly the description for Margaret Trudeau.

Ted Kennedy, incidentally, is no different from other members of the Club. Handsomer, perhaps, but they can keep up with him in the "Hill and dalliance" department. At least he is able to hang on to his marriage. Let me tell you what happened in another case.

This particular Senator had a female top aide who was desperately in love with him. I knew her well and listened sympathetically as she wistfully told me of the Senator's promises to marry her some day, after he had gotten safely reelected for another six years and could dump his wife. I had heard that before but didn't tell her that the chances of any Senator divorcing his wife to marry someone else—unless she was rich or famous or both—were very slim.

I saw this girl's chances get even slimmer as she put on a lot of weight, started hitting the bottle, and developed an unhappy face.

Sure enough, the Senator suddenly added a new girl to his staff, and Number 1 found herself sharing his poor overworked "bod." I thought Number 1 would simply give up and get another job or another love, but she hung on, explaining to me that Number 2 was stupid and the Senator would soon get tired of her. And besides the Senator simply couldn't manage without her. But just to be sure, Number 1 went on an intensive diet to get her own "bod" back in shape.

The plot thickened when a particular lobbyist, working for a manufacturer in the Senator's home state, decided to have a party for the Senator. The fact that they needed the Senator's help with a problem, of course, had nothing to do with it.

The lobbyist worked with me on the plans for a party, a big bash involving some 700 or 800 guests, and I thought something was rotten in Denmark when I was told they had hired a caterer to help me and take charge. When I saw the caterer, a well-stacked blonde who knew nothing about catering but everything about pleasing a man, I could understand their reasoning. I learned that they were paying her $5,000 for the event, and I was also told that, before the night was over, she had earned it.

The food she insisted we prepare for the party was very complicated to make and totally unsuitable. So was her outfit—slinky, low cut evening pajamas that made it obvious she was not wearing a bra. She was also hanging around the Senator, looking after his needs.

I couldn't believe that the Senator could be interested in her type, but obviously I was wrong. As the party was just getting nicely started, I became aware of a loud commotion. The Senator's Number 1 girl, already in her cups, was screaming at the skimpily clad caterer for the way she was dressed and how she was "on the make" for the Senator, and the caterer was delivering as good as she got.

I had a sick feeling that this could develop into a hair-pulling contest that would get the Senator's name in the paper—about the only thing Senators worry about. I rushed around and found a couple other members of the Senator's staff, and they pulled the two screaming females apart.

Number 1 went home in a huff, the caterer stuck with the Senator and went off with him after the party was over—

supposedly to another big bash given elsewhere. But the real winner was the new girl that Number 1 had labeled "dumb." The Senator did get a divorce, and he married her.

So she wasn't so dumb after all.

Oh, did I forget to mention it? Number 1 was fired the morning after the party.

The list of playboys in the annals of the Senate is as long as your arm. Some are no longer there to wear their laurels, but stories about them are still told around the Club when old friends meet.

Stories of old Carl Hayden, trying to rip the clothes off a sweet young thing. Tales from another young Hill lady, who bragged about her conquest of HHH right in his own apartment, while his wife was out of town.

Stories of LBJ when he was Senate majority leader, would reach halfway around the world—his interest in black girls and white and his closeness with young men. It had been said so many times on the Hill, that I get bored when I hear it. But that makes it no less true. When Lyndon got tired of a girl, he would marry her off or thrust her into the arms of the first convenient young aide around and say, "Here, why don't you take this little filly home to her corral? She's too high stepping for me." Then he would give her a big hearty kiss, as if he were just overwhelmed with the big sacrifice he was making and having one last moment.

Because Senator Ted Kennedy was so handsome, so rich, and a scion of such a distinguished family, it was natural that all eyes were on him. And his name would be mentioned first when Hill staffers bragged about their distinguished playboys. But he was no better and no worse than a lot of others on the Hill—George Smathers, who used to cat around with Ted's brother Jack; Alan Bible, Estes Kefauver, Jennings Randolph, Norris Cotton, Russell Long until he remarried, John Tunney, Strom Thurmond until he remarried, Robert Kerr—said to be the richest man in the Senate when he died at age sixty-six in the early '60s, still pursued by every money-hungry eager-beaver girl around the Hill. And finally, among the top Senatorial playboys, Harrison Williams, who was the wonder of the Hill, because if he saw a pretty girl, he could not keep his hands off. "Probably from force of habit," the Hill wags said. But not anymore—marriage to a member of his staff settled him down, again to the amazement of Hillites.

That about covers most of the real playboys of the exclusive Club I served. Not that others didn't play around, or experiment one way or another, but the rest were more cautious or reserved.

And, wonder of wonders, some Senators really didn't care to play around—men like Hugh Scott, and J. Glenn Beall, James Allen, John Pastore, John Stennis, and Abraham Ribicoff.

There were rules and standards older Club members tried to instill in newcomers—"If you want to play, stay away from your own secretary. Pick someone else's secretary. And if you want an office full of strife, pick a file clerk for your office wife."

These words of wisdom were not always taken, and every now and then, there would be great upheavals in someone's office because the Senator was playing footsy with a girl of lower rank than his own secretary.

The life of the *chosen* girl would be picked to pieces, and many's the time I've had to sit listening to a private secretary tell how the boss had taken up with this little slut, who had come into the office looking for a job. And, "I'm getting ready to quit the son of a bitch."

The Senator was lucky if his disgruntled ex-girlfriend simply left quietly. I remember some harrowing times when jealous girlfriends managed to let the wife know what was going on, and sat by virtuously while the storm broke.

I could be a rich man if I had accepted the money offered to play detective. And it wasn't always the wife who wanted the information. Sometimes the private secretary wanted to know who the boss was taking to a party or meeting at a restaurant or in the private hideaway. Other times, it was the lobbyist, who was willing to pay for information.

I have never blown the whistle until this book.

Even now, I hesitate to tell who does what. But what I can say is that oral sex is so important on Capitol Hill that Club members have a way of letting each other know whether a "new discovery" among the pretty staffers will perform oral sex.

"She's all right," they may comment to each other, even in front of the girl in question. "She does windows." To convey the opposite meaning, a Senator might say to another, "I'd like you to meet Dora. She's a lovely girl but she doesn't do windows."

It sounds like fun party talk to the girl, who laughs along with the Senators, not dreaming of what they have really said.

But even if the girl does windows, some sexual adventurers around the Club are just not interested. They have other needs.

It was said around the Hill that the worst thing that could happen to a politician was to be caught in bed with a dead woman or a live man.

Capitol Hill is riddled with homosexuality and kinky sex. Members and aides romp together. Graffiti in the men's room would give the initials of someone who was looking for a good homo romp in the hay. I always wondered if any Senators copied down the telephone numbers of these outsiders and young aides, looking for a connection.

There was a story that made the rounds of Capitol Hill about a Senator who refused to open his luggage at National Airport. The metal detectors had picked up something, and the security men wanted to have a look inside. He pulled rank, and they did not get a look. On the Hill, it was said that he was carrying some devices for a fun time away from his home base.

Once I heard that a certain Senator known to have homosexual tendencies went out of his way to help a fellow from the gay community get a job on a committee. The fellow had barely started working before he was invited to attend a party in the Senator's hideaway.

The fellow was faithful to his male lover and did not show up at the party. The Senator was furious and went to the chairman of the committee to get him fired.

"On what grounds shall I fire him?" asked the startled chairman.

"Incompetence!" thundered the angry Senator.

One day, Judy Cameron who with Alice Warrick took the place of my best friend in the restaurant, Marie German, called in tears. An administrative assistant to the manager of a big restaurant toughens up pretty fast. So I knew this had to be pretty serious.

"What in the world's wrong, Judy?" I asked.

It seems someone was saying I was a queer because I shared a house with another man. There had been a conversation in the restaurant, and she had overheard it.

I said, "For Christ's sake, why are you crying? Do you feel that I am?"

She said, "No, I don't think that at all. Or I wouldn't be telling you."

I said, "Well, we had a woman named Nora living with us too, and that didn't mean I was having an affair with her either. It has always been, and still is, just a business deal and a friendship. None of us could afford alone what we could afford together. But each of us had our outside friends and romances.

"When Nora died, we just kept everything going. And as you know, with my eyesight, I have to have someone drive me and write checks. So, I'm lucky to have a friend who will bother."

Judy said, "What should I tell them?"

I said, "I don't give a damn what you tell them. You're not going to change anyone's mind anyway. Anybody who knows me knows I can't be gay."

It was not the first time or the last someone had assumed Penny and I had to be homosexuals. The most embarrassing evidence of this mistaken identity would come about when someone would invite me to a male sex party on the Hill, assuming I was one of the boys.

Several Senators played around with male staffers, and I didn't want to act holier than thou, but I didn't want to attend to find out what happens, either.

One of the parties I was invited to was in the hideaway of Lyndon Johnson when he was still a Senator. Staffers, who claimed to be among his playmates, said that LBJ was very fickle. He liked young men and easily tired of them. And he liked young girls and easily tired of them. "He's got no sense of loyalty," one complained—a slim, tall, young man.

Every now and then, after Johnson was President, I would hear about some of the revelry on the Presidential yacht, involving young people of all races. The joke around the Hill was that at least LBJ wasn't prejudiced—he screwed anybody.

With all the bisexuality around, it was a refreshing relief to deal with the playboys who just liked plain sex and thought they were very naughty if they merely chased a pretty girl half their age until they caught her. Or she caught them.

Senator Sam Ervin was a ladies' man, old as he was. He didn't think he was old. He was a good dresser, did very little entertaining, except for a pretty girl here or there, and was very well liked by his office staff. In the restaurants, he was always fair and considerate.

One of the most powerful men in the Senate was Carl Trumbull Hayden—president pro tempore of the Senate when I came to work on the Hill, as a matter of fact. I used to think, Wouldn't the nation be surprised if they could see the Carl Hayden I saw instead of the one they were reading about in the dull political write-ups in their newspapers?

I had to admire the old boy. Though in his eighties, he was pursuing the girls as avidly as a drugstore Romeo of twenty. At a Capitol Hill party, he would sit with his drink waiting for a secretary or other young girl staffer to get within arm's length. His trick was to draw a girl near and drape his arm around her shoulder, so that his hand lay across her breast.

Some of the girls would gently take his hand away. Some would just have a smirk on their faces and say coyly, "Now, Senator, you know you don't want to do that in public." And they'd not move. Finally, he would take his hand away. He was a complete reprobate when it came to the ladies.

Even when he became the beloved "relic" of the Senate, hitting the age of ninety, he was still at it. All the staffers around the Hill and his own colleagues got a kick out of seeing him operate. Some were envious because he was so nonchalant about it. He didn't bother to be discreet.

Sometimes staffers expect a Senator to be altruistic and a good family man and are terribly disillusioned to find he's not. Usually such staffers haven't been long in Washington.

Ernest "Fritz" Hollings of South Carolina was a good dresser and heavy drinker, who liked the attention of young ladies. He had a favorite expression, which he would tell me as he waited for his luncheon date: "If you fatten them up and booze them up, they're bound to come along."

Two of his male staffers once told me they were quitting him because he was getting a divorce and they objected to the way he was treating his family. As it turned out, he married a lovely girl who was a member of his own staff, Peatsy. Peatsy was good for the Senator because she slowed down his drinking.

In his early days in the Senate, Birch Bayh had been a ladies' man, and one socialite, a young beauty known for her wittily acid tongue, had been completely smitten by him. It was rumored around the Hill that the gal was serious and hoped that some day the handsome and debonair Senator would divorce his wife and marry her. Then came word that Marvella Bayh had cancer, and suddenly Birch was a changed man. He dropped the beautiful socialite immediately and went back to being a faithful husband.

Several years went by and the young lovely played the field, but still carried the torch for Birch. She told her friends how she was suffering but got little sympathy because everyone admired the gallantry of Marvella in fighting the dread disease in public and setting an example for the world.

Senator Allen Ellender was easy to get along with. He was strictly a ladies' man, who wasn't happy unless he had a pretty lady to eat with. He frequently came to restaurants with pretty girls not from his own office. He had a great trick for stopping pretty girls. He would carry a pocketful of pralines that he had made with Louisiana pecans. He would pause to pass them out and get acquainted.

He also kept the elevator operators and policemen happy by the same beneficence. He never gave me anything, but then, I could not afford the time to dig up any young ladies.

Jacob Javits of New York was always called Jake or Jack around the Hill. It was hard not to like him. He was warm-hearted and generous and led quite a social life, apart from his wife. Senatorial wives were not happy to hear Marion Javits quoted as having said she didn't care to spend her time in Washington among the peons, but wanted to be around the creative people in New York. They left the elegant Marion to her own devices, and so did her husband, the Senator, to a great extent.

I don't know about her life, but I did know that the Senator had a liaison with a particular female friend and was very happy in her company. I would sometimes find myself at her apartment, helping them throw a party for friends.

Jake really asked very little of life, just to do a good job for his state and his nation, and to sit around with his lady love and their Hill friends, talking and eating. His wife, Marion, on the other hand, liked a grander style of life and once chartered a plane to take a group to a party in the Virgin Islands.

Whenever Marion Javits came to town and it fell my duty to help her with a party on the Hill, I could never please her. In contrast, Jake Javits was always happy with how I handled his parties and more than once sent me a $100 bill.

I recall once he had a lady friend who got married. He gave her generous gifts, including a fur coat, according to members of his staff.

While virtue may be its own reward, the discard of virtue, especially with the right people, pays better. One hard-working, bed-climbing young woman, who catered to the Hill crowd, finally got her just desserts—a high-paying Senate job, a magnificent home, an expensive car, and the most fashionable clothes. Not bad for a girl who had started only a few years before, with a tiny job, paying about $5,000 a year.

Finally, I who had been so proper, decided to make the most of a friendship I observed. For years, I had been pleading with Everett Jordan to let me get new carpeting for the Senators' dining room. It embarrassed me to have to serve dinner in such a shabby-looking room. But the Senator seemed not to notice. Then I decided to put a bug in his friend's ear.

Taking the chairman's current sweetie by the arm, I pointed out the worn spots, observing that it was really a shame that such a chic girl had to spend time in such tacky surroundings. "You're right," she replied. "I'm glad you came to me. Let me take over."

Very shortly afterward, I was asked to join the Senator and the girl in the dining room for a cup of coffee. "What's this I hear," he said, in a tone of utter amazement, "about your needing new carpeting, and not being able to get it?"

"Senator," I said, trying to look as innocent as possible and pretending that the two of us hadn't been batting around the topic for over six years, "I realize that you're bogged down by vastly more important legislative concerns. But if you could just take a moment away from your national concerns, and look around, you'd notice that the dining room is on the shabby side."

He said, as if it had just come to his attention for the first time, "Well, it does look like the carpeting needs replacement. While you're at it, you might as well do it right. The drapery could stand replacement too." Meanwhile, his girlfriend stared at him in apparent admiration.

Magnanimously, the Senator volunteered, "I'll call my friend at the carpet institute right away, and have him bring over some samples that we can pick out together."

True to his word, with his adored one still in attendance, the samples arrived pronto-pronto. The Senator stood by while his girl and I selected a carpet with an attractive design that would not show soil. Then we picked drapes in a slightly lighter color to match.

Everett just smiled, showing a friendly interest in our choice. Then he himself walked the samples down to Lewey Caraway's office as soon as we finished, telling the superintendent of the Senate office buildings to order it immediately. The whole transformation took only three weeks—from ordering to putting down the carpeting and installing the drapery.

Never underestimate the power of a woman! Here, a young lady was able to accomplish in minutes what I couldn't in six years.

Now I was happy. For we had a room suitable for the Sweetest Little Club in the World. G 211 in the Dirksen Building blossomed and became one of the most pleasant rooms on the Hill.

The wife of another Senator complicated my life by having an affair with a member of my personnel. It was a bad situation to have an employee thus involved. But there was nothing I could do about it. She would even wait for him in the dining room. When he was through working after a meal, she would leave, and he would sign his name to her check as if he had been eating—so she wouldn't have to pay.

The situation was further complicated by the fact that her lover was black. Because of the tenor of the times, she would be careful not to be seen even walking with him. She would march down the hall, and he would follow at a discreet distance.

They had a rendezvous place at a certain Virginia high-rise building, where a friend of his had an exotic-looking apartment—or so it was described to me.

I could understand the lady's predicament, because her husband had his own offbeat affairs that kept him away from home. I would be amused to see him at parties making a big fuss over all the young girls and attractive wives, giving them little kisses and huge compliments, while his wife played femme fatale on the other side of the room.

What I was amused at was that the Senator wasn't going to relate to any of those girls he was making a fuss over, raising their hopes, because his interests were off the Hill. Nor was his attractive wife at all interested in the male Senators and their aides she was fussing over, for she was perfectly content with her stud. In fact, he would show me expensive gifts that she had given him. And once it was a $100 bill that was the sign of appreciation.

I said, "What are you going to do with it?"

He said, "You'll find me with the ponies tomorrow. Don't say a word, it's my day off."

I said, "I'm not going to say anything to anyone, except you. I hope you know what would show up in the newspapers, if you both happened to be coming out of that apartment building together at the wrong time."

"Forget it, man," he said. "That's the least of my worries. I go my way, she goes hers. I don't know her, and she don't know me."

And nothing ever did surface in the newspapers. For all I know, they may still be an item. I used to wonder how many people besides myself figured out for whom the Senator's wife was waiting in the restaurant. It was so obvious, the way her eyes followed him, and she seemed almost to be drooling.

Now and then, he would pause at her table to have a word with her, and she acted very solicitous and dignified. But she would grab his arm and laugh too animatedly. Maybe I've been in the restaurant business too long, or maybe he was just a better actor than she. But to me it was all very obvious.

Once I did think of warning the Senator's wife, in a very indirect way, but I figured she was old enough to know what she was doing. I tried to remind myself not to be so personally involved and would tell myself that, if she didn't find fault with his performance, why should I?

And she certainly didn't, from what he told me. But what she didn't know was that he was not being faithful to her in his dalliance! She was the only Senator's wife he had, but he was proud of his position as a Senate jock, with a half-dozen female aides waiting their turns for his favors.

I once asked the great performer whether the Senator and his wife intended to get a divorce. He said, "Hell, no, man. They've got the perfect marriage. She's got her freedom, and all she has to do is walk into the room with him at a party, so everyone will think everything is nice and normal."

It was one of those perfect Hill marriages.

The public would be amazed at the violence that some Congressional wives must put up with or get out. When the Hill was considering a bill to help communities set up shelters for battered wives, one Washington, D.C., doctor brought it out into the open.

"We have had instances of Congressional wives being beaten," Dr. Saul Edelstein, director of the emergency room of George Washington University Hospital, testified before the House Select Education Subcommittee, "and they have admitted it to a nurse, but only on the condition it would not be written on their chart."

And why didn't the wives go ahead and blow the whistle on their tormentors? "Because it would be harmful to their husbands' livelihood," the doctor explained. From my own personal experience with Hill wives, I can certainly back him up.

To switch from too much attention to too little, how remote from each other Senators and their wives get! Muriel Humphrey heard it first on TV that HHH was running for president. She sent him a telegram that was half humorous, half bitter: "LET ME KNOW IF I CAN HELP."

I remember hearing Muriel Humphrey once, scolding the Senator in the dining room, saying, "I can never find you. Why don't you keep me informed of where you are so I can talk to you occasionally?" Since he didn't want her to know where he was, he couldn't give her the number of his girlfriend's apartment, where she could find him.

Most Senate wives know if their husbands are ladies' men but just refuse to face it. Their lives are busy and pleasant and full of reflected glory. They are treated like queens. But to be an ex-wife takes them off the glory train.

Betty Talmadge told me, "You have to close your eyes and ears if you are married to a Senator." At that time, Herman Talmadge seemed to be after every gal he could get. After their divorce, the Senator changed his act, no longer drinking or flirting and started arriving at his office with clothes nicely pressed.

I was sort of a confidant of Humphrey through the years and I knew who his girlfriends were. However, for years, there was just one girl who meant a great deal to him. They would meet frequently early in the morning in the cafeteria, and they liked me to join them—I suppose so it would seem a more casual thing—so I would spend quite a bit of time with them.

But in private, Humphrey did not hide his feelings about this girl in front of me. Both considered me a personal friend, and they would even invite me over for cocktails with them at her apartment, where the Senator spent considerable time.

Since Hubert was so open and aboveboard with me, I was the same with him, and he asked me once, before he was Vice-President, what would happen if he ran for President. "How would you vote, Lou?"

Both of them waited for my reply, and I could see that he meant it merely as a rhetorical question to massage his ego.

I said, "Senator, I'm sorry. There is no way I could vote for you for dog catcher. No offense personally, but our interpretations of what is intended for the average American in Constitutional government just don't match. There's no way we can see eye to eye."

I had never seen Humphrey look more startled. Then he laughed and said he admired me for being honest.

His girlfriend laughed, too, but with a bitter edge and said she would never invite me again to join them, if I was going to insist on being so honest.

Humphrey looked at me and said, "Well, how the hell are you going to answer her on that?"

I turned to her and said, "He's heard worse things before, and it's nothing to what he'll hear if he runs. Anyway, I'd rather tell a friend the truth to his face than to his back."

Humphrey's girlfriend worked on the Hill but not in his office. I had known her for some time. She had been the girlfriend of someone doing business with the government, until she met and fell in love with the bighearted Minnesota Senator. In fact she had had a drinking problem, and with the help of Hubert she had gotten her drinking under control.

She herself told me that Hubert was maintaining the apartment she lived in, within easy walking distance of his office. He would slip away when he got his work in hand, and if the Senate was still in session, he would arrange to be called at her place. One particular person in his office knew where he was. He'd come racing back, zip into the subway, and be back at the floor of the Senate within five or six minutes.

The Capitol Hill area is convenient for those who indulge in illicit affairs. There are apartment buildings and houses right across the street from the various office buildings. And row on row of them.

After the day's Senate session was over, Humphrey would join his girl for cocktails and sometimes dinner at her apartment. And, as I've said, sometimes I would be included.

One day she called and invited me to come a little ahead of time and keep her company because the Senator was tied up and would be late. I got there at 5:30 and who came to the door but HHH in his shorts.

He said, "Jesus Christ Almighty, what are you doing here at this hour?"

I looked at him, and he was not smiling. I said, "—— asked me to come by for a drink. Good-bye." And off I went down the hall almost at a trot.

When I was there at the apartment having a few drinks—this was back in the days when I drank my share—it was never dull. Humphrey had a great sense of humor and always had something funny to say about what was happening on a bill or about someone who had come in to see him that day. He had a terrible time remembering an off-color story, and he would tell it as quickly as possible while it was still fresh in his mind.

They had a tender, but also a kidding quality to their relationship, and she would call him "Hubert baby" in a soft voice, even when in the next breath she was going to needle him.

Though the Senator was always completely dressed when I was there as a guest, she would frequently be wearing a beautiful lounging robe. They were very expensive and beautifully cut to show off her good figure. She had once been married, she told me. One of her many girlfriends, whom she would talk to me about, was Carol Tyler, who was Bobby Baker's girlfriend and who lived in a house owned, or partially owned, by Baker.

It was ironic that after Humphrey died in office, a woman filled his place—his wife had won the final round. When he was hale and hearty, HHH had not had his wife, Muriel, around his office too much. I don't know if she knew about his girlfriend, but his girlfriend was jealous of Muriel, and in a way I felt sorry for both of them. Mrs. Humphrey would occasionally join the Senator at the Capitol. If the Senate was going to be in session till nine at night, she would come down for dinner, stay around for a while but not too long.

When the Senator died, I wondered if Muriel found any evidence of his dual life around the office. But knowing how much the Senator truly respected and had affection for his wife, I was almost sure he would have left no telltale traces.

Anyway, the whole affair was over. It ended a few years before he died. What happened to the girl? A new man came to town. She fell in love again and left when he left, to follow him. But not to marry him. "I'm no hypocrite," she said. "I couldn't promise to stick forever. I've been on the Hill too long."

7

Relatives, Relatives, All— All Is Relative

"If President Carter doesn't make it back to the White House for a second term," said one of my buddies on the Hill, "he can thank his relatives—Billy, Ruth, Gloria, and his mother Miz Lillian."

"I can understand Billy and his boozing ruining his brother's image, but what about the others?" I asked. "They say Sister Ruth acts almost saintly."

"That's just it," said the Senator. "She acts too damn sanctimonious for his own good. And she's made it a paying proposition. Selling books, running a religious spa."

"What about Gloria?" I asked.

"Just the opposite," he said. "Got in trouble in a beer joint for refusing to quiet down. She should have been a little more sanctimonious if she wants to help her brother."

"Well, what about Miz Lillian?" I demanded. "I thought she was everybody's idol—nursing the lepers in India and all that senior-citizen Peace Corps stuff."

"I could have used a mammy like that myself in my last election," he said, "but she blew it when she said yes, she would vote for Ted Kennedy. Any way you look at it, it's a bummer. In the first place it's disloyal to her son, and in the second place, it sounds phony as a three-dollar bill.

"But worse than that was the way she hinted that something might happen to Kennedy if he ran for President. Hell, the Secret Service had no choice but to get a lot of protection around him right away."

"So what's the answer?" I asked.

"The answer is what Lyndon Johnson said. He said it, and he was damned right and his widow, Lady Bird, is still quoting it: 'A President should be born an orphan.' But if he isn't lucky enough to be born an orphan, he should at least throw a muzzle over them."

I'm sure that many a time Lyndon must have wished he could throw a muzzle over his brother, Sam Houston.

It was not easy for Lyndon Johnson to have a brother who could not hold his liquor. Sam Houston was always in LBJ's hair at the wrong time. LBJ would be having an important meeting, and his brother would walk in, sit down and start chiming in on what he thought should be done.

When Sam Houston had a job in the garage, he would wander away and end up in Lyndon's office. LBJ was too important for anyone to complain that Sam Houston was not looking after the cars properly.

Sam Houston Johnson was all over the place when Lyndon was majority leader. You couldn't miss him. He was a free-wheeling drunk. He would come into the Senate restaurants or the cafeteria, or even the carry-out corner, without a cent and loudly proclaim, "I don't have any money, but I don't need money, honey. You just put this on Lyndon's bill."

We did. And we never heard a murmur out of Lyndon, because he was embarrassed about this member of his family.

Lyndon kept his account in first-class shape and simply paid the bill and shut up, no matter how outrageous his brother was. And Sam Houston could be pretty outrageous. He would suddenly become the big shot, inviting a string of guests along to lunch or dinner, and run up a considerable bill for his famous brother.

Suddenly he would take a notion that everything in the restaurants should be free, that we shouldn't charge at all. "Nothing should be sold," he would rant. "The country owes it to the Senators. *My* brother works very hard." He would stand around arguing drunkenly. And what about you, pal? I would think. But, of course, we never voiced that question.

Sam Houston would make a nuisance of himself, walking around the restaurants, introducing himself, telling everyone who would listen that he was Lyndon Johnson's brother. The one thing that most irritated me was that he would never refer to Lyndon as anything but the Kingfish. Kerr had been called the Kingfish before him, and Huey Long before Kerr.

"The Kingfish is my brother, and he's going to straighten this country out," Sam Houston would declare. Democrats were not cheered by this. Nor were they cheered by his appearance. His clothes would be all disheveled, and obviously he had slept in them.

I was told that when he was sober, he was quite an intelligent man, and that Lyndon occasionally even took his advice. He was always giving LBJ advice. When Sam Houston returned to visit on the Hill, after Lyndon was in the White House, Sam Houston acted as if he were helping his brother run the country.

On the Hill, we heard that the worm turned after Lyndon died. The story around the Texas delegation was that Lady Bird did not put up with her brother-in-law anymore, and she cut him off.

We also heard she cut off others, who had been hanging onto Lyndon's coattails, even in his retirement. Suddenly, their bills were their own. I gave her credit. She was a remarkable business-woman and much respected on the Hill, for how hard she had worked to build the ranch and the TV station in Austin, which had freed her husband to pursue his political career and reach the Presidency.

As if I didn't have enough problems with besotted brothers, temperamental Senators, wives, special diets, and the restaurant help, I also had to wrestle with religious dietary restrictions of Senatorial mothers. Senator Richard Bernard Stone of Florida, for example, would eat some things that weren't kosher as long as his mother, Lily, wasn't around. But when he brought her in, every-thing had to be kosher. We used glass plates, silverware, and food brought in from a delicatessen, since the chicken had to be killed by a rabbi.

He was not permitted to eat shellfish when his mother was there. We would serve them salmon steak, swordfish steak, kosher beef, or corned beef and potato salad which had come from a kosher delicatessen. The Senator would put in his order in advance for a party at which his mother would be present. At both Stone's parties and Jake Javits's, some of the men would wear yarmulkes on their heads.

When Stone's mother was coming in from Florida, one of Stone's secretaries would come flying into the office and say, "It's that time again. The boss's mother is coming. You know what that means!"

I would answer, "Yeah, order from the delicatessen, use the glass plates—strictly Orthodox."

Richard Bernard Stone would amuse me because he catered to his mother more than any Senator I knew. His wife, Marlene, didn't seem to mind. She was a petite, jolly person in sharp contrast to her tall, solemn, Senatorial mate.

Abe Ribicoff was more liberal, reformed, or casual. The only Senator I knew who was more or less kosher was Jake Javits. At Passover, Javits asked the restaurant for matzos. Other times, whenever he got a yen for them, he'd put in an order for bagels and lox. We got them from the market that supplied kosher delicatessens.

Javits was an extra nice guy, easy to please, although he was a millionaire. His wife, Marion, on the other hand, was a pain in the elbow. "Washington is a cow town" was her favorite comment. And her nose was in the air whenever she put in an appearance on the Hill, often arriving late and angry.

She would come to my office to make arrangements for a luncheon. One of her favorite meals was stuffed avocado with crab meat or chicken salad. Another of her favorites was Chicken Princess, which is breast of chicken, deboned, on top of a slice of ham, broiled, and served with a champagne sauce. I wondered if she realized she was eating ham. But, then, the Senator ate ham too. Senator Stone also enjoyed Chicken Princess when his mother wasn't around. Perhaps you might be interested in the recipe we used on the Hill for champagne sauce for a large party.

CHAMPAGNE SAUCE

Take equal parts of club soda or sparkling water to champagne. For a quart of champagne and a quart of sparkling water or club soda, use ½ cup brown sugar and ½ cup butter.

Put the butter and sugar on the stove first, dissolving the sugar in the butter. After that, pour in first the club soda or sparkling water, and then the champagne. Bring to a slow boil. Pour over the 30 to 40 breasts of chicken, garnish with paprika, and serve immediately.

At least Marion Javits was thoughtful enough to stay out of our kitchen. Some Senate wives made themselves so at home around the Senate that they invaded the kitchens to give orders.

Mrs. Mark Hatfield, wife of the Senator from Oregon, was such a person. Though her husband was one of the easiest men to get along with, and one of my favorites of the whole Senate, his wife almost drove me wild. She was always bad news. Antoinette Hatfield would go right into the kitchen to see the chef and tell him what she was dissatisfied about, when she ate with the Senator or his staff, or when she had a ladies' luncheon.

The Italian chef would come out sputtering, "Mr. Hurst. I am getting bats in the belfry. Keep that woman out of my kitchen. She thinks she is the chef, and she has yet to take her first lesson." He would wring his hands and appeal to the heavens, "She is trying to teach me to cook."

Mrs. Vance Hartke was another pain in the neck to the chef. She would not take my word for anything but would march right into the kitchen to tell the chef what she had told me in order to hear his assurances, too. But that wouldn't be the end of it. He would become furious because she would not rely on his word either, and would go back again and again to remind him of what he had promised to do.

Mrs. John McClellan, wife of the Arkansas Senator, was another worrywart. She needed the chef's personal assurance that something would be ready on time. She had never had a bad experience but was afraid there would be a first time.

Mrs. Herman Talmadge, wife of the Senator from Georgia, also worried the hell out of the chef and saw him often, because the Talmadges did a lot of entertaining. She would want to know exactly how a thing would look. She was very concerned about colors—would the colors look right and go together? She even tried to dictate the color of the doilies and underliners that would be used, wanting them in colors that would give the food a brighter look.

A gentler person in dealing with the chef was Mrs. James Eastland, wife of the Senator from Mississippi. She at least had the courtesy to be very diplomatic and apologetic about wanting to deal with the chef. She was not at all arrogant and just assured the chef she felt more secure hearing from him how he was going to prepare something. The long-suffering chef would listen and say that he would fix it the way *she* wanted.

Many Senate wives insist on eating in the Capitol Building rather than one of the lovely rooms of the Dirksen or Russell Senate office buildings. Mrs. John Sparkman, for one, considered it beneath her to eat at the Dirksen Building where her husband had his office. Only lower echelon ate there.

She, like many others, preferred to see and be seen under the Capitol dome. And insisted her parties be staged in the Capitol building itself.

The wives for reasons of prestige seemed to feel to be seen in the Capitol itself had special significance. There was no use telling them the best chef was in the Dirksen Building. It was the address they care about.

Ivo Sparkman was one of the most determined women I have ever met. Once she had made up her mind, nothing could change it, and I long ago learned to "go along to get along," as Speaker Sam Rayburn was famous for saying.

Even the opportunity to save money did not change her mind. And once this stubbornness cost her a pretty penny. That was when her husband, the senior Senator from Alabama, through seniority, was elevated from the chairmanship of the Banking and Currency Committee to the most prestigious committee of them all—Foreign Relations.

Mrs. Sparkman, the inside story went, had pressured Sparkman into switching into the more social committee because she liked the grand atmosphere of the embassies and hobnobbing with ambassadors. According to those who knew Senator Sparkman best, he hated taking the Foreign Relations post and loved his Banking post because his whole background had been in banking. But when Bill Fulbright was defeated, Sparkman's wife saw the chairmanship as a golden opportunity to enjoy a richer social life. So he eventually acquiesced to please her.

I came into the picture when Mrs. Sparkman wanted to have a tremendous party to celebrate John's new chairmanship and get the maximum amount of publicity. What could be better than to throw the party at the National Press Club? The only trouble was the Press Club turned her party request down explaining that she had to find a Press Club member who would sponsor it.

I was told that Mrs. Sparkman had tried to become a member of the National Press Club to qualify. It didn't work because it would take time.

I had estimated the party she wanted would have cost around $2,500 if she had held it in the Sweetest Little Club in the World. By insisting on holding it at the Press Club, she ended up with a bill that came to something like $4,000. I had the last laugh when a staffer told me the Senator had hit the ceiling when he found out what that little jamboree had cost.

The word around Sparkman's office was that John was very unhappy with his new committee, and this was a consideration in his decision not to run for reelection. There was no way out and no way John Sparkman could kick someone out to take over his old committee. As they say on the Hill, "You don't go backward." There was no place from up but out.

I almost felt sorry for Mrs. Sparkman when I heard how hard she was taking the news that she had, in effect, outsmarted herself. It was breaking her heart to give up social Washington and their magnificent home in Georgetown, that was said to be worth $2.5 million.

So it was good-bye to the prestige and luxury of Georgetown and hello to Huntsville, Alabama!

When Ivo had pleaded with her husband to run for office again, he was said to have retorted that he had lost all interest in running because he was not that interested in the field of foreign relations and he did not care to hear anymore.

Mrs. Sparkman had the last word, telling him she knew she would simply die of frustration away from the world she had grown accustomed to.

But old John was like a rock. He could not be budged. He did not choose to run. He did not choose to hang around Washington and pretend to be busy, or swing into a new career at his age and really work his tail off.

I'll never forget when one Senator's wife seemed to be making me her scapegoat and blaming me for her husband's problems—

Maryon Allen, wife of the Senator from Alabama, James Allen.

She called me not too long after he had been elected to the Senate and told me that it was my fault that on his way home the night before, he had gone into diabetic shock.

I couldn't believe my ears. I asked what she thought I could have done.

She said, "Why didn't you send a glass of orange juice to him?"

I said: "I didn't know that one had been ordered, nor did I know he was a diabetic."

Maryon Allen said, "He certainly is, and you people should always have a glass of orange juice for him when he speaks on the Floor."

I said, "Oh, did he speak on the Floor yesterday?"

She said, "Oh, yes, he was speaking last night. Don't you pay attention to what is going on there?"

I thought to myself, I must be losing my mind. Since when is it any of my damn business who is speaking on the Floor? But since this was the Club, I said, "I try to keep in touch with Floor proceedings in a general way, Mrs. Allen, but I'm kept pretty busy around the Senate restaurants."

"Well," she said, "I am telling you now that any time he speaks, he is to have that glass of orange juice handy."

I said, "I'll be glad to take care of it."

I hung up, wondering how in the hell I was going to follow up on that. I did the logical thing and arranged for Allen's office to let us know when he was going to speak on the Floor so we could rush that blasted orange juice over to him.

As fate would have it, when Allen's time came to meet his Maker, during his second term of office, it was a heart attack that took him, and orange juice had nothing to do with it.

I confess I heaved a sigh of relief when I checked and found that insulin shock had not been the cause of death.

One of the easiest wives to get along with was Muriel Humphrey, wife of HHH. She never made a fuss and seemed so timid that I sometimes felt she would be afraid to make a fuss even if she didn't like something. From all I heard and saw, she was the compleat house wife, happiest when she was sewing for herself or her home. Not once, out of the hundreds of times that I saw her, did I ever hear her complain.

But the opposite was true of Humphrey's sister, Frances Howard. She would call me on the telephone and raise hell, expecting the same service she claimed she was getting at the State Department, where she had a high position.

She wanted special linen. She did not like the silver plate and wanted solid silver. She wanted bone china instead of the regular Syracuse china we used, which was an unattractive brown-and-beige modern with the Senate seal. I had to agree with her, though I didn't say so, that this was one of the ugliest and most inappropriate chinas I had ever seen.

I had been dumbfounded when I arrived at Capitol Hill and saw what I had to serve the people on. In this beautiful eighteenth-century dining room, with its cut-glass chandeliers and sconces to match, the tables look like those of a cheap nightclub. The tablecloths were frequently pulled out of shape, and sometimes the place was downright dingy. And then there was that china. It looked almost plastic. As a collector of fine glass and china, I would cringe at least once a day.

Using the clout of having a brother who was one of the most powerful members of the Club, Mrs. Howard would call me and reserve a table, bringing with her guests from all over the world. After lunch, she would charge it to the Senator—I don't know what their financial arrangement was. I never knew Muriel to call and reserve a table. Nor to my knowledge was Muriel ever at one of her sister-in-law's luncheons.

When I visited the Senator and Mrs. Humphrey's Harbour Square apartment, Frances Howard was not there. I gathered, from what staffers said, that they did not travel the same circle but did meet at other parties around town and maintained an outwardly friendly relationship.

The contrast between the two ladies was marked. Muriel was low key and very quiet, and Frances was exuberant and demonstrative, like her brother but with a bit of an imperious air.

When I first came, Senator Hubert H. Humphrey's kids were young adolescents, running wild around the Hill. They became friendly with the pages, and between the two groups, we were kept traumatized in the dining room. They would dump catsup on the tablecloths, reverse the salt and pepper, or dump them together so that those who wanted salt got both.

But worst of all to the harmony of the restaurant, the kids switched the salt and sugar. Customers would send the food back with angry words about the cooking. Naturally, we were eventually reported to the Rules Committee. "Why in the hell don't you get someone who knows how to cook?" I was asked.

I answered, "We have three chefs who all know how to cook."

We never did complain to Humphrey. When I suggested it to the general manager, Diamond said, "Are you crazy? The minute you complain about one of the family, no matter who might be in the wrong, *you're* the one in the wrong."

Senator Stephen Young from Ohio caught Jordan in the dining room. Young had just gotten a steak, and instead of salting the steak, he had sprinkled it with sugar. Not realizing why his steak had tasted so unusual, he asked Jordan, "Why don't they get someone who knows how to cook in this damn restaurant?"

Jordan called Diamond and me to investigate. We soon discovered that the Humphrey kids had sneaked in again. When I reported back to Jordan, he laughed and said, "Well, you know, we've got to raise good politicians for the future. They've got to raise hell one way or the other to be known." And that was the end of it. Jordan phoned Young to say it was a youthful prank of some of the pages.

Even with this, we could not bar the Humphrey kids from the door. But we did try to keep an eagle eye on them. And the minute HHH went to the Vice-Presidency and the White House, Walter Mondale came along with the same kind of kids. Again, the switching of sugar and salt, the spilling of catsup on the tablecloths. I could only assume this was a Minnesota tradition. I don't know of kids from any of the other states who do this.

The children of Senator Henry Jackson of the state of Washington were little angels in comparison. Anna Marie, born February 1963, and Peter Hardin, April 1966, would act more adult than most adults, sitting back with their mother, Helen. The children's manners were perfect. They sat straight, used their silverware properly, even though they were only seven and ten years of age. When people talk about not being able to do a thing with their children's manners, I think of Helen Jackson and what she was able to do.

Little children, little troubles. Big children, big troubles. Even a family like the Kennedys are not immune. I would sometimes hear through the grapevine that Ted Kennedy was very worried about the sons of his dead brother, Senator Robert Kennedy. And he would go rushing out of the Capitol sometimes to spend time with them and play substitute father.

But even so, they got into scrapes. The most serious perhaps happened in 1979, when Robert's twenty-four-year-old son, David, was beaten up in a seedy Harlem hotel. What looked at first like a simple mugging that netted $30 turned into a drug case. Twenty-five envelopes of heroin were found in a hallway of the hotel. The Kennedy family eventually admitted that David had a problem with drugs and that he had been hospitalized at the age of twenty-three for rehabilitation.

Robert Kennedy, Jr., also worried his family by flaunting tradition to take up housekeeping with a twenty-two-year-old girl sans marriage.

I remember when Joy Baker used to come to the Senate restaurants with her mother to visit Joy's father, Senator Everett Dirksen. Joy didn't appear to drink to excess. But her mother did, and so did the Senator himself. There was a saying on the Hill that Dirksen drank like a fish, and never dropped a drip. Neither he nor his wife showed their liquor. They probably were adjusted to it.

I'm not sure that Joy was already married to Howard Baker when I first met Senator Dirksen. His friends did not call him Everett, but "Eez." In my presence, his wife called him "Senator," seeming to feel the need to keep reminding people she was married to a Senator. I didn't need help in remembering that this woman was one of my many bosses.

Most people don't remember that Senator Baker's father was in the House, Representative Howard Henry Baker, Sr. When Senator Baker's father died in January 1964, Baker's stepmother, Irene Bailey Baker, was elected to fill out the Congressman's term. However, she did not choose to run for election in 1964, the same year. She only served from March 10, 1964, to January 3, 1965.

Howard Baker, Jr., served his first term as a Senator beginning January 1967. Senator Dirksen, I remember, ran all over Tennessee, helping his son-in-law raise campaign funds. A better father-in-law you couldn't get.

Senator Dirksen told me how dearly he loved his daughter Joy—actually, worshipped the ground she walked on. All he wanted was for her to have a happy, successful life. That's why he worked so hard for his son-in-law, and that's why I felt so bad when Senator Baker got up and told the world about his wife's drinking.

If Senator Dirksen had been alive, he would have given his son-in-law a real tongue-lashing. As a matter of fact, I wouldn't be surprised if he turned in his grave that day, during the 1976 campaign.

Possibly, Baker felt that President Ford would admire his bravery in standing up and blabbing about his wife's problem, which was all in the past. Maybe Baker believed that Ford would reward him for his bravery by offering him the Vice-Presidency, instead of Dole. It didn't work that way.

The Senate ladies had formidable power, and the Rules Committee never dared deny them anything they told me they wanted or needed. They had free use of a committee room to hold their big annual party for the First Lady—a sitdown affair for 90 to 110—in the caucus room of the Russell Building, Room 318.

Besides that, they had two rooms all to themselves, which could not be used by anyone else without special permission of the Rules Committee. The permanently assigned rooms were also in the Russell Building—154 and 155.

In these rooms, they met every Tuesday that the Senate was in session, rolling bandages for the Red Cross on oblong tables, and companionably eating lunch together in little clusters. It was interesting to see how they approached lunch. Some, refused to spend a cent, and brought their own sandwich and beverage like school kids. Others ordered the most expensive luncheons they could find in the Senate restaurant menu and had them delivered to them, then didn't tip. Some overtipped.

There was a little pantry with a hot plate where the ladies could make coffee—usually very weak—and heat up soup. Some who brought their own sandwiches sent to the restaurant for the coffee, which was almost strong enough to stand a spoon in it, Navy style.

As I've said the restaurant dreaded the call to serve these "angels of mercy," and my staff would end up muttering to themselves.

Most active among Senate ladies were Marvella Bayh, Antoinette Hatfield, Martha Elizabeth Hansen, Caroline Long—who relished belonging to the Club because she had come up through the ranks as Senator Sam Ervin's secretary—Peatsy Hollings, Betty Talmadge, and Mrs. J. Bennett Johnston.

Some Senate wives—like the Kennedy women—wouldn't show up for fear they would be bored rolling bandages. Others truly were interested in helping the Red Cross, and still others came to make a mark for themselves in this highly social group. There were many who were on an ego trip and were simply there to put on the dog and get a bit of recognition.

It's a long time since Hattie Caraway was a Senator on Capitol Hill—35 years to be exact. But a relative of hers is still there. He is Lewey Caraway, her nephew.

Hattie, whom I met when I came to Washington, was the wife of a Senator from Arkansas, who died in office in 1931. When she was appointed, and then elected, to fill her husband's seat, she wanted a member of the family near her, and brought her nephew to be an elevator operator at $1,000 a year. When she left office in January 1945, John McClellan became her nephew's sponsor.

Slowly, through his own ability, young Caraway rose to become the Senate's building superintendent, which he is today, with an income in excess of $40,000 a year.

I remember Joe Tydings would bring his stepmother, Marjorie Merriweather Post, in for lunch. She wore a lot of jewelry. Hair in tight rolls on her head. She had lovely features. She was very pleasant, very gracious, and many Senators would visit her table. But they would not sit down. She obviously wanted just her stepson to eat with her.

I recall that Joe Tydings did not entertain on the Hill. He didn't spend money needlessly. When alone he would eat in the carry-out shop and the cafeteria. To my recollection, I never saw him bring in anyone other than Mrs. Merriweather Post.

Fathers and sons don't always get along—even if they are both serving in the houses of Congress.

The point on which the Senator and his son, Congressman Barry Goldwater, Jr., did not see eye to eye was Susan Goldwater, the Congressman's wife. The Senator thought she was wonderful and a great mother to his little grandson, Barry Goldwater III. When the marriage did not hold together the Senator continued to see his daughter-in-law and attended many gatherings with her.

Eventually, after a divorce, Susan married an American ambassador, and the senior Goldwater attended her prenuptial parties. At least he had sense enough not to let her out of the family.

Susan was indeed a charmer. I admired her for her conduct during her difficult marriage when all the Hill buzzed with rumors of the Congressman's activities with many glamour girls about town. I also admired the way she set out to earn her own living, after the marriage was over, first trying her hand at real estate and then starting a new program for CBS in Washington, called "P.M. Magazine."

Where other such interview programs had only endured a short time, hers was so different and informative that it was still going strong with its co-host Henry Tannenbaum, at the helm, when she went sailing off into the sunset with her new husband.

The instance of Susan Goldwater shows that even with a change of husbands and a change of political party—from Republican to Democrat—one can keep one's political relatives happy.

A Funny Thing Happened on the Way to the Senate Forum

Not all Senators curse, and not all Senators have to.

The ultimate Capitol Hill curse does not need cuss words: "May you take a two-week vacation in the Bermuda Triangle."

Nowhere is the clever put-down so applauded as in the Sweetest Little Club in the World. Members who are expert at the delicate art of insult are much honored and quoted from one end of the Capitol to the other.

Whatever happens, be they Democrats or Republicans, the members of the Sweetest Little Club in the World stay cool. Sometimes they laugh till it hurts. Example:

Senators did not lie down and want to die during the Watergate scandals, even if they were Republicans. They just quipped along and kept smiling. Even Barry Goldwater was heard saying, "I don't know when I go to the White House whether they are going to be playing, 'Hail to the Chief' or 'Bail to the Chief.' "

Democrats, of course, found the proceedings even funnier, and chuckled as their colleague, Senator Joseph Montoya of New Mexico, commented that Nixon was substituting Opera Breakfasts for his Sunday Prayer Breakfasts because his staff was *singing* so eloquently. "In fact," Montoya added, "they're getting so famous you don't know where you're going to find them—one week they're on the cover of *Time* and the next week they are *doing* time!"

When Democratic running mate Senator Thomas Eagleton of Missouri confessed that he had had psychiatric troubles and had required the services of a shrink, Democratic Senators still managed to see a little humor, even as they groaned that there went their chances at the White House.

"Can you imagine confessing he's been on a couch and had a psychiatrist?" said my good friend, Senator Hubert Humphrey. "Now if they'd had Ted Kennedy as the candidate and he confessed he'd been on a couch, at least you wouldn't have to worry about his mental condition."

Some fellows on the Hill were commiserating with a Senator whose combination secretary-girlfriend had quit her job because of his chasing around. The Senator's AA, who knew the whole score, said, "Well, it isn't as if you've lost everything. You've still got your wife."

The Hill gang had a field day when President Carter insisted he had been attacked by a rabbit. He swore he was sitting in his own boat, minding his own business and trying to catch a fish, when this rabbit with blood in its eye came after him, swimming out for the attack.

The poor President had had to fight off the rabbit with his paddle.

My own favorite animal story is my memory of Ethel Kennedy coming grandly into the Senate dining room with her dog, Brumus, a huge monster—which no one else would be permitted to bring in—and appropriating Senator Scoop Jackson's table. The part he wasn't using.

Jackson is not fond of dogs. And he is not fond of uninvited guests at his table. He did not say a word, but I will never forget the grim look on his face as he sat stiffly enduring the fact that Ethel's dog had not only settled itself under the table but was comfortably sitting on his foot.

As I said, Jackson was a perfect gentleman, not saying a word of rebuke to the lady—but what he said to me on his way out!

When President Jimmy Carter was in Vienna on the SALT talks in 1979, the word came back that the Russian leader Brezhnev had slipped, and Carter had grabbed him and kept him from falling.

Wags on the Hill speculated on what other Presidential types would have done under the circumstances: Johnson would have pulled Brezhnev up by the ears; Nixon would have pushed him out of the way; Ford would have fallen with him; and Teddy Kennedy would have waited ten hours to decide what to do.

Jimmy Carter's sense of humor left something to be desired, and Gerald Ford's lost something in the translation. The real humorists of the 1976 campaign were the two Vice-Presidential candidates—Mondale and Dole. Seldom has the country been lucky enough to have such evenly matched wits. They had both received good training on the Hill.

Dole lost no time in saying that "the Democratic platform leans so far to the left that it ought to be inspected by the OSHA—the Occupational Safety and Health Administration."

Mondale came right back with the observation that Ford was campaigning on a "laundry list." He thought they were a list of issues. "Someone handed him the list, and he didn't know the difference."

Dole commented that he'd been passing through the Senate chamber recently, just in time to hear Mondale saying, "Let me tax your memory."

At that, he added, "Teddy Kennedy jumped up and shouted, 'That's a great idea. Why haven't we thought of that before?' "

Mondale countered by taking off his hat to the Republicans. "They've finally done something that's never been done before. They've given us *two* Presidents and *three* Vice-Presidents in two years—with only *one* election!"

Bob Dole wasn't all bad. I always thought it was a pity he was a Republican because he had a Democratic sense of humor. He used to go around saying, "I'm the only four-letter word around here that you can use." And now and then he would complain that he was not a household word, except in Hawaii.

But what the Hill appreciated most was what Dole said when Bill Fulbright got mad at him, claiming he was taking credit for introducing an amendment Fulbright had already introduced. The Hill doesn't know we are not in the agrarian era anymore, and members of Congress are always using cows and other farm animals to make a point. Senator Fulbright was saying that "stealing a man's amendment is like stealing his cow."

Dole attempted to placate his Democratic colleague by saying, "I didn't steal his cow. I just milked it a little."

Candidate Senator George McGovern, whose pursed lips gave him the nickname around the Hill of "Sweet Lips," was pretty good at throwing in a bit of barbed wit during the course of his campaign to wrest the Presidency from Richard Milhous Nixon. My favorite was his quip that President Nixon taking credit for Congress upping Social Security benefits was the equivalent of Scrooge taking credit for inventing Christmas.

One of the Carter gang, who had a mischievous sense of humor, was Bob Strauss, which is perhaps why Carter did not fire him in the famed Thursday Massacre, but kept him as one of his top aides.

With Senator Edward Kennedy breathing down his neck as his greatest contender for the Presidency, Carter needed laughs, especially those centering on Teddy Kennedy.

The story came back to Capitol Hill that one day Bob Strauss was in the West Wing of the White House on his way to confer with Carter, when he passed an open doorway and saw some of Senator Kennedy's aides consulting with the President's domestic-policy aide, Stuart Eizenstat.

Strauss yelled in, "Hey, Stu, that Kennedy really isn't as big an ass as you said he was," and then he darted away.

It takes a relative to know how to put a politician down. I sometimes wondered whether Jimmy Carter appreciated the barbs brother Billy tossed at him in the guise of humor—especially when in his cups. But even after Billy had gone to the same military drying out "spa" as Betty Ford had, he still hadn't kicked the barbed-wit habit.

Billy was trying to tell why he was sure his brother was going to run for reelection. "I was in Washington two weeks ago," he said, "and I found out Jimmy has bought four new suits. And tight as he is, I'm sure he isn't buying four suits unless it is for something serious. There's no way he won't run."

Billy Carter seemed to have a compulsion to put everyone down, but even staunch Republicans commented that maybe Brother Billy had finally gone too far when he cast a humorous aspersion at Chappaquiddick, on the Tom Snyder TV show, "Tomorrow."

Ted Kennedy might make a good President, Brother Billy allowed, "But he couldn't get a job teaching driver education in Georgia."

Senators could joke about Teddy's misfortune but Presidential families are supposed to be like Caesar's wife and very prim and proper.

The stories that make the rounds of the Hill can be pretty raunchy. And sometimes they are perfectly true.

One day Senator Norris Cotton had his fly open. It was called to his attention. Not a bit bothered, he said, "Listen, anything that can't get up can't get out."

Senator Alan Simpson of Wyoming is one Senator who doesn't take the office too seriously. "You know the difference between a horse race and a political race?" he asks. "In a horse race, the entire horse is running."

You frequently hear a Senator giving a punchline to his table companions with a straight face, "The problem with leadership is that it's hard to tell whether the crowd is following you or chasing you."

Or this sage bit of advice: "Don't argue with a fool—people might not recognize which of you is the fool."

The work of the Hill revolves around statistics, and staffers are always running around or phoning cross-country to find statistics that will back up the position their Senator has taken on some subject.

Though they all act very grimly serious about these findings that make such-and-such bill necessary, with a few drinks in them, Senators and staffers like to quote what Mark Twain said on the subject: "There are three degrees of lies—lies, damn lies, and statistics."

The ultimate use of the statistic, a staffer once told me, is the proof that beds are dangerous—"Most people die in them."

Will Rogers' spirit also still lives on Capitol Hill. When the hundredth anniversary of his birth took place in June 1979, Senators Henry Bellmon and David Boren, both of Oklahoma, hosted a party for Rogers' fans among the Congress and important Oklahomans. The walls of the Senate caucus room were decorated with Will Rogers photos and political commentary.

Boren, a Democrat, pointed out that the job of President was just as tough in Rogers' day as it is now, and quoted the humorist as saying, "We shouldn't elect a President; we should elect a magician."

Senators are always proud of anything that makes their state look good. Senator Sam Nunn of Georgia was ecstatic when a bushel of Georgia peaches was auctioned off at the Porter peach festival for $3,500. It wasn't just any bushel of peaches but that judged by the festival to be the Grand Champion bushel.

Nunn had to take a little ribbing, however, because evidently no Georgian could afford them. The winning bid came from Oklahoma men—representing Tulsa TV station KTUL and the Razor Clam Restaurant of Tulsa.

When Carter traveled to Japan and met the Emperor, who was cast in the role of the heavy after Pearl Harbor, the tale came back to the Hill about an exchange between Carter and Hirohito.

To make conversation, Hirohito is supposed to have asked Carter where he was going next on his travels. Carter told him he was on his way to Hawaii to see Pearl Harbor.

As the story goes, Hirohito smiled and said, "Well, you know the best time to get there is early in the morning."

The man who will probably go down in Senate history as our greatest raconteur is the beloved Sam Ervin of North Carolina, whom everyone around the Hill respectfully referred to as "Senator Sam."

Senator Sam was very concerned about the good health of the Democratic party, and when he heard that someone—maybe it was Harry Byrd, Jr.—had left the party to become an Independent, he told this story:

There were two boyhood playmates in Morgantown, North Carolina, who did everything together and even got religion at the same time and joined the church together. And they made a mighty vow that every night they would get down on their knees and pray for the other one as long as they lived.

They drifted apart, and one of the fellows, known as Uncle Billy Hallyburton, became the magistrate of the town and a leading citizen. One night Uncle Billy was awakened in the middle of the night by a loud knocking.

"Who's disturbing the peace at this ungodly hour of the night?" shouted Uncle Billy out the window."

"It's your old boyhood friend, Carlton Giles," the figure below shouted back. "I heard a foul slander against you tonight, Brother Billy, and I hitched up my horse and drove right over."

"What slander? What you talking about?" shouted Uncle Billy.

"The foulest slander," shouted Carlton Giles, "and I want to hear a denial from your own mouth. I heard you have left the Democrats and taken up with the Populists."

"Go on home, Brother Carlton, that's no slander," shouted Uncle Billy. "That's the truth."

There was a long pause and then Carlton Giles's voice came wafting up again: "Brother Billy, do you remember when we joined the church together and promised each other we would get down on our knees and pray for each other for as long as we lived?"

"I remember," came the loud reply.

"Brother Billy," yelled his old boyhood friend, "Brother Billy, I have kept my part of the promise. And every night I have gotten down on my knees and prayed to the Almighty for you. And Brother Billy, do you hear me? From now on you can do your own goddamn praying!"

As for political platforms, Senator Sam called them "the ultimate exercise in hypocrisy." But the Bible-loving man saved his best punch line to blast Ford for pardoning Nixon before seeing what action the Watergate special prosecutor would take—pointing out that the President was more powerful than God, because he could pardon a man who had not confessed his sins.

When Jimmy Carter got the Democratic nomination, in 1976, Sam Ervin, who had retired from office, was asked what he thought of it. With his usual candor he said he would support Jimmy Carter "because he and I are both Democrats, and I hope, as the campaign goes along, he'll give me some more good reasons."

I remember when John Fitzgerald Kennedy was a Senator, telling Irish-wake stories, his favorite brand of humor. His place has been taken by another Irishman, Senator Daniel P. Moynihan of New York, who always enjoys a good Irish-wake story, especially this one.

It's a story about a fellow named Paddy, who happened to take on a wee nip on his way to the wake of a friend. When Paddy came weaving into the room, he failed to focus on the casket, and instead knelt before a maple upright piano.

After staying on his knees a suitable length of time, he got up and started to make his way to the door when he spied his friend Mike's grieving widow. "Sure and it's a grand wake," Paddy said, taking the widow's hand to comfort her. "I did notice that Mike's complexion was a little bad, but his teeth sure held up."

In view of all the expletives deleted in the Nixon Watergate tapes, it is amusing to look back to 1960 at how candidate John Fitzgerald Kennedy handled the fact that his opponent, Richard Nixon, was expressing great shock at the salty language ex-President Harry Truman was using:

> One of the inspiring notes that was struck in the last debate was struck by the Vice-President [Nixon] in his moving warning to the children of the nation and the candidates against the use of profanity by Presidents and ex-Presidents when they are on the stump. And I

know, after fourteen years in the Congress with the Vice-President, that he was very sincere in his views about the use of profanity.

But I am told that a prominent Republican said to him yesterday in Jacksonville, Florida, "Mr. President, that was a damn fine speech." And the Vice-President said, "I appreciate the compliment but not the language." And the Republican went on, "Yes sir, I liked it so much that I contributed a thousand dollars to your campaign."

And Mr. Nixon replied, "The hell you say."

However, I would not want to give the impression that I am taking former President Truman's use of language lightly. I have sent him the following wire:

MR. PRESIDENT: I HAVE NOTED YOUR SUGGESTION AS TO WHERE THOSE WHO VOTE FOR MY OPPONENT SHOULD GO. WHILE I UNDERSTAND AND SYMPATHIZE WITH YOUR DEEP MOTIVATION, I THINK IT IS IMPORTANT THAT OUR SIDE TRY TO REFRAIN FROM RAISING THE RELIGIOUS ISSUE.

PART III

President, Anyone?

Neither Fish nor Fowl- The Vice-Presidents

The Senate is one place where nothing is sacred—even death. When former Vice-President Rockefeller died under rather mysterious circumstances, with only trousers and no undershorts on, and a certain fogginess existed about how many females, associates, guards, and others were around, the word quickly spread on the Hill, "Rocky's fluctuating blood pressure finally caught up with him—seventy over anything from eighteen to thirty." His proclivities were well remembered.

But forgiven. Because a Vice-President is very special there, even though the public may view a Vice-President as neither fish nor fowl. Vice-President Humphrey himself used the label, adding that a Vice-President is required to act like a President yet have the humility and modesty of a vestal virgin or a novice nun.

At the Club we call the Senate, Presidents are not the most honored of men. Vice-Presidents are the most honored. Nowhere around the Capitol will you find statues of all the Presidents. But what you will find are busts of past Vice-Presidents. As I am writing this book, two more have been installed on the second floor of the Senate side of the Capitol. They happen to have been Presidents as well—but that is secondary. Richard M. Nixon and Lyndon Baines

Johnson were honored for all eternity for having presided as presidents of the Senate.

Because the Senate is very conscious of protocol, the statues are installed in turn, and still to be placed, at this writing, are Hubert Horatio Humphrey, Spiro Theodore Agnew, Gerald Rudolph Ford, Nelson Aldrich Rockefeller, and Walter Frederick Mondale.

A Vice-President has a formal office off the Senate floor facing the Senate chamber. His office is on the right-hand side and the President's office is on the left-hand side. The President uses it when he comes to make State of the Union addresses. They are separated by the cloakroom.

Even though the President and Vice-President might not be there for weeks or months on end, the two rooms are kept under very strict security because they are considered a part of the Senate Chamber. Even when the building seems deserted, night and day the two rooms are under guard.

When I first saw Nelson Rockefeller, I did not dream that one day he would be presiding over the Senate or that I would know about his private life and would be treating him almost like an old shoe around Capitol Hill.

It happened not too long after he had married Happy, and he was still being talked about as a possible President. I was having dinner and cocktails at the Sheraton Hotel with two family visitors, my mother and my first cousin, Lucille Goodgame, the head of the mathematics department of the State Board of Education of Mississippi.

Rocky suddenly entered the room with a sexy-looking girl, who was even younger than his bride, who was not along.

I said to my mother, "Boy, the governor sure does keep nice young company."

She gave me a dirty look and said, "You might call it company, but where I come from, we call it something else." From his behavior, it appeared that Rocky was romantically interested in the lady. I more or less forgot about it—mature men keeping nice young company on Capitol Hill is hardly a novelty—until the ex-New York governor arrived on Capitol Hill in his new position as Vice-President to Gerald Ford.

I had several good friends among the staffers of the Senate Rules Committee, which assigns space to new men on the Senate side and explains the rules of protocol. What I learned was that Rockefeller had barely hit town before he had stolen away the beautiful girlfriend of one of the first men he had dealt with in his new position.

One of the men connected with the committee warned the new Vice-President that this was one of the most dangerous things a Hill man could do—get involved with staff members. The new Vice-President retorted that he did not need any underling staffer's advice to guide his personal life, that he made friends with whom he damn pleased.

Then he let loose a bombshell. He said he planned to find a place for the young lady on his own staff.

My friend who had been dumb enough to give this advice came down to the restaurant and told me, "To hell with this guy and all his money. I can just see what life is going to be like up here with him around. I'm going to look into retirement this very day. I'm going for my forms."

I couldn't believe my ears. "You're going for your forms?"

"You heard me. I'm going for my forms right now."

My friend took an early retirement, and I kept in touch with him, and we exchanged bits of information about how the new Vice-President was conducting himself.

Rocky chose to ignore the advice he had been given, and it was common gossip that the Vice-President was involved with one of his employees. As all the Hill experts on staying out of trouble knew, if you're going to play around, you should keep it off the Hill. The reason Wilbur Mills got away with his girl chasing for so long was because it was off the Hill.

Even though the lady of Mills's choice was a stripper and actually lived in the same apartment building he did, he suffered no bad publicity until heavy drinking dulled his judgment so much that he ended up attracting the attention of the police on the night his lady love jumped into the Tidal Basin quite far from Capitol Hill.

Around the Hill, Mills was the kind of man you could find nothing to gossip about except his drinking.

Rocky didn't seem to care that he was seen too much in the company of one female. He would take her to dinner at the Hill "in" spots like the Monocle. Or they would disappear at long lunches at the prominent hotels. At one hotel, he had his own dining room and private rest room and even a private bar in an adjoining lounge. He had his own bartender and his own waiter. He maintained his own supply of liquor there.

I know that at the Hill parties he drank Chivas Regal on the rocks with just a dash of water. But his girlfriend told me he drank nothing but champagne with his meals. Since liquor is not served in the Senate restaurants, we seldom saw him there at mealtime.

I had almost a front-seat view of this romance because Rocky's girlfriend was a good friend of mine in a nonromantic way. Since she didn't trust her girlfriends not to try to take him away from her, she turned to me as the friend she could confide in.

Supposedly, according to her, he had been a perfect gentleman to this point. Only tender and romantic. Nothing more.

One day she called me full of excitement, asking whether I had time for a cup of coffee. I said, "Sure. Come on down to the dining room."

She said, "This is very confidential. I've got to talk to someone but I don't want anyone around to overhear me."

I said, "Meet me in G 211, Dirksen Building. It's time for the dining room to close and I'll be at the back table—Senator Jackson's table—with a cup of coffee for you."

She finally came out with it: "I have my suitcase in the office, but I don't know what to do. I'm terrified."

Rocky had just invited her to visit his estate in the Virgin Islands—Caneel Bay. She would be leaving in his private jet that afternoon. It was a Friday.

"My God," I said, "are you going alone?"

"No, he'll have his maid and houseman and pilot and copilot, and of course he'll be there. Just one happy family."

I laughed. "More power to you and get the hell out of here. If you have to get to Andrews Air Force Base before the plane leaves at four, you haven't got much time." It was then a quarter of three.

She was so excited that she was partially crying and laughing again. "I'm so scared. I had thought of maybe giving his chauffeur a note that I couldn't make it," she said. "He's sending his car for me, so I don't have to worry about catching a cab. But now I'm going." She laughed, "I've had to fight before, and if I have to fight Rockefeller, it will be an enjoyable fight."

She jumped up and I grabbed her arm. I said, "Hey, you've been crying and your makeup is streaked. Let me walk you to the ladies' room before the gossips see you."

I was pleased to see, on her return, that my old friend was smiling broadly. She came to see me on the following Tuesday morning at my office.

I said, "Well, wha' hoppen'?" My assistant was in the office so she didn't want to talk. She said, "I prefer to have lunch with you—my treat, of course. I have so much to tell you."

"In the meantime, can you lend me a million bucks?" I joked.

She laughed hysterically. "I'll have it for you next year, you damn fool. I'll see you at eleven thirty in G 211."

I chuckled to myself as I reflected how this gal was an ardent Democrat and Rocky was Republican Vice-President.

This time we honored Senator John McClellan's table. He was the chairman of the Appropriations Committee for the Senate and never arrived at his private table till 12:05.

I had ordered her lunch and mine, and it was on the table when she appeared, hardly seeing where she was going or what she was eating. Her head was in the clouds.

She was so excited, she walked right by the hostess without saying where she was going, almost causing an incident in this protocol-laden room.

The first thing she said was "What a man, what a man. This man's got everything. Lou, I can't tell you the type of home he's got. And I was waited on hand and foot. Being a poor southern gal, I never dreamed I would see such treatment. It's like in the movies. The environment. The private golf course. The shrubbery. The immense gardens. It's thirty acres. I can't believe it."

Again she began to laugh and cry with enjoyment. And said, "I feel so free. I feel no obligation to anybody. Do you blame me?"

I said, "I told you. You'd be a damn fool not to see the good life. What happened? What kind of a lover did you have?"

At first she hesitated, saying, "Oh, nothing happened while I was on the island. I had my own room, with my own maid." She told how the maid had helped her choose clothes to wear from a fantastic wardrobe that was there and even included suits and cosmetics. And expensive French perfumes.

"Would you believe," she said, "he gave me a bottle to take

along and told me to quit wearing the junk perfume I've been putting on." She shook her head as she remembered.

Then she added, "Guess what. I was not allowed to even open my suitcase, and I had enough clothes along to last the weekend. A brand-new bikini, and I never got to use it."

"What happened to your suitcase?" I asked curiously.

"You can't believe it," she said. "When we landed at the private airport, a limousine was waiting, and the manager of the estate met us. Then a butler took my suitcase when we got to the mansion, and I never saw it again.

"Mansion?" I asked.

"Yes, I guess you'd call it a mansion," she said teasingly. "It had thirty-five or so rooms and twelve bathrooms. Though we had adjoining bedrooms, we had separate baths."

"So you had adjoining rooms but nothing happened?"

She threw back her head and laughed. "I guess he had to rest up a day or two from his other activities. Because he made up for it on the plane ride back."

"You're kidding," I said.

"No, I'm not," she said. "That's when it finally happened." It had been romantic and beautiful and had taken place in one of the two bedrooms on the plane.

I must admit that, though I heard a lot of things on Capitol Hill, even I was a little startled. Ah, love!

She really seemed carried away. Then came the leveling off period. She would come back to the Hill to see me now and then—she told me that she knew she was not the only extracurricular love in Rocky's life. "I know I'm one of five in addition to his wife. And he really does care for her, too."

"Doesn't it bother you," I asked, "the competition?"

"No," she said. "I'm just happy that he needs me too and feels that I can make him happy as well as do a good job for him in the office. It's a wonderful closeness."

She commented that Rocky was not aware that she knew about the other girls in his life and was sure he would be embarrassed to find that out, as most men would be. As for his wife, Rocky had told her that he really loved and respected her but could only feel intense sexual excitement with a young woman of prime child-bearing age.

That was the way Rocky had stated it. Then she had restated it in her own words. "He has to feel he is knocking a girl up. That's his sexual hangup."

Meanwhile, life with Rocky presiding over the Senate went on serenely enough, and we had a friendship of sorts.

I knew Rockefeller was a good tipper because the help were hiding their tips. If a Senator or Vice-President was a cheapie, they made fun of him behind his back. If he was exceptionally generous, they would clam up but fight to take care of him.

Happy Rockefeller rarely came to the Hill. I was told by Rocky's office staff that he discouraged it. Mrs. Ford as First Lady would be seen around the Hill more often than Rockefeller's wife.

My friend continued to pretend, when she was with him, that she didn't know about his other dalliances. But as time went on, she would sometimes be a little sad, as she would tell me the things she was learning.

I would try to bring her out of it by telling her straight stuff: "Come on now, grow up. You've told me yourself you know this can't be a permanent thing. You're in it for what it can do for your career and what it can mean monetarily. On that basis, you're way ahead of the game already."

She admitted that I was probably right but that it hurt anyway, not knowing how long it would last. It did last long enough for her to vacation on the Riviera and even to meet a princess once in Paris—a high-water mark for her.

But meanwhile, according to her, Rocky would also indulge himself with other young women, the younger the better. And every one of them seemed to come out the better for it. He'd buy them clothes, set them up in fancy apartments, make sure the furnishings were in good taste, take them to New York and turn them over to a dress designer.

Rocky would have someone make them over—tell them what to wear, how to fix their hair, how to apply their makeup. Just as they did for movie stars. They would even be instructed in the colors they were to wear. In other words he wanted them first-class in his presence.

My friends told me that Rocky had picked up a young gal and sent her abroad to finishing school. When he had developed her potential fully and had a suitable companion, beautiful and sophisticated, he put her on the payroll at six figures a year and all expenses to look after him during some of his trips.

My friend was aware of this and even when the companion was visiting in Washington. "When you become his girlfriend, he owns you," she told me when I asked her why she didn't play around too. She was afraid to be anywhere but where he could reach her at any time. For a time, she had to share him with another girl whom he would take to the same supper clubs he took her to.

My friend had cleverly cultivated a friendship with several of the employees at Rocky's eating places so they could keep her informed. She found it grimly amusing that Rocky was trying to be fair by dividing himself equally between them—alternating evenings.

I was told that one of Rocky's "graduates" eventually became a personage in communications. He had become enamored of her beauty and in this case had sent her to a finishing school in the East.

When my young friend got too sad, I would also remind her that she could afford to share the wealth. Rocky had been very good to her, she admitted, and had moved her from her small apartment to the commodious place she owned, with a live-in maid, in a fashionable section of Washington, D.C.

When Rockefeller's term as Vice-President was about over, my friend came to talk to me about all the decisions she had to make: Should she move to New York? Should she stay in Washington and get a job again on the Hill? Should she just be Rocky's girlfriend or let him get her a job in New York as he wanted to. And what should she do about her Washington place?

Before we were through talking, she had decided to hang on to the place, in case Rocky shunted her aside for someone else. But she was going to hang on as long as she could.

I told her to keep in touch with me, even though I was no longer on the Hill, and she did. She purchased an attractive dwelling in New York and urged me to stay there any time that I came to New York. She seemed quite pleased that she had gotten what she called a "confidential job" and was being paid a great deal a year.

She said that I should feel free to call her collect any time, and she would tell me where to pick up the key, and I could just make myself at home, whether she was there or not.

Then one night she called, sounding rather agitated and depressed. She wasn't sure she was going to be happy in New York after all, she said. And if I was going to come visit her, I had better hurry up and do it.

I didn't do it, and eventually I was shocked to read of the bizarre circumstances under which Nelson Rockefeller died in his town house in New York off Fifth Avenue. The person with him at the time was not my friend. That was someone else—Megan Marshack—about whom I know nothing at all.

As for what happened to my friend, I am happy to say she has since found happiness and has a new and different life.

Not all Vice-Presidents played around. Jerry Ford and Fritz Mondale didn't care for extracurricular women. The bottle was good enough. However, both men held their liquor well and were never obviously loaded.

I knew the Gerald Fords for many years—through the time Jerry was Congressman, then House Minority Leader, then Vice-President, and finally President of the United States.

In fact, I knew the Fords better than they realized. A relative of mine was the Fords' baby sitter on occasions when they had a night out on the town. It was nothing unusual for them to come home in their cups, and decide to take a 2 A.M. swim in the pool of their Alexandria house. One such night, when they got home, Jerry wanted to go swimming, but Betty said no, she just wanted to keep drinking.

Jerry put on his swim trunks and kept telling Betty to put her suit on. Betty said, no, she was going to sit and drink no matter what he did.

Grumpily, Jerry got into the pool. But, suddenly, he reached up over the rim, grabbed her by the leg, and pulled her in with her clothes on, drink and all.

Before they were so surrounded by Secret Service men, the minority leader and his wife would come to the parties on the Senate side. It was known and accepted on the Hill that both were heavy drinkers. Betty Ford had a good reputation of being able to hold her liquor. Even though she drank her liquor straight, she never seemed under the influence to me.

Staffers always commented on how Betty Ford refused to act

her age, and seemed to be working at appearing young and frivolous. She would be flirtatious with the men, and I must say, they responded to her.

Through the years I got to observe quite a few Vice-Presidents on a day-to-day basis and must say they certainly were different from their public images. Nor did I necessarily go along with public opinion. I confess I liked Nixon's first Vice-President, Spiro Agnew. He was one of my favorite people.

I was really shocked when I learned Agnew was in trouble and was being accused of misuse of influence. After he chose not to contest one of the charges and resigned the Vice-Presidency, other nations chose to trust him enough to help them do business with Americans.

I choose to remember him as he was on the Hill. He wasn't an excessive drinker. He had a few drinks socially and was clever about getting out of taking another drink without hurting anyone's feelings.

And he wasn't a lady chaser. He was as fond of his wife, Judy, as it was possible to be. They were inseparable. I enjoyed seeing them together.

I would hear the outrageous things Spiro Agnew would say about the press, of course, but I didn't develop the hate toward the man that others did. I found his comments only amusing. I was used to Senators making insulting comments about the news media—didn't everyone?

The only difference was Agnew let himself be quoted. His words like "effete snobs" seemed milk mild compared to the names others used—"press" and "son of a bitch" were almost synonymous in the inner-sanctum dining room.

I recall that among other social events, I catered four Christmas parties for Agnew and his staff. He gave them a Christmas party every year, and it was even a family-style party where they exchanged gifts from names pulled from a hat. I never saw anyone get drunk at these parties.

Nixon, who was much more powerful in his position as Vice-President under President Eisenhower, gave no such parties on the Hill.

Incidentally, everyone wanted to wait on Vice-President Agnew. I never heard any complaint about him. In fact, he was held in great affection in the Senate restaurant because he was one of the very, very few bigshots on the Hill who talked to everyone from the busboy to the porter who did the sweeping and vacuum cleaning.

For this reason, the restaurant help called him "the male Lady Bird." It was a compliment. Lady Bird Johnson was beloved around the restaurants for the same reason—she made the humblest person feel important and noticed.

I felt even sorrier for Judy than for Spiro, when her husband's job on the Hill came to a screeching halt. They had just bought a home in Montgomery County, Maryland, and had moved out of the Sheraton Park Hotel where they had maintained an apartment.

Their whole dream, Judy Agnew told me, had been to have such a house—colonial style with stately columns. There had been stories around the Hill about how much the Secret Service had spent on building a wall around the back of the estate to protect the swimming-pool area from curiosity seekers and give the family privacy for the first time.

At the last Christmas party Spiro and Judy gave for his staff, I had a long conversation with Judy about her newfound happiness—how much they were enjoying the house, and how she had never dreamed when she was a little girl that she would grow up to live in a house with columns like Mount Vernon.

Judy had assured me they were eventually going to have an open house and my name would be high on the mailing list. It never happened. Before it came to pass, all the problems involving Agnew had hit the papers, and he eventually had to sell the place.

Now they have a home on the Eastern Shore of Chesapeake Bay, and I wish them happiness.

People ask me if I learned any good Greek recipes from Vice-President Agnew and whether he gave us a hard time over money. Agnew did not flaunt his Greek origin. He didn't serve Greek food when he hosted parties on the Hill. Whatever he did, he never haggled about the price. He would tell me, "We're planning on having a party for X number of people. Will you plan me a menu and tell me the price?"

When I worked it out and went back to tell him, he never complained or commented. He just accepted it. I have letters I received after many of his parties, complimenting me on how well it had gone.

In comparison, Fritz Mondale questioned every price, through a member of his staff, whom he would send to talk to me. By the time he was Vice-President, I had retired, but I remember Mondale well from his Senatorial days.

I remember Fritz was appointed Senator from Minnesota on December 30, 1964, after Humphrey had been elected Vice-President to serve with Lyndon Johnson. Humphrey resigned in order to give Mondale seniority over the new members to be sworn in on January 3, 1965.

Fritz Mondale was the razor-sharp kid in college, who hitched his wagon to a star and helped his old Macalester, Wisconsin, professor friend, Hubert Horatio Humphrey, get elected to the Senate in 1948. Mondale knew talent when he saw it and was convinced that simply being mayor of Minneapolis was not a big enough job for HHH.

With a man like Hubert Humphrey, old favors were not forgotten, and when Hubert resigned his Senate post in December 1964 to become Lyndon Johnson's Vice-President, he helped boost Mondale into the Senate to serve out the remaining days of his term.

Humphrey probably also deserves the greatest amount of credit for boosting Mondale into the Number 2 slot as running mate with Carter, by recommending him most highly to the Democratic candidate.

Back to December of 1964, when Mondale was the new man in town, I remember that Doris Fleischer, his secretary, came to see me so many times over the swearing-in party to ask why they were being charged so much for this and that item that she was very embarrassed. She apologized.

I told her not to worry, that each Senator had his own way of handling things, and we adjusted.

Probably, as the result of the shock of paying for a party with liquor and hors d'oeuvres, after that the Mondales usually managed to entertain at breakfast parties, rather than lunch or dinner.

I would give many menu suggestions, but almost invariably they would choose the least expensive breakfast on the catering menu—creamed chipped beef on toasted cornbread, served with orange juice and coffee, $1.25. The only thing cheaper was a Continental breakfast, which was rolls, juice, and coffee.

I was told that Mondale and Birch Bayh were about the poorest guys up there, financially, in the Club, rubbing shoulders with the multimillion-dollar boys. So I did not mind that Mondale tried to keep his expenses down. It really takes a lot of money to keep up appearances on the Hill.

The Mondales didn't seem too concerned about their public image in those post-Jack Kennedy years when the nation had gotten accustomed to the elegance and formality of Jacqueline Kennedy's attire and were still following it. Therefore it was natural that what struck me as unusual was the casualness of dress of the Mondale family when they came to the Hill for lunch. The kids would have shirttails out. The girls wore blue jeans and so did Joan Mondale. They wore open sandals and no stockings on a summer day.

Joan Mondale was an active member of the Senate ladies Red Cross Association and rolled bandages weekly. I don't know if she continued that actively as Second Lady.

As a couple, Joan and Fritz were poor tippers. Once a waitress complained in the dining room that when she served Mrs. Mondale at the Red Cross luncheon, Mrs. Mondale, among others, left no tip.

After Fritz Mondale became Vice-President, the word around the Hill was that, aside from having a free Vice-Presidential residence, Mondale had been better off as a Senator.

Because of his poverty and lack of power, Mondale was treated more like an office boy by Carter, including running errands up to Congress. He was not even allowed at Camp David. When he was entertaining, he did it at the Old Herbert Hoover camp down in the Blue Ridge Mountains.

Agnew had had Camp David privileges and would frequently go there with Nixon.

Under Lyndon Baines Johnson, Humphrey was treated like Mondale. He, too, was not allowed at Camp David, and just before he died, it brought tears to my eyes, when Humphrey, looking frail and at death's door, thanked Carter for having invited him to the Presidential retreat for a weekend. He had never seen it before.

Incidentally, I heard that when Mondale used Camp Hoover, he had to pay the National Park Service for its use. I seem to recall it was only $40 a day, but it was the principle of the thing that bothered me. If a President can use Camp David without any charge, why shouldn't his second-in-command have something similar graciously provided?

I was pleased to hear that at least Mondale maintained a sense of humor about his inferior position. Mondale himself told the story of the man who lived near Three Mile Island who had been assured that the area was safe from radioactivity because the *President* had visited it.

"What makes you think that proves it's safe?" the man had demanded.

"Because," Mondale quoted the expert as saying, "if it wasn't safe, they would have sent the Vice-President."

We no longer have the famous Robert Kennedy pool parties where Congressmen get pitched in with all their clothes, but the Mondales are at least a little bit colorful. At some Mondale gathering, as the Hill crowd heard it, a member of the Mondale family had mentioned that the windows of the Vice-Presidential mansion were made of bullet-proof glass. Someone—slightly giddy—decided to check this out and threw a lamp at the window. The report on the Hill was the window was breakproof—spiderweb lines appeared, but the glass did not break.

Every now and then, HHH, when he was Vice-President, would sit and tell me how he hated to go to the White House, and how terrible it was for his ego to go there. "I meet that jackass in the hall, and he runs right over me and doesn't even say hello, good morning, or acknowledge I'm alive."

I was happy that Humphrey could relax enough with me to call a President a jackass, because he always had to go around projecting his image of the Happy Warrior and a perfect gentleman.

He was "damn sick" of LBJ's attitude, he told me, and once even commented that he was "the most unhappy man in the world." I thought wouldn't the world be surprised to hear their smiling Vice-President had said this.

I asked why Lyndon Johnson had picked him if he didn't like him.

Hubert said, "Lou, you're not dumb. Surely you must know Johnson picked me solely because he didn't think he could handle the Negro vote without a liberal." Then he looked at me and said something that really shocked me: "There's no way in the world these people can ever be put on the same economic or social or scholastic level with the average American because of their inability to accept the generosity that has been shown them in picking them up and pushing them forward. No way till they change their attitude. Maybe it will take a hundred years."

Hubert Humphrey was not the saint he was made out to be, but he was one of the dearest people I knew on the Hill, and one that I cannot get out of my mind. Such a good actor was Humphrey in posing as the happy-go-lucky legislator, that few people ever got to see the man inside.

I did and I think it is time to tell the truth. At least the segment that I know.

For example, I'm sure that most people don't know how bitter he felt about the way Mondale ignored him in his latter years. In private conversations, after he had been operated on for cancer and returned to the Hill, Humphrey talked to me about the pain of helping someone rise to power and then being ignored by him.

Humphrey told me several times how he had helped Mondale get into the Senate and had been his mentor and then Mondale had treated him like dirt—ignoring his existence. After I was gone from the Hill, he had even had a talk with Jimmy Carter and recommended Mondale for the Vice-Presidency. He could have recommended someone else, but didn't.

When Humphrey died and was buried in Minnesota, Vice-President Mondale made a very moving speech about how Humphrey was the greatest man that lived, and that he had taught the world how to live and how to die.

Mondale had cared. Had appreciated. But it was too late for the man who loved him to know.

HHH was a giant among men, who helped everyone who showed the slightest inclination to help himself. I saw him do that until the time he died.

One of the last persons he took under his wing was a young man from Minnesota who came to the Washington area and wanted to be in the aviation business. When he met Humphrey, he had just one plane and flew private individuals. Humphrey took a liking to him and gave him all kinds of advice, and today he owns a fleet of small planes and runs a charter-airplane service.

The young pilot's father had been a friend of Humphrey's in Minneapolis, back in the days when Hubert was running the family drugstore. The pilot told me his father had had a hard time raising a big family of kids, and Humphrey himself had helped out the pilot's father. And he helped the future pilot get through college and counseled him on getting ahead in business.

I don't know the details but the pilot loved HHH like a father. Muriel Humphrey resented the close relationship but hid it well until her husband died.

Hubert Humphrey had helped the young pilot meet important people on the Hill, who became his clients and passengers, and the young pilot had never let Humphrey down—the bill for these parties had always been paid before thirty days were up. The Senator never got a bill for the parties because they were always paid currently. Anything over ninety days was considered to be in arrears.

Once, after I had handled a party for him, under the sponsorship of Senator Humphrey, the young pilot came to pay the bill. He said, "Lou, I've got to make a trip to St. Thomas and the Dominican Republic over the weekend. I'll only have one person. Would you like to go along?"

I would have, but my dear friend Nora, with whom I shared a home for so many years, was sick in a nursing home and depended on me to be near. I was especially sorry I didn't go because I would have gotten to talk about Hubert Humphrey, one of my favorite subjects.

Because this young pilot was with Humphrey a good deal, especially in the latter days, I got to know him very well and liked him for his dedication to the Senator, who was more than a little lonely in his last days, but hiding it under a grin.

When Humphrey was in the hospital being operated on for cancer, the young pilot was there. And when Humphrey was in his last days on the Hill, the pilot was there. In fact, he went around getting blood donors lined up in anticipation that there would be need of it.

As it turned out, the donated blood was not needed. Humphrey deteriorated gradually, and I could see the change from month to month as he just faded away.

Humphrey died almost a pauper by the standards of the Club. But most of all, what bothered him was his disillusionment, because of his years with Lyndon Johnson. This was uppermost in his mind in one of my last talks with him in the Senate private dining room.

I remember how drawn and thin he looked. At this point, he

was taking chemotherapy, and his once luxuriant hair was falling out and had turned white. He was in a talking mood, and I sat and talked with him. He said, "You know what a raw deal I've gotten from my own party," he said. "You know I didn't get the backing. With backing I would have made the Presidency. But of course they were getting their orders and taking their cues from Johnson. I never believed that Johnson would be as small and petty as he was. All he had to do was speak up."

I walked Humphrey to the subway. It was as he stood beside the subway track, waiting for the little trolley to take him back to his office, that he told me that everyone was going to be surprised some day, and that he would eventually win out and be credited with all he had accomplished, and exonerated for his mistakes made during the Vietnam War.

As he stood there, Hubert said he had been opposed to the war, but he simply had to be a team player, echoing what his commander in chief wanted.

He had a faraway look in his eye as he told me he was leaving instructions for the type of funeral he would like, someday. I told him it was a long way off, and he pulled himself together and laughed and buoyantly agreed.

Former Republican Congresswoman Clare Boothe Luce of Connecticut shares a party-time joke with current Senator Charles Percy of Illinois.

Raquel Welch, beauteous movie star, shares drink with Senator Larry Pressler, who shocked other, more staid and conservative members of the Club by announcing in 1979 that he was running for the Presidency in his very first term of office as Republican Senator from South Dakota. He also made news when he virtuously declined a bribe in the famous FBI-ABSCAM caper.

Senator Russell Long loves to tell stories about his daddy, Senator Huey Pierce Long, at parties, and here the wife of Chief Justice Warren Burger is among his eager audience. The Senator's daddy, Huey, used to be a guest at my house in Mississippi, and I listened to his stories at my kitchen table.

Joan Kennedy leans down to hear Eleanor McGovern better at a party, as Senator George McGovern of South Dakota listens in with a small bemused smile.

Rich man, poor man. I have to smile as I see one of the poorest men of the Club, Senator Birch Bayh of Indiana, shaking hands with one of the richest, Senator Lloyd Bentsen of Texas—both Democrats. Birch might not have had worldly goods, but he long had the love of a good woman, here looking up adoringly at her husband, some time before her death.

Liz Taylor arrives at a Hill party with husband, Senator John Warner of Virginia, and is immediately served a drink, befitting her rank of cherished guest wherever she goes. Her favorite drink, however, is champagne.

Senator Ted Kennedy walks with his mother, and wife, Joan,
trails behind. Ted is the perfect son, always giving his mother his first
attention. Rose is the perfect political mother—the nicest kind of
relative a politician can have.

Senator Edmund Muskie of Maine and Mrs. Pat Boone, wife of the singer, get a kick out of a story spun by Lloyd Hand, center, who was President Johnson's chief of protocol for a time.

For some reason, singer Glen Campbell was the special pet of the Senate wives. Here he gives Joy Baker a big smooch right in front of her husband, Senator Howard Baker of Tennessee, who peers between them pixielike.

Strange alliance in the old Senatorial days—the Nixons and the Johnsons arrive at a party together. The general public would be surprised to see how much Republicans and Democrats hobnob together on Capitol Hill, especially if there are no cameras around. I often think the voters take the political parties much more seriously than the politicians do.

Senator Scoop Jackson of Washington dances with the beautiful, statuesque Madame Alphand, wife of the French ambassador. After twenty years as one of the most eligible bachelors on Capitol Hill, there was much gnashing of teeth among the devastated females when Scoop married Helen Eugenia Hardin.

Senator William Fulbright of Arkansas gallantly fishes for an ice cube for his dinner party companion. Fulbright, as chairman of the Foreign Relations Committee, was one of the most sought-after guests of Capitol Hill, and you would see him, here, there, and everywhere.

The Hubert Humphrey few people knew—a fellow who let his hair down and clowned around and could even take a tumble romantically. I used to visit with him and his girlfriend.

One man who really liked to laugh was Senator Jack Kennedy. Here he is yakking away, probably at something Mrs. Barry Goldwater has said. She was more fun than most Senate wives and a wealthy lady in her own right.

Jackie Kennedy, as a young Senator's wife, also laughed a great deal, and here she wrinkles her nose at some delicious bit Senator Frank Church of Idaho is sharing with her. As her husband progressed in his career, Jackie became much more inhibited in her behavior in public. But she would let her hair down and fling off her shoes with me.

Bobby Kennedy, Senator from New York, in a soulful tête-à-tête with Lady Harlech. When she died, the rumor around the Hill was that Jackie Kennedy would marry Lord Harlech and renounce her American citizenship to become an English peeress. At least they were right when they guessed she would marry a foreigner.

The husband Congressional wife Arlene Crane is kissing at a party is—her own. He's Philip Crane, Mr. Conservative of the Congress and a candidate for the Republican nomination for President. Arlene does not wear her heart on her sleeve. She does better than that— right on the front of her gown.

Head table for one of the most posh luncheons given annually on Capitol Hill, the Hearst Foundation salute to young scholars, always in the beautiful Carl Hayden Room of the Dirksen Building, Room 1202. This time there was a jarring note in that the apple pie with cheese had to be placed on the table before the first course had even been eaten. It had been ordered served that way by the Secret Service who said that Vice-President Agnew would have to eat and run after giving a little speech. At the table, from left, are Senator Howard Baker, Republican of Tennessee, Judy Agnew, and Mr. and Mrs. George Randolph Hearst, Sr., sitting on either side of the Vice-President.

This is the most private and sacrosanct area of the Club, the Senate private dining room. It is out of bounds for photographers and only a Senator can arrange for a picture to be taken here. But when you have the clout of the men at this table, you can understand why you are looking at a picture of this off-limits room. From left: Senator Edmund Muskie, Senator Edward Kennedy, actor Douglas Fairbanks, Jr., Senator George McGovern, sports star and broadcaster Sunny Jurgensen, Jerry Gereau of the Senate Rules Committee staff, and Eleanor McGovern, the Senator's wife.

This is what a salad for 150 people looks like. We made them all the time. That's Belgian endive on top. Senator Frank Church of Idaho is being served, and his wife watches in the background.

Two of my many bosses—Joseph Diamond, general manager of the Senate restaurants, and Senator B. Everett Jordan, chairman of the Senate Rules Committee, Democrat of North Carolina. I'm the man trapped in the middle, as it was in real life, since I was assistant general manager. When my good friend Joe died on Christmas Eve, 1974, I was offered his job, but said I preferred to head up the catering service exclusively. After nine years, I had had enough of overseeing twenty-six Senate food operations, including that of catering Senators' private parties. However, for some months I did serve as acting general manager until a suitable replacement could be found.

My "kitchen cabinet," as I called them, on Awards Day, receiving certificates from Senator James Allen of Alabama, chairman of the Rules Subcommittee on Restaurants, for their long and faithful service in the Senate restaurants. That's Joe Diamond, general manager, to the right of me—I'm on the end—and Jim Allen in the center. Of course, this was only a small fraction of my "cabinet"—Joe and I supervised 222 employees.

This is Penny—Nemrod Pinard, my housemate, who is my eyes for fine print and also my driver, because my eyesight never has permitted me to have a driver's license. He, too, works at the Capitol, as subway-car operator.

Tiptoe through the gladiolas—Republican minority leader Senator Dirksen kisses Jermaine Magnuson, the wife of Senator Warren G. Magnuson, Democrat of Minnesota. Jermaine was one of the loveliest and gentlest Senate wives, and I always enjoyed seeing her, especially since she always thanked me for taking such good care of her husband. My old friend Dirksen was one of the kissingest members of the Club, and he didn't care which political party a lovely woman belonged to.

Presidents-
Whatever Happened to
Mr. Nice Guy

It would be funny if it weren't so sad to see every time how a gullible public starts treating a man as if he's headed for sainthood, just because they are about to vote for him for President. They will fight to defend his every word.

Even sadder is what happens to the man himself. Every man I have seen become President starts out as a sweet humble guy for about a hundred days. That is the length of time he can pull the wool over the eyes of his adoring public and of a Congress eager to get along and get some legislation passed.

If the sainted President hasn't gotten his projects passed or well on the way to passage in those golden hundred days, always referred to on the Hill as "the honeymoon," his title around the House and Senate changes to "that son of a bitch in the White House." Or for those rare legislators who don't swear, "That clown, that clod in the White House." The public gets furious because campaign promises are not fulfilled. The insults begin flying toward the White House.

Then four years later, it's back to idolatry of some other candidates and a mighty vow to get rid of the incumbents: "Throw the rascals out."

As it turns out, the slogan more accurately should have been "Throw the rascals in!"

I've known a parade of Presidents close up, and not one escaped having one or more of the three fatal flaws—bad judgment, laziness, greed. The nation is lucky if, as in the case of Eisenhower, the flaw is merely laziness. At least the nation is safe from impulsive moves—and the worst thing that happened with the Eisenhower White House is that his Vice-President had to do much of the work and got none of the credit.

It was said on the Hill that Richard M. Nixon was the last "working" Vice-President. And Ike was the last "reluctant" candidate. He was the hero general who didn't want the job, and all he promised to do was the best that he could. So he was in the clear. He could grin his famous grin and hit his little golf ball around the White House putting green and come out of the Presidency as the last "good guy" President.

Senator Robert Taft, who ran for the Presidential nomination in 1940 but lost to Wendell Willkie, spoke of this inability of most new Presidents to get anything passed through Congress that would please the public. As Ken Hoyt, his campaign publicity director remembers it, Taft said a new President always reminded him of a certain army recruit who was learning to fire a rifle.

His officer came by and asked if he was hitting anything.

"I don't know," said the recruit, "but the bullets sure leave here with a hell of a bang."

Jimmy Carter is the most recent example of a President whose promises left the gun with a bang but missed the mark. He had made so many promises that the nation had been led to believe he would be an extra special marksman. What they heard instead was a series of inconsequential pops followed by a brutal broadside at his Cabinet.

The more angry Capitol Hill got at Carter for his policies and his firing of his Cabinet, the more brutal their humor became.

"Don't criticize Carter," Republican Senator Percy told some Democratic colleague. "He's doing the work of two men—Laurel and Hardy."

How does a new President start losing friends? With Carter, it started early by taking two steps forward and one step back—claiming to be pure, then saying he lusted in his heart; saying LBJ was a "cheat," then calling his widow, Lady Bird Johnson, to apologize.

Nor did Carter get over the bad habit. In the early precampaign days of 1979, he publicly pointed out how he had never panicked in an emergency, then sent a note to his top competitor, Ted Kennedy, apologizing and saying he had not meant to refer to Chappaquiddick. "Like fun he didn't," said the public.

I can tell you of one voter Carter antagonized in his very first year of Presidency, Sylvia Stewart, a Virginia housewife and mother who gave permission for her story to be told in this book.

As Mrs. Stewart tells it, "Carter was such a friend of the people during his campaign that I almost worshipped that man, and I felt that at last we were in good hands.

"I telephoned Jimmy Carter at his home in Georgia just after he had been elected but before he had taken office. I wanted to discuss a national health policy with him.

"First I spoke with his mother, then his brother, and finally to the President-elect himself. Each time I explained the need for a national health plan to help people like myself who have had cancer and therefore cannot obtain a hospital policy, or who simply cannot afford private health insurance.

"At that time, Mr. Carter told me, 'I cannot do anything about it right now but call me after I am in office and make an appointment to see me.'

"I was filled with joy. 'You mean that you will see me in the office of the President?' I asked.

" 'Yes,' said Jimmy Carter. 'Just call and tell them I told you to call for an appointment.'

"I was in awe of this man. He was really going to see me and discuss a health plan—or so I was foolish enough to believe. But once he was in office, I could not get an appointment to see him or talk to him. I doubt that he even remembered. So I called Jody Powell to make an appointment and explained it all to him to explain to the President. But I wasn't able to get an appointment to see him either.

"I was determined not to give up, to get my message across to Carter somehow of this great need of people like myself. I began to write letters—to Senators, Congressmen, HEW Secretary Joseph Califano. Anyone I thought might listen and do something about it. In all the letters I used myself as an example of a person who was ineligible for ordinary health insurance because of having had cancer.

"I had just written to Senator Ted Kennedy when, in a few days, I got action—but not the kind I was looking for. It was the White House calling, and a feminine voice said, 'This is the secretary to the President, and he has asked me to call and see what kind of hospital care you are in need of.'

"I quickly explained that I was not ill and did not need care at this time, but that even if I did, it would do me no good because I couldn't get it—being ineligible for insurance and so forth and so forth.

" 'Well,' said the voice impatiently, 'if you need care, Mr. Carter will see to it that you have the best of everything. But he wants you to stop writing these letters to everyone and stop making waves. You are causing trouble, and right now he really doesn't need that.'

"I was so hurt that I couldn't think of what to say, and I was afraid I'd start to cry and make a greater fool of myself, so I simply thanked her for calling and hung up.

"As I see it, Carter has turned from a nice down-home guy to an SOB—the job of President has gone to his head."

What happened to her campaign for a national health policy? Did Sylvia Stewart give up?

"No, indeed," she said, "I went to see Senator Kennedy and gave him all my thinking on the subject, and I was gratified to see that part of my thinking is incorporated in his national-health plan. I pray that someday he can bring it about."

Had Carter kept his promise and seen the lady for three minutes, she would have been singing his praises to all her friends. As it was, she joined the ABC Club—Anyone But Carter.

The first time I met Jimmy Carter was when he was governor and attending a party Senator Talmadge gave for influential Georgians. I was not too impressed. He did not seem a firebrand in those days but was playing very humble. Bert Lance was also there.

I remember this meal very well because of how furious I was with Senator Talmadge and his wife, Betty. They had pulled a fast one, getting use of the kitchens to prepare all the food that was being donated by people back home in Georgia.

This meant that the Senate restaurant would operate at a loss, receiving nothing for the food and having to keep staff members on duty, including myself. It was a typical Georgia meal—black-eyed peas, turnip greens, ham, and fried chicken. There were over two hundred guests, most of whom, I am sure, thought that Herman and Betty were footing the bill.

With that crowd, it required seven dishwashers among others. Thinking of the restaurant deficit, I took matters into my own hands and dared charge the Talmadges for the cleaning-up job!

Years later, when Carter moved to the White House, I was not too surprised that I started hearing low grumbles from Congressmen and Senators who had been invited to break bread with the Carters at the White House. He had dared to serve the same food they might have gotten at a small-town church social—chicken a la king. He seemed to have learned from Senator Talmadge and other Georgia politicians how to save money.

And they were even more alarmed later to learn that the President had broken with tradition in seeking contributions for a dinner party for the visiting Israeli and Egyptian chiefs of state—Begin and Sadat—and that he pocketed all the surplus left over from his entertainment budget at the end of the fiscal year.

Though some Senators may do such things, they expect better from the commander in chief of the nation. They determined to enact legislation to make it mandatory that any leftover funds from entertainment must go back into the Treasury's general fund—for the common good of all taxpayers.

As a matter of public record, President Carter used only a small portion of his $50,000 a year allowance and turned a neat profit of over $85,000 for his first two years in the White House. In all fairness, it should be pointed out that Vice-President Fritz Mondale operated with a different set of standards and did return about half of his $10,000 expense allowance to the Treasury, both years running. He, too, could have kept it and counted it as earnings, had he wanted to.

There were two dinners early in 1979 at which private "donations" helped the White House with its entertainment of foreign dignitaries. First, when friendly relations were resumed with China, members of the National Council for U.S. China Trade chipped in $1,000 apiece to pay for entertaining Vice-Premier Teng Hsiaoping at the Kennedy Center with such performing stars as the Harlem Globetrotters, John Denver, and Eubie.

This went so smoothly that Carter was inspired to solicit contributions of $5,000 from corporation executives who would be attending the Begin-Sadat dinner. According to Betty Beale, society writer for the *Washington Star,* one corporation chieftain told her he had "turned down the request to contribute and did not receive an invitation."

When bad publicity resulted from this gouging of guests, President Carter, through his mouthpiece, Jody Powell, had a quick answer—other Presidents had done it first. Ford's friends had built him a swimming pool, and Kennedy admirers had contributed authentic period pieces for redecorating the White House. The Hill crowd laughed and said they could have warned him that he'd have to think of a better excuse.

At least Carter learned one lesson well from the Hill boys— make a good impression in front of the press. So, he decreed that no hard liquor would be served at White House receptions. But he didn't promise no hard liquor would be served upstairs in the family quarters. That's where Carter and his friends hoist a few in the White House. Presidents can change.

Carter started out playing a spartan, tight-fisted role, acting contemptuous of creature comforts. He would invite Congressmen and Senators to breakfast and feed them only rolls and coffee. Soon they didn't bother coming. He might be President, but every Congressman is a king. Carter found out the hard way that you must feed and booze them. Otherwise, even if you are President, you won't get them to come to your party.

Soon the Congress had the President nicely trained, and when next he had legislation that he yearned mightily to get passed, he invited a group of Congressmen and Senators for evening cocktails. There was a full cocktail service, as usual. In fact, my friends told me there were two bars in the East Room of the White House and a marine orchestra playing soft music for dancing. Carter fed

the Senators and Congressmen well. They came away saying the
President might be a little slow, but he was trainable.

And what else was the Hill saying about the President? That he
did, indeed, lust in his heart.

It was not too long before I started hearing that Carter did have
a roving eye—and the younger the better. The word was he had
started paying attention to a girl who works at the White House. Or
at least flirting. The Senators said, "More power to the Old Man." A
President is always called the old man. That's because he's supposed to represent the tradition of the father of the country. On
the Hill when they say the old man is coming today, they are
referring to the President.

When this nation, under God and Jimmy Carter, went into a
panic in the summer of 1979 over the gas shortage and the humilia-
tion of waiting in long lines to beg for $5 worth, I immediately
thought of the Trilateral Commission Report. I first heard about
this report on the Hill, and couldn't believe my ears when I was told
that, as long ago as 1972, the financial powers of the Rockefellers
were laying plans for everything that was to happen, including the
Presidency of Jimmy Carter.

There are those who say, "David Rockefeller invented Jimmy
Carter." Wherever insiders talk about how strange it is that a
relatively poor and obscure man became President, the subject of
Carter's Trilateral connection comes up.

I am not writing this book to give a lesson in history and the
behind-the-scene manipulating of politics, but I do think the report of the Trilateral meeting of 1972 should be required reading.
It's not cheap. I paid $35, and it was not easy to get.

The Trilateral Commission was the brainchild of the Rockefeller family, especially David. It was set up with the rationale of
solving the nation's problems, domestic and international. A think
tank with clout. The greatest brains of the nation would be tapped
to solve the problems of the world.

Henry Kissinger and Zbigniew Brzezinski were both closely
allied with the Rockefeller Foundation, which set up the Council on
Foreign Relations, which in turn set up the Trilateral Commission.

To be a part of the commission was almost a solid-gold pass into the highest echelons of politics. Both President Jimmy Carter and his Vice-President, Walter Mondale, were Trilateralists. The man on the street does not know that, years before he ran, the Trilateral Commission picked Jimmy Carter as the man they wanted in the Number 1 job. Or that more than a dozen of the men Carter would bring to Washington would be part of this group: Brzezinski as his National Security Council director, masterminding the most delicate international policies; Cyrus Vance as his Secretary of State; Harold Brown as his Secretary of Defense; Michael Blumenthal as his Secretary of the Treasury; James Schlesinger as his energy expert; and on and on.

I'm not saying that we have become a nation controlled by a financially powerful nongovernmental organization, but I am saying that there is a lot of hidden power that we know nothing about, unless we are on the inside or have an ear to the keyhole.

I know that every four years there are any number of little groups joining together to work for the election of this man or that for the Presidency—but they do it openly, in the public eye, shouting their preference. What worries me is when the greatest financiers and money trusts get together, very quietly, and decide they must capture the Presidency, because their judgment is best.

Another thing that most men on the street do not know is that the heads of Who's Who of top corporations have a very private Club they call the Business Roundtable, which carries tremendous lobbying weight.

Representative Wright Patman of Texas, who was chairman of the Banking and Currency Committee, as well as a member of the Joint Committee on Defense Production, worried about the Roundtable's secrecy. On the floor of the House, Patman rose and said:

"Mr. Speaker, I do not oppose the right of the fat cats to lobby. But I think it is important that this activity be out in the open so that the public will know what is happening to its business."

It would also be a boon if the public could know all there is to know about the behind-the-scenes wheeling and dealing of the men they are electing President. I happened to be within earshot at a party at which a lobbyist was buying Senator Robert Kerr's vote on some important legislation, while Lyndon Johnson stood nearby pretending he didn't know what was going on.

Kerr got a promise of X thousands of dollars. He moved over and talked to Lyndon. I heard Kerr tell Johnson, "Don't worry, I'll take care of you."

Kerr moved back to the lobbyist, and I heard the lobbyist say, "I need a guarantee."

Kerr said, "I'll guarantee it."

I would often hear that "money talks with Lyndon." There is no way I could have called this to the attention of the voters. In the first place I would have been fired. In the second place no one would have believed me. And in the third place, Lyndon was not elected to the Presidency, the first time. He lucked into the job through the death of another President.

And it was at another party that I heard something so ominous that I still get the shakes when I think about it. I only hope that I was wrong. It was soon after John F. Kennedy had been inaugurated into office and a group had gotten together at an off-the-record party to toast the new Vice-President. Kennedy was not there, and it was a big noisy party with a lot of lobbyists and representatives of big industry. Or so I was told. I did not recognize the faces.

It was a stag party, and a raw bar had been set up at one end and the booze at the other. Lyndon was sitting at a table near the raw bar, and people kept coming over and hovering over him and then moving on.

I was idly listening to this cluster of men and that as I stood watching the waiter at the raw bar. Anyway, suddenly I realized some voices were talking about the fact that Ike had severed relations with Cuba before leaving office and how Kennedy would never be able to handle it. And all the money it was costing because of Castro nationalizing our firms. The voices sounded very angry about the money.

Then came the line, "We are going to have to dispose of him." I thought the word "dispose" was strange so it went over my head at the time, but it came back to haunt me after the assassination. What had I heard? A vow to get rid of Castro or Kennedy? There seemed to be an agreement that this thing must happen prior to the '64 election, or Kennedy would dump Johnson.

So it had to mean Kennedy.

At the time, I wondered idly how someone got rid of a President before an election. The moment I heard of the assassination of Kennedy, I instantly saw myself at that bar scene and broke into tears.

They had talked of the future of Lyndon—the kind of President he would make. He would be renominated by the Democratic convention and would escalate Vietnam to take the heat off Cuba. That was a mystery to me too—how would that take the "heat" off Cuba?

Of course I said nothing at the time or even later—until now. What could I have done? Busted into the conversation of five or six men huddled together at a party talking and say, "What's going on here?"

Anyway you hear so much wild talk and braggadocio, if you work around Hill parties, you discount it or pay it no mind unless something happens afterward to make you remember.

Did Lyndon Johnson know what was going on around him that night? I don't know. I often wonder. I also wonder who these men were.

When I came to the Hill, Lyndon Johnson was majority leader of the Senate. I found him very demanding, but I was not the only one he pushed around.

One Sunday morning when I was arriving to do catch-up work, the Senator was in a state of nerves. I was told by others that he had discovered there was no elevator operator to take him to his office—he would have to operate it himself.

Lyndon called the sergeant at arms, Joe Duke, at his home and demanded that an elevator operator be put on the "Senators only" elevator closest to his office in the Capitol Building seven days a week, twenty-four hours a day, 365 days a year.

As a result, Lew Caraway, superintendent of the Senate office buildings, was obliged to spend the extra money for a full-time operator even though the elevators were self-operating.

I understand it was a lonely time for the sole operators on weekends because very rarely did any Senator—including Lyndon Johnson—arrive on a Sunday or after noontime on Saturday.

Lyndon was always entertaining this group and that. For example, LBJ had a real love-hate relationship with reporters. But after he had stayed angry long enough over some story he didn't like, he would decide to woo a couple of reporters and plant some stories more to his liking. Sometimes the stories would be planted in advance by someone like Bobby Baker, and the party would be a follow-up.

I would prepare all the food, or supervise the preparation, but the party would be completely closed. Someone on his staff would give me the order: "Hurst, the boss wants a nice buffet with everything served on silver. You know, silver chafing dishes—the works."

When I heard that we were to use a lot of silver, that meant that LBJ would be there in person, and probably the photographer would take some pictures. Otherwise, china would be used or whatever came to hand.

If LBJ was buttering up some reporter or TV man or a group of them, he would not want our waiters around. We would all clear out, and LBJ would have one of his own trusted staffers to do the serving.

Much of the time when LBJ was giving an intimate party, he didn't even want his own Senate staffers to be there. Sometimes, it was not a press party but just some male or female whose presence at the party he was protecting. Even so, the next morning I would hear from some policeman or other employee—maybe a clean-up man—that there had been a pretty wild party in LBJ's hideaway.

If someone were to ask me who was the most unforgettable character I have met, I would have to say it was Lyndon Baines Johnson. I suffered with him, and he suffered with me through the latter part of his career as majority leader and his years as Vice-President, when he presided over the Senate, from January 1961 to November 22, 1963.

And then, when he was President, I would be involved when he came back to the Hill on various occasions. When he had finally been elected President on his own and was back on the Hill for his swearing-in ceremony on January 20, 1965, as is traditional, an inaugural luncheon had been prepared for him in the Capitol building, easy to get to from the inaugural stands outside.

I had helped set up Room S 207 for 110 Hill leaders and other VIPs. They had ordered a most impressive three-piece bouquet of flowers to cover the entire marble mantel.

Just as Johnson was getting up to say a few words to the guests on the loudspeaker, the center section of the flowers and base fell and hit the President smack on the back of the head. The Secret Service men ran to him to make sure he was not hurt or the victim of foul play. I just smiled.

I remembered what he was like in the Senate restaurant—hell on wheels. Waiters and waitresses hated to wait on him, because of the fear that he would explode and embarrass them in public. He never said, "Relax, I have time." He was always in a hurry, always impatient and a perfectionist. Service had to be perfect.

And believe me, it was. Only he didn't think so.

Once in the dining room, a waitress brought him a menu without the glass of water he always wanted. He exploded at her. "Get the hell on the ball," he told her, berating her for several minutes for not knowing what she was doing.

Another time I entered the dining room to hear LBJ in an uproar, demanding that the tablecloth be changed. I went over and asked, "What is the trouble, Senator?" He was majority leader at the time.

He said loudly, "If we can't get better linen, you'd better the hell get a different laundry."

I looked at the tablecloth, and it did indeed have a worn spot, but nothing really serious. However, I didn't say a word. I quickly told two busboys to change the linen and reset the table. Other Senators looked at him askance but said nothing. They were used to him. I noticed no one tried to join him.

Much of the time, LBJ was a loner as majority leader. He would come into the restaurant alone. Even as Vice-President, he would usually come into the dining room alone except for the Secret Service.

LBJ had a salad that he habitually ate when he was Vice-President. All the waiters knew what it was—and so, I'm afraid, did all who had to deal with him—lettuce, a heap of raw onion rings, and tomato with oil and vinegar. He loved onions. Some said he ate them to get rid of the smell of booze, but he smelled like an onion factory so I don't know which was worse.

When LBJ said he would not run again for President, there were no tears on Capitol Hill. I heard nothing but cheers around the dining room. And many Senators voiced the opinion that he had wrecked the economy by escalating the Vietnam War and could not even be elected buck private, let alone commander in chief.

In a way, Nixon was a lot like Johnson. They both were most at home in the company of males. But Nixon was much more uncomfortable than Johnson in the company of females—even that of his wife.

Nixon would go with male friends whenever possible. It was the talk of the Hill how he would leave Pat behind. Even knowing about his life, I voted for him, because he still was a dedicated public man and politician and a knowledgeable man. If he hadn't started cutting through the Bamboo Curtain around China, Carter and Ford would never have accomplished what they did.

Carter got the credit for reestablishing diplomatic relations with China, but it was really Nixon's triumph, and the Chinese Vice Premier acknowledged it by insisting that Nixon be invited to the White House when the Premier came to Washington.

I remember when the quip on the Hill was that the best thing that could happen to Nixon would be to be found in bed with some woman. He seemed to keep all women—including his wife—at arm's length, so to speak. Yet he did have a sense of humor and, as one of his close friends told it, the friend and Nixon had played a trick on another fellow. They invited the fellow over and had a "girl" in bed ready for him to see—only it wasn't a real live doll.

What it was was a flowing wig on a styrofoam head showing from the top of the covers and two inflatable legs sticking out from the bottom of the covers.

Also, for some strange reason Nixon seemed to get a charge out of hearing about Jack Kennedy's love life, and several people have told me Nixon would chortle when he heard of JFK's exploits and ask questions about them.

As the Vice-President, Richard Nixon had a hideaway in the Capitol building itself, but he rarely made an appearance there because he was too busy serving as the unofficial President—because of Ike's "inability to function." That was the word on the Hill. Eisenhower simply did not know how or was unable to operate as a full-fledged President.

Republicans and Democrats alike scoffed at Ike, even though many of them were obliged to support him for a second term. As a matter of fact, the question was often asked around the Hill in those days, "What if something happened to Ike and Nixon became President?"

To which the answer was, "Hell, what if something were to happen to *Nixon,* and *Eisenhower* became President?"

Nixon as Vice-President was one of the busiest men I knew. He maintained his Vice-President's office in the Capitol. The only person there was his secretary who would go home early. Nixon would sometimes stay there in the evening with a male friend.

When Vice-President Nixon was at the White House, he had a hideaway that he really used in the Executive Office Building. He even had his own private dining room there, so he would not have to eat at the White House. He also had a suite of offices at the Executive Office Building, where he did most of his work.

Nixon was not known for his generosity when he was a Senator, and he did very little entertaining. His colleagues had an expression for it. They would say, "The check was too heavy for him to lift." If he was with others, he was one of those who would let the check sit there until someone else eventually paid.

Even as Vice-President, Richard Nixon did not get carried away when he ate on Capitol Hill. When he ate alone, which was usual, a 25¢ tip was standard. Once a waiter complained to another waiter about this, and was told, "What are you talking about? That's princely on Capitol Hill." It was true that many Senators left nothing behind but hot air.

An amazing thing to me was that, when he was Vice-President, Richard Nixon didn't impress me as being a very religious man. But when he got to the White House, Billy Graham was practically a family member—frequently holding Sunday services. And when he wasn't there, other ministers and rabbis presided at religious services in the East Room for which there were printed programs.

Nixon was a Quaker, but you wouldn't know it. He drank. Swore. Had a bad temper. His patience was very short. He was a nervous man and perspired a lot.

When he was Vice-President, he played it grand. His entourage of Secret Service men was more in evidence than for other Vice-Presidents. Already he seemed to like pomp and ceremony.

I was standing with some Senators, watching a Nixon entrance, when one of them said, "I would not be surprised to see him brought in some day, sitting crosslegged on silken cushions, high on a pagoda-type throne with four men at the corners."

Any man who aspires to be President must have a certain sense of pride, but in the case of Nixon, his vanity meant that another man, Rogers Morton, could never achieve his dream—to become Vice-President. Instead Nixon made him Secretary of Interior but it was not the same.

Rogers' career had been closely tied to Nixon's. He had helped Nixon in every way. He had even been floor manager for him at the 1968 Republican Convention. There was only one thing he wanted—to be Nixon's running mate.

Nixon considered it, but he had an ego problem. He was conscious of his size and hated to be surrounded by tall men. Rogers Morton, at 6 foot 7, simply hadn't a chance.

This was confirmed in a conversation one day with an old friend of Morton's, George Mathieu, a PR man at DOT (Department of Transportation), who knew him on the Eastern Shore, where Morton lived and Mathieu vacationed. George said Morton never got over the disappointment.

I must confess I knew in advance that Nixon was going to resign as President and that Rockefeller would be chosen as the new Vice-President. Again, I overheard it at a party—the place where more business gets done than in committee rooms.

The way I pieced it together had to be right, I told myself. I was at the bar where Vice-President Jerry Ford was standing as a guest and listening intently as he was being briefed on what was going to happen. He was going to name Rockefeller, and he would have no trouble getting it through the Senate.

Well, for Ford to appoint Rocky meant that he would have to become President. And to become President meant that Nixon was about to resign.

I looked at Jerry, and he was looking very pleased. It passed my mind that he couldn't care less whom he was supposed to nominate as Vice-President—he seemed overcome at the thought he would soon be President.

As I see it, Nixon was calling all the shots before stepping down from office, with Rockefeller as part of his price for stepping down. With Rocky there, he'd be protected.

The Hill people were not so naive as to think the pardon had not been worked out in advance. I would hear Senators talk of it among themselves, saying, "That was quite a deal Ford had going for him." They would ask each other, "Would you have gone along with it to be President?"

Only a few protested that they "would not have pardoned the son of a bitch no matter what the deal was." But the realistic ones quoted Sam Rayburn's rule: "You have to go along to get along."

I knew Jerry Ford as minority leader of the House, because he was one of the most prodigious partygoers. If there was a Republican wingding anywhere on the Hill, he was there. He was not the perfect guest, showing himself to be ill-tempered and impatient, and always with the belligerence of a couple of drinks under his vest.

Ford would be very annoyed if he walked into a party, and the bartender did not know what he was drinking. He took it out on me, telling me I ought to have my bartender trained by this time. I said, "But, Mr. Ford, you may not have noticed, but it's always a different bartender at each party."

He still thought, he said, that I ought to train the bartenders to know what he wanted. I could not resist telling him, "I happen to be in the business of serving Senators, not *Congressmen*. It's enough to know and memorize the eating and drinking habits of a hundred and one members of that Club without memorizing the drinking tastes of their guests as well."

Seeing that he could get nowhere with me, he stomped away. But it gave me a little shiver of apprehension when not too long after that encounter, President Nixon anointed him heir apparent, and Jerry Ford as Vice-President was the 101st member of the Club, presiding over the entire Senate.

Candidates-
Few are Chosen
and
the Chosen Few

When Ed Muskie was making his desperate primary-to-primary fight for the Democratic Presidential nomination, Senator Clifford Hansen, my friend from Wyoming, was convulsing his Republican friends with a story of how a big Democratic leader was giving a talk to a small group of faithfuls, including Muskie.

"I am looking for a great leader to lead us all into the White House," the influential man said, "a great thinker, a charismatic campaigner."

Muskie jumped up and said, "Hey, here I am!"

"Good," said the speaker, "you can help us look."

And when you get through laughing, let me assure you that isn't as funny as it sounds. Insiders said from the beginning that Muskie didn't have a prayer. And it wasn't just money or the lack of it.

Gerald Ford didn't have a pot to pee in as a child, or a window to throw it out. The same goes for other Presidents I have known.

The point is, any time you see a man progress fast in Washington like Nixon or Ford or Lyndon Johnson or Eisenhower, the powers have gotten behind him, and money is no object.

I've already mentioned the Trilateral Commission, one of the pyramids of power. Their man Carter was not Washington but he was closer to it than he let on.

I was told by Hill insiders in the Republican policy committee, talking to me off the record, as far back as 1973, that James Carter—he is listed by his full name in the rolls of the Trilateral Commission, and not as "Jimmy"—was being groomed for the Presidency by two men closest to Rockefeller. The men mentioned were Henry Kissinger and a fellow I had never heard of before, Zbigniew Brzezinski.

I couldn't believe it. I thought it was a joke. Why would Kissinger, a Republican, be helping a Southern totally unknown governor? And who the hell was Brzezinski?

And why would this powerful organization pay attention to this little guy from Georgia? "A Democrat has to win sometime," I was told. "Better one of their own."

Time moved along, and in 1975, in the late summer or fall, the word around the Hill was that Nelson Rockefeller was totally disgusted with Ford and his administration and planned to leave at the earliest decent interval—the end of Ford's fill-in term for Nixon.

What Rocky was mad about was Ford's lackadaisical attitude toward oil and other energy problems and the world monetary situation. According to my sources in the Republican policy committee, Rocky had told his Trilateral friends that he would be too old to run for President in 1980, when Ford would finish his elected term. Rocky had informed them that James Carter would not make it the first time because an unknown could not beat an incumbent, but 1980 would be the year of James Carter.

Of course, what Rocky could not have foreseen was that the combination of Dole and Ford was a do-nothing mix and that the country was still so angry about Watergate and Ford's pardoning of Nixon that even an eager-beaver unknown *could* make it the first time.

Of course there's many a slip twixt the cup and the lip—or else Nelson Rockefeller would have made President himself somewhere along the line! The unknown factor is the public. Sometimes the deaf, dumb, and blind voters can be led, and sometimes they can't. If they think they are being pushed, they can't be led. They shove back.

If they think someone is trying to buy his way, he's out. Rocky's money actually worked against him. The way the Hill boys saw it, Rocky might have overcome the fat-cat image, but when he flouted the average homemaker's standards of moral integrity by divorcing a wife of many years and marrying a younger woman, he really blew it.

Not that Happy Rockefeller wasn't a great gal. I met her and liked her. The point is simply that though we are not that morally upright ourselves, we expect our national leaders to be ideal—especially our President.

The way the Rockefeller brothers were explained to me was that David was the worldwide man and the kingpin of the Trilateral Commission—the egghead. Nelson was the authority on domestic issues and the family politician—the glad hander. They made a good team in influencing national policy on any subject in which they had an interest.

One hears many things on Capitol Hill about how campaigns are run. And how Presidents are made. The story of 1976 that you hear on Capitol Hill is different from what you read in history books.

On the Hill the story was that Ted Kennedy was sponsoring Birch Bayh for President, and that Bayh wouldn't even announce without the blessing and help of Kennedy. He didn't have the wherewithal, and he didn't have the clout. That was the common gossip on the Hill.

Then Kennedy did the same with Muskie, as insurance. When Carter ran his folksy campaign against them, neither one made out worth a damn in the primaries. They said around the Hill that the game plan was for either Bayh or Muskie to pave the way for Kennedy the next time around. For after all that help, if he wanted them not to run for a second term, could they say no?

The Hill crowd smiled when, with great pomp and ceremony, Ted Kennedy "went to the mountain," and came back saying his dear mother had given him "permission" to run for President in 1980. That was the best-orchestrated entrance into the Presidential running, they said, since Eisenhower had to be begged to run.

Birch Bayh remained the darling of the Kennedy family, and when, in the fall of 1979, he started to fear that his enemies were ganging up on him for his reelection in Indiana in 1980, the family went all out.

Ethel Kennedy threw a fund raiser for which 150 guests paid $1,000 apiece to get, Ethel said with a giggle, "three minutes with a noncandidate, and a walk through the downstairs of Hickory Hill."

The noncandidate—Ted Kennedy—arrived an hour and a half late and gave not just the usual lip service praise of a candidate but told how Birch Bayh had literally saved his life by pulling him from the burning wreckage of a plane crash.

Ted also told how his brother, the President, had been a friend of Birch and had been in Indiana, campaigning for Birch when news came to him of the Cuban missile crisis.

The Hill crowd got a big chuckle over the fact that the richest candidate in American politics, Nelson Rockefeller, with his estimated worth of $200 million and a yearly income of $5 million, couldn't get into the White House while a peanut vender like Jimmy Carter, who was barely a millionaire, could.

These days personal wealth alone is not enough, they explained. It takes the backing of organizations with supercolossal wealth and clout to aspire to the White House.

As for the candidates who win, they have to be team players, a part of a committee, good at taking subtle orders. Why would the powers back a man who wasn't going to help them?

Richard Nixon had to go through fire and failure before he got backing strong enough to catapult him into the White House. And many segments of the business world prospered in his administration—the dairy industry, the wheat commodity market, the oil industry, to name a few.

On the Hill, when the public screamed that Nixon was unleashing a monstrous inflation by letting milk prices go up and permitting a tremendous sale of wheat to Russia, members shrugged and said Nixon was just paying his dues.

I used to wonder what would have happened to the country had an earlier Republican candidate of a very independent nature become President. A millionaire only several times over, but married to a woman possibly richer than he—Peggy Goldwater is the daughter of R. P. Johnson and niece of C. S. Davis, founders of Borg-Warner Corporation—Barry Goldwater had one of the sharpest minds on Capitol Hill.

I used to talk with him a lot. He was like an old shoe, absolutely unimpressed with titles and people trying to put on the dog. One of

Goldwater's pet peeves was the military—and I deduced that he was not too pleased with the performance of General Eisenhower as President.

"The poorest politicians are the military," he would tell me. "There is no way military men can be politicians because of their training in the academies. It's waste from the time they start school till they leave. They're weaned on a bottle of waste."

I listened to the Senator make this little speech over and over and never cracked a smile. But it amused the hell out of me because of his pride in being a general of the 9999. These were the men who kept their so-called military standing on Capitol Hill by logging a certain number of hours in military airplanes, and formed a very elite Senatorial side club.

Barry Goldwater was known for his excellent sense of humor and his quick temper. He rubbed enough people the wrong way to make them wish he would retire. Around friends he would cuss like a sailor. I liked him because he was such a colorful character. In addition, I appreciated his philosophy of owing nobody. He didn't believe in deficit spending.

He was among the Senators who ate in the staff cafeteria, waiting in line with the rest, avoiding recognition, just looking around.

The Senator would sit with his staff. When he had guests, he shocked them when he took them to the cafeteria. An unpretentious man, he seldom entertained.

When he was running for President in 1964, I frequently worked near him as he waited in line. The day after he lost, he said, "There's only one thing worse than a politician." I asked, "What's that?"

"A losing politician," he retorted. Goldwater added, "I just hate to lose to a goddamn jackass from Texas!"

Good and loud he announced that he was disgusted. Most of the people in the cafeteria were Democrats, and everybody heard him. He couldn't have cared less.

Had Barry Goldwater been elected, we would have had our first tattooed President—not heavily tattooed, just a nice discreet arm tattoo.

Another Presidential candidate out of the past—1948—but very much in evidence around the Hill today is Strom Thurmond, whom my restaurant staff labeled as "tight as a tick."

Senator Strom Thurmond was a good dresser. He beat Proxmire in getting a hair transplant. He may have been a poor tipper, but he was the proudest daddy on Capitol Hill. He liked to brag about his kids—how smart they were, and didn't they look like him.

It was Penny, who shares a house with me, who may have finally triggered Strom's hair transplant. Penny, who is very outspoken, and the Senator used to eat breakfast together. One day when the Senator had some new pictures of the kids and was telling again how smart they were and adding, "And don't they look like me?" Penny shot back, "There's no way of knowing with that bald bean of yours."

Thurmond looked startled and was soon into hair transplants.

I don't know what triggered Proxmire to follow suit except his own vanity. He is a good-looking man—but knows it.

Robert Dole was a surprise candidate, announcing in 1979 that he would be "available" in 1980. But then I shouldn't have been too surprised. He was one of the most ambitious men on Capitol Hill.

I don't know why Dole and his first wife were divorced. She had been a nice woman, a fine woman, the helpmate who, as a physical therapist, had devoted herself to helping him overcome the ravages of his World War II combat injuries, or so I'd heard.

After his divorce, he found a perfect combination of political acumen and physical beauty in Mary Elizabeth Hanford, a member of the Federal Trade Commission. They said he gave himself a Christmas present when he married her in December of 1975.

The Robert Dole that I knew was a very ill-tempered man. However he had a way of turning his acid tongue into a barb aimed at the hide of another person. This sometimes passed as humor.

President Ford chose him as his Vice-Presidential running mate in 1976. Ford had thought Dole would inspire the Republican Senators to go out and really work for his election. But Dole was not that popular, because his sharp tongue had cut gashes in many of his colleagues. Nor had he been a greatly effective Senator. As some Senators told me, with some bitterness, "The man doesn't fight for causes, not even veterans' legislation, though he's on the Veteran's Committee. He'll be no asset to Ford."

One reason Ford looked to the Senate for a running mate was that he needed to show that he could get legislation through Congress. He had become known as the Veto King, and Congress had lost patience with him.

Dole had promised to curb his tongue during the campaign. He had also promised to maneuver legislation through Congress. He didn't succeed in either.

And when Ford lost his fight to hang on to the job that had been handed to him by Nixon, the same men said, "No wonder Ford lost—he was on the *dole.*"

Jerry Ford finally admitted he had made a mistake. When Rocky died, the Hill crowd wondered aloud what would have happened had Ford continued with him as his running mate during the 1976 election. Would they have won, and would Rocky still be alive today?

More than once I felt Dole's ire. He was hard to please on food and service. Nothing ever arrived soon enough to suit him. One day toward the end of Nixon's first term, a hostess he was complaining to told the Senator that he should have his own waiter.

He tried to get her fired, reporting her to the Rules Committee. Chairman Jordan called Joseph Diamond and me to his office.

Jordan started out on a sympathetic note, because he knew how hard Dole was to get along with and what a hard time he gave us. But then he fixed me with stern eye and said, "Louie, you tell that hostess to curb her tongue, no matter how mad she gets. Stuff some of your Mississippi cotton in that damn mouth of hers."

Everyone else on Capitol Hill called me Lou or Hurst, but Senator Jordan and Senator Jennings Randolph called me "laboring Louie" when they were in a playful mood.

I went back to the restaurant and told the hostess, "You know, this man might just be our next Vice-President. That's Nixon's pet. Nixon made him Republican Committee National Chairman. Maybe you had a good idea. Let's give him his own damn waiter, and say nothing more about it."

So for the duration of Dole's dream of the Vice-Presidency, he was waited on hand and foot whenever he set foot in our restaurants.

After Nixon announced Agnew would again be his running

mate, we returned to reality and the old way of doing things.

I recall that Dole's temper influenced one staffer to leave soon after Dole took office as U.S. Senator in 1969. That was his personal secretary, whom he inherited from his predecessor, Frank Carlson of Kansas, on whose staff she had been.

The woman was a personal friend of mine, and I was shocked one day when she came to my private office in distress to tell me that she could not take it any longer and was going to retire.

"Senator Carlson was the kindest, most reasonable man in the world," she said. "And I never had any trouble pleasing him. I've worked for him for years with never a harsh word directed at me. But now, with Senator Dole, I think I'm losing my mind. There's nothing I can do that pleases him. I have done my best and strained to do whatever he wants, but it still isn't right. Nor is he the kind of gentleman Senator Carlson was, when he wants something a different way."

My friend decided it wasn't worth the hassle. She had been on the Hill long enough to get partial retirement pay, and simply retired, settling for that.

Senator Dole, from the moment he arrived in the Senate in 1969, played the cocktail circuit, and gave every sign of wanting to become a part of high society. That costs money. He didn't reciprocate with expensive parties. I never knew him to do any large-size entertainment.

Dole was known as a minor playboy on the Hill, who preferred young women, whom he could bring to the Senate restaurant for lunch or dinner and also to the Hill parties.

I never saw him with his first wife. I do not even recall seeing him with her on the day of his swearing-in ceremony. Though he did not give a big swearing-in party of his own—he was not one of the wealthy members of the Club—he did attend the parties of other members, making the rounds.

In spite of the fact that Senator Dole would show up at parties, he still gave the impression of being a loner. He would stand alone and wait for others to come to talk to him. He was a handsome figure of a man, tall and blessed with a full head of dark hair, and with brooding, intelligent eyes. Women, especially, were drawn to him, feeling sympathy because of his partially crippled hand. His constituents told me they admired the way he had come up from adversity, twice wounded and twice decorated as a platoon leader in Italy, in the 10th Mountain Division.

I also well remember Senator Edmund Muskie. Around the Hill he was known as a real steady drinker, who made good use of his hideaway in the Capitol basement. No one could look in—it was windowless. He didn't complain.

He liked women. I know that some of the pretty girls who shared his hideaway with him got claustrophobia, but it didn't bother him. He served them a couple of drinks and a steak. He always fed them well—he wasn't cheap. Anything a girl wanted. And dessert.

We kept an extra waiter for him. He almost always ate his lunch in his hideaway. Muskie liked to invite girls around the Hill, but avoided those from his office, as far as I know. That made him smarter than many.

Muskie was also noted for having guests stay on at night— serving them the same meal. Dinner was steak, lunch was steak. Occasionally he switched to lobster if we had it. He tipped very well, drank bourbon. Kept his own supply.

His attendance record on the floor for voting was very poor. His ability to speak out with determination and originality about legislation was practically nonexistent. He was always backing someone else instead of being a front runner. That's why I said he'd never attract the kind of backing needed to make President. He'd do as well as what we have now, however.

One of the most brilliant and dedicated Senators is Frank Church.

I heard Frank Church give the stirring keynote address at the 1960 convention that nominated John F. Kennedy. He was such a powerful speaker that it was hard to believe that I was seeing the same man in the Senate restaurant.

He was acting like a pipsqueak. He made a very poor impression on me with his dress, his manner, his talk, his ability to converse with people.

The poor man was putty in the hands of his wife and one female staffer, who frequently ate with them. The two ladies gave me a pain. They were in charge, he kept quiet, and they talked.

His wife, Bethine, was not very popular in Hill circles, because she was considered too bossy. When Church started to be talked about as an alternative candidate to Carter in 1980, the Hill crowd laughed and said, "If he gets in, that will make Bethine our first woman President."

Of all the candidates' wives, the most retiring one I've known was Joan Kennedy, and the most blatantly outspoken and publicity-mad was Arlene Crane.

What a wife is or appears to be is tremendously important to the women voters. Women's lib notwithstanding, the shy and retiring wife is still an asset on the campaign trail—just as long as she is there on the platform to smile, wave, and say she just might vote for the man she's married to.

Rosalyn Carter, for example, did her husband's candidacy no good when she came on like gangbusters in Chicago early in October 1979. As she came down the steps of the airplane at O'Hare International Airport to be greeted by Mayor Jane Byrne, she hit the lady mayor with the question of whether she was going to support Jimmy Carter.

Caught off guard—since this was supposed to be a Columbus Day celebration—Mayor Byrne said she did support Carter, and the First Lady chortled at making news that the Chicago mayor was supporting Carter for reelection. But sly tactics beget sly tactics, and as soon as she could, Jane Byrne issued a clever diplomatic retreat that proved she was not one to be taken advantage of. She said she did "support" Jimmy Carter "the President of the United States." However, she said, she was not ready to state whom she endorsed for the Presidential election of 1980.

The Kennedy forces grinned broadly and around the Hill, word was that the First Lady had been left with egg on her face and maybe should relax and just await developments instead of pushing so soon. "It's not becoming a First Lady," they said.

Within days of the unfortunate incident, President Jimmy Carter flew to Chicago to mend his fences, appearing at a $100-a-plate fund raiser to help Jane Byrne. Carter waxed eloquent about the millions of dollars Chicago had received in federal grants for this project and that. And he came bearing new gifts—especially a plan to expand O'Hare Airport on adjacent Air Force land.

But still the smiling Mayor Byrne played it coy, praising President Carter to the heavens as "the savior of the nation's big cities," but still adding, "It would be premature and presumptuous of me tonight to say that I believe the Democratic Party ought to renominate our present leader for another four-year term."

True, as she spoke, Byrne had already received a message from another political suitor, Ted Kennedy, in the form of a telegram reading "JUST REMEMBER I HAVE KNOWN YOU AND LOVED YOU AND CHICAGO LONGER," but savvy politicos said that wasn't the only thing holding her back from pledging to support the incumbent President.

And in a few days, Mayor Byrne announced her support for Ted Kennedy. To show how quickly things change in politics, Jane's own growing unpopularity became an albatross around Teddy's neck by the time of the Illinois primary. But we are talking about wives of candidates and how the public perceives them.

So aggressive did Mrs. Carter seem to one seasoned Washington reporter, that she was quoted as saying of her, "She could have marched in Hitler's army."

No one will ever be able to say that about Joan Kennedy, who was the most sheltered wife of Capitol Hill. She maintained a low profile and was happiest when nothing was written or said about her. Still, the press sought her out.

Eventually they really had something to write about when Joan was charged with hitting the car ahead of her near her home in McLean, Virginia. Her fine was $200. It wasn't the money that was so embarrassing. It was that she had been hauled to the police station where she had failed to pass the sobriety test.

The theory around the Hill was that the Senator's playing around had so shattered his wife's self-confidence that she had fallen into a nervous state. For a time she sought help at two private sanitoriums, Silver Hill and Capistrano-by-the-Sea.

In the autumn of 1979, when Ted Kennedy was wrestling with his courage and conscience over whether to become a candidate for the Presidency, Joan was celebrating the triumph of two years of sobriety. She told friends she thought she was ready to help her husband in the campaign. Not to make speeches but just to be there at his side.

Stories are told around the Hill of Joan's kindness and gentleness. For example, how she once kept smiling for cameras and did not let on that a strange child had accidentally given her a sharp clout on the head with a stick in playing. Joan was afraid the child would be punished and did nothing about first aid until she got home.

Stories are told, too, of the put-down treatment she received from her sister-in-law, Ethel Kennedy. Before Joan and Ted were married, Ethel and she were friends, and it was almost an aunt-niece relationship. But eventually, after the marriage, they hardly spoke, because Ethel not only became bossy but started making fun of her glamour-girl image—as if being plain was beautiful and beautiful was ugly.

I have to smile when I recalled how Representative Philip Crane of Illinois labeled himself Mr. Conservative Republican, among the candidates for President.

He may have voted conservative, but he drank very liberally, attending parties held by conservatives and liberals alike, be they Democrats or Republicans. It mattered not the color of their politics, as long as the liquor had the right color and aroma.

Crane was one of the most handsome men on Capitol Hill, even pitted against Ted Kennedy, with whom he had something in common. In fact, in their mutualness, Crane had Kennedy beat in some ways. Whereas Ted would put his arm around a girl in an elevator, or give her a little pinch on the rear, continental style, Crane, at private parties on the Hill, after the more staid guests had left, would pull a girl down on his lap, as the evening wore on.

Of course Crane's behavior was a little different when he was accompanied by his wife, Arlene, who was called "the Watchdog." Arlene could behave like a jealous wife. For a time, Philip developed a reputation for stealing other members' staff gals. He would hire them away at a big salary but tire of them after a while and let them go.

I remember once when Phil Crane got very obstreperous because I would not physically wait on him when he was attending a Senate side party. I told him I was the manager and not a waiter, but that I would get a waiter for him. When he grew loud and profane, I told him I worked for the Senate and not for Congressmen. Eventually, I simply walked away.

Mrs. Crane was also a noisy drinker. With a few drinks she would start talking about how she was "all woman" and how other women envied her. But from the account of one girl who found herself in a nightclub party with Arlene Crane, the Congressman's wife was not as sure of herself as she proclaimed.

The girl came away shocked because, she said, Arlene had given her "a mean pinch on the arm because she thought I was muscling in on her territory—the man who was escorting her."

Candidate Jerry Brown, governor of California, without even being married, had to face the problem of whether his candidacy was being helped or hindered by his lady fair, a rock singing star, Linda Ronstadt. When they went on an African vacation together, sour notes drifted back to the States instead of the dulcet tones expected of a dedicated candidate's helpmate. Crabbing that he was more interested in desert water projects than in her, Linda took off on a passing camel and left the workaholic governor sitting high and dry.

Back in the States, they made up, but the public image of a sweet and lovely show-biz gal as First Lady was shattered—could the White House fence fence her in?

The closest thing we have had to a husband-wife Presidential candidate was Senator Fred Harris and his wife, La Donna. They came to Washington with a bang from Lawton, Oklahoma, and they made a striking couple. He was very distinguished looking. She was a full-blooded Indian, who often came to parties in tribal costume with her beautiful long black hair dressed in Indian fashion. It was interesting that Harris came first, not as an elected legislator, but to fill the vacancy caused by the death of Senator Robert Kerr in 1964. Club members smiled and said it was a matter of the poorest man coming to fill the shoes of the richest man of the Senate.

Senator Kerr was indeed acknowledged to be the man with the most millions on the Hill. I don't know how poor Harris was, but after winning his own election in 1966, he and La Donna decided he was ripe for the Presidency. Indian rights was one of his important planks, and this attracted a lot of young people. But, unfortunately, the young did not have much money to help the Harrises as they campaigned side by side in 1968.

In 1972, Fred and La Donna did a lot of entertaining on Capitol Hill, in search of the Presidency and backers for their campaign. They ran up big accounts, throwing cocktail parties for important people who could help raise money. I was happy to see they did pay their bills up, but the Democratic nomination eluded this colorful couple. I sometimes wonder what it would have been like to have La Donna in the White House as First Lady. She was a lovely lady and a *true* native American.

In my twenty-one years in Washington, rubbing elbows with the top political leaders, I saw a lot of Presidential timber drift down the river. I decided long ago that I liked most of them better as friends than as Presidents, and that the difference between Republican and Democratic candidates is the great American myth.

There ain't no difference worth speaking of. Parties are alike—individuals are different.

George McGovern was as American as apple pie, even though he lived in a Japanese house. He was a very pleasant man to talk to. He and I had something in common—an interest in Meals on Wheels. The Senator was instrumental in getting it started. It does a lot of good. Senior citizens pay if they can, and a hot meal comes to those who need it.

McGovern was not a typical political candidate, because he didn't have a string of parties on the Hill to make new friends as other hopefuls had. As it turned out, he could have used a few more friends in 1972. Also a more conservative platform. A guaranteed income, indeed! He was really far out.

In the political world there are resigned losers, and there are sore losers. McGovern was an angry loser. He sued seven big corporations for $1.09 million damages for allegedly making illegal contributions to Richard Nixon's reelection campaign. The suit dragged along and was eventually dismissed.

Eventually McGovern did lighten up and learned to joke about his disastrous campaign, saying, "Frankly, ever since I was a boy, I wanted to run for President in the worst possible way—and I sure did."

I got to hear a lot of another loser's witticisms. HHH was best when he made up a quip to suit a given situation, instead of telling a long-drawn-out story.

I remember when Humphrey was running for the Presidency against Nixon, he said, "Some people say he will be a hard man to beat. But I say between the old Nixon and the new Nixon, the old model and the new model, the low road and the high road, the juvenile delinquent and the statesman, he will be a hard man to *find!*"

And when we would be sitting around the apartment of Humphrey's girlfriend, Hubert would smile as he delivered this punch line about the communist problem: "Well-fed communists are less dangerous than hungry ones." What he was always saying one way or another was that a prosperous nation had nothing to fear from communists boring from within.

But the most surprising story, coming from Humphrey, was the unexpected one he told to a bunch of Senators to illustrate how hard it was to remember all the things a candidate was supposed to remember.

The way it went, a mother was having trouble potty training her little boy. "Johnny," she said, "if you don't stop doing your business on the floor when company's here, I'm going to have to lock you up. I'll tell you what. From now on, you come in and hold up this finger if you have to pee-pee, and this other finger if you have to do a job."

The little boy said, "Yes, Mama."

The next Sunday, when there was company, the little boy came rushing in with one finger up. His mother got up and took care of him.

An hour later he was back, dancing around and shouting, "Mama, Mama, I've got to shit, too, but I can't remember which finger."

Every four years I would hear the Hill crowd indulge in the same punch lines. Every time someone would announce that So-and-So was going to run as a favorite *son* from his state, some detractor would mutter, "Why don't you go ahead and finish that sentence?"

And if a candidate dared to pretend he was only running because he was responding to the call from all those wonderful people out there, someone would comment, "I didn't know he was a ventriloquist."

Former ardent candidate Mo Udall said it best not long ago:

> If you arrive in Washington and you're under the age of 65, you're considered a Presidential candidate as long as you are not under indictment, detoxification, or living in sin. This disease, candidacy, cannot be cured—but as we've seen in the case of George McGovern, it can be controlled.

The Hill crowd hates coyness, much prefers a candidate who comes right out and says he's running because he wants the job and thinks he has a chance.

At least they liked that about Jimmy Carter. He knew what he wanted. But as the early campaign days moved along, and Carter's image at the polls in 1979 didn't, some claimed he was behaving "just like a goddamn cat—licking himself with his own tongue."

Campaign years bring out the wildness in otherwise solid citizens, guaranteed to pep up the proceedings and bring a grin or a grimace to even the most jaded politician. The '70s saw a pig running for office. For the 1980 election, one candidate running for governor of Louisiana, prepared by changing his name to "None of the Above."

A sixty-four-year-old mule skinner went campaigning for the 1980 Presidential nomination. His campaign promise? A return to "a little common mule sense."

The Presidential candidate guaranteed to make the biggest waves, however, given the million-to-one-chance he got anywhere in his reach for the 1980 Presidency, was Fred Weiland III. His platform called for cutting all millionaires down to size—permitting them a net worth of only $1 million and using the rest to pay off the national debt.

Log-cabin childhoods are out, but some modern campaigners are trying to capitalize on the moral equivalent—Congressman Philip Crane, the conservative Republican candidate, bragging about his childhood in a home made of two railroad passenger cars, and fellow Republican candidate Benjamin Fernandez topping him with the story of his childhood home—a renovated railroad boxcar.

Hubert Humphrey couldn't come up with a log-cabin childhood either, to help his Presidential candidacy, but he could tell over and over how his dear wife, Muriel, had made and sold sandwiches to students to help Hubert get through graduate school.

Now and then, members of the Sweetest Little Club in the World would talk about campaigning techniques of the greats. Churchill was always cited as the most elegant put-down artist of history. The story was retold of how Churchill, in his earlier days, was on the platform campaigning for office and trying to ignore a female heckler. Finally she succeeded in getting under his skin when she shouted, "Mr. Churchill, I like neither your politics nor your moustache."

Churchill replied, "Madam, you're as likely to come into contact with one as with the other."

But when it came to stories of low-down campaigning, they agreed LBJ was the master. Lyndon would tell of the time some Texas politicians were sitting around trying to think of a campaign issue that would guarantee their candidate got elected.

"Let's spread the word," said one, "that the opponent screws pigs."

There was a stunned silence before one of the roundtable gasped, "But you know he doesn't do that."

"Sure, sure," said the idea man. "You know it, and I know it. But let's make the son of a bitch prove he doesn't."

PART IV

Please Don't
Steal the Silver

12

Party Time in the Sweetest Little Club

I still have a recurring nightmare. It is almost time for the party, and I can't get the apple into the mouth of the fatted pig.

Then I wake up and remember a real-life nightmare when I was pressed into helping Caroline Long, wife of Senator Russell Long, prepare her food for a party in her home. She had brought in a ham to have it baked and decorated. It had turned out beautifully, but because I had forgotten one thing, she almost had my scalp.

When I wrote up the order for baking and decorating the ham, at a $5 charge, I neglected to make out an additional slip for the carry-out biscuits. I forgot the order completely. The bake shop was already closed, and all I could offer her was bread. She left in a huff.

I thought she would never get over her mad. Eventually, after I had apologized over and over, she said, "Well, we're still friends, but I'm still mad at you about the biscuits." It mattered not that I had saved her a mint of money.

Just to show you the difference between having food prepared by a good private caterer and the equally good catering of the Club, here's an illustration. The average high-quality caterer—equal to the Senate restaurant's service—charges $25 just to bake a ham. If you want it decorated, it will cost $40. Should you want it sliced and put back together with toothpicks, the cost will be $75, because of the amount of work going into it.

Our charge to the Senator's wife for baking and decorating the ham was only a piddling $5. So, even though she had the inconvenience of going to a bakery to pick up rolls or biscuits, she still had a rather good deal for her money. A hell of a good deal!

I want to mention just one incident which shows the power of the Senatorial wives, even when it comes to wasting a lot of taxpayer's money. It's well known that every year the Senate ladies, who roll bandages for the Red Cross, have a luncheon for the First Lady.

When Betty Ford was First Lady, Senator Mark Hatfield's wife, Antoinette, was in charge of the luncheon. She got it into her mind that she wanted all French service, which meant that everything was to be served on silver, even to individual salt servers.

I tried to discourage her, pointing out that the Hill was only equipped for china service with the food already on the plate, American style. She demanded to see the architect of the Capitol, one of my top bosses, and wanted *me* to summon *him*. When I carefully explained that *I* could not *summon* my boss but would be happy to escort her to George White's office, Antoinette grabbed my phone and summoned the architect herself. Before she was through with White, who did indeed hurry to my office, the architect did agree to rent the whole silver service so that the meal could be served French style. It cost the taxpayers $400 and in fact closer to $500.

The problem with Senate wives is that their sense of importance escalates along with their husbands' seniority. I liked preparing parties for the wives of Senators who had not yet let their husbands' positions go to their heads.

Naturally, I had not been hired to cater to Senatorial wives but only to their husbands. However, I was well aware that if you made an enemy of a wife, you might have a Senator ready to kick your ass.

The husband-wife situation became more tangled when the wife drank. Few Senators approved of their wives tippling no matter how much they themselves drank. And it was drinking which was at the root of my problems with the wife of one very influential Senator—Everett Dirksen.

Louella Dirksen was what we called "an angry drinker." She would get very abusive to me when in this condition and call me "a damned bastard," even as I was trying to help her.

Maybe it was because the Senator was annoyed with his wife over her drinking. At any rate, for some reason, he continually left her name out of his biography in the Congressional Directory, while inserting his daughter's name in each year's edition. The biography, which he, like every other Senator, had total control over, merely said, ". . . married and has one daughter, Mrs. Howard H. Baker, Jr."

I knew that theirs was a stormy life, because he told me about it now and then. Occasionally, in a semi-embarrassed, offhand way, he would ask me to have forbearance in dealing with her.

Everytime I failed to please Mrs. Dirksen, I would end up climbing the walls and determined to refuse to deal with her anymore and let someone else handle her parties. But time would pass, and I was so fond of my good friend Dirksen that I'd get involved all over again.

I remember one time Louella Dirksen got so angry at being kept waiting a few minutes for the food to arrive that she accosted me in front of her friends, saying loudly, "You damned bastard, if you can't get the stuff here on time, I'll never talk to your silly face again."

Stunned to the quick, I said, "Madame, I couldn't care less, and you can report me to any one you please. I'm giving up my Sunday afternoon, without pay, to take care of you and your friends."

I looked over and saw Senator Dirksen pretending not to hear what was going on. Mentally I cursed him for his cowardice in not helping me handle his wife.

My crime, it seemed, was that the two waitresses who were going to serve the food had gone to change clothes and were now five minutes late. Mrs. Dirksen's guests had arrived and were waiting but chatting happily. It was a Sunday afternoon, and I had come in to work especially to please the powerful Republican Senator. I knew he would be there, and it was a way of making brownie points with him. He, in turn, was there to make brownie points with his wife by letting the ladies meet a Senator.

There were 150 or so guests, and from the first, Mrs. Dirksen had given me a hard time. I had tried to plan a nice food spread for her, but she had insisted on cutting corners. And all she was serving was a few finger sandwiches per person, cookies, and coffee.

The Senators' staff had set up their own bar to cut costs. Dirksen was not a big spender, either. We would be making no profit on the party, but it was good public relations for me to be there, seeing that everything went well.

Just at the moment Louella Dirksen had finished blowing her stack at me, the two girls in uniform arrived with their trays heaped with the goodies. It had not been easy to find girls willing to work on Sunday. Their wages were $15 each.

Mrs. Dirksen had given me a hard time about this, too. She had said, "Anyone would be tickled to death to serve for five dollars. I can get all the help I want."

I had stopped short of suggesting that she get her own waitresses, nor did she offer to. She did pay the $30, but added no tip.

After the blowup, a few guests sidled over to me, and tried to make me feel better. One said softly, "Don't worry, Mr. Hurst, I know her. She's just talking."

I thought I had weathered the storm when the Senator, looking sheepish, signed the check. I left immediately, just to get away, and lick my wounds.

But that wasn't the end of it. The next morning at 11 A.M., Senator Jordan sent over a Xerox copy of the letter Mrs. Dirksen had sent him, telling him that he should fire me and that *I* had ruined her party.

A little while later, I was surprised to see Senator Dirksen himself enter the Office Building restaurant—the same building that would be named for him after death. I was surprised because he always had lunch in the Capitol's Private Dining Room on the Senate side. I wondered if he knew that I had seen the letter. I realized he was there to see me, but it was a delicate situation.

I decided to take the bull by the horns, and said, "Senator, you know me well enough to know I'm straightforward, and I'll never embarrass you and your guests in any way. I'd like you to know how sorry I am that Mrs. D. was so abusive in the presence of your guests."

I could see he was relieved I had brought the subject up first. He said, "You know about the letter?" And I said, "Yes."

He said, "Don't pay any attention, and don't be concerned. There wouldn't have been any letter, but Lou got up this morning and called my secretary and told her exactly what she wanted her to write. We had a hell of a row at breakfast. She wanted me to bring her notes to my secretary, and I wouldn't. So, she phoned it in."

I had to laugh at this, and Dirksen chuckled too, as we both mulled over the thought of his outraged wife dictating her complaint.

"Well, Louie, I must say she was very efficient. She told Eleanor, 'I want this in Jordan's hands no later than nine thirty.' "

I started to say again that I was sorry about the whole thing. But he lifted his hand to stop me. "Louie, she's bitchy, and there's nothing *I* can do with her. So what can *you* do with her? I don't want to hear another damned word about it." He raised his hand again, and started to move off, but stopped. "But just remember," he said as he turned back a moment, "if you need, I'll defend you with Jordan."

As he walked away, I shook my head, thinking, who would believe the irony of this situation—a Senator's office sends a complaint aimed at getting a man fired, and here is the same Senator promising to defend the man's job.

I went to the phone to call Jordan and tell him the heat was off. Before I could say a word, he said, "What the hell goes on around here on Sunday?"

I told him that Dirksen had just left and gave him the Senator's version of the story, including his offer to defend me.

Jordan laughed and said, "I knew there was no problem with the lady—other than the usual—but I thought you'd better see what she had written."

He laughed again, as at some great joke, and hung up.

I stood, looking at my phone. No wonder my nerves went raw sometimes.

Not long after, I received a little gift from Senator Dirksen. No note. Just a bottle of my favorite bourbon. It was hand-delivered by one of his aides.

It was not exceptional for the restaurant staffs to have to cope with Senators or their wives who could cast a pall over a party if they had already gotten into the sauce. They were case-hardened and would not bat an eyelash when Senator Talmadge, for example, would come reeling into a party in a belligerent mood.

Employees dreaded to see Senator Ernest Hollings of South Carolina and his wife, Peatsy, arrive at a party if they had already had a few drinks. Before they cut down, both were heavy drinkers, and neither held their drinks well. Peatsy would, under the influence, take offense at something another guest was or wasn't doing. I have even heard her berate a guest for not pledging the size donation she expected for her husband's reelection campaign.

Still, I was very fond of Peatsy Hollings. I was one of many who had watched her romance with the Senator blossom into marriage. Hollings' wife, we were told, had not come to join him in Washington, preferring life in South Carolina. So it was natural that he was attracted to a bright young girl who was an aide in his office.

In the early days of the romance, Peatsy would eat in the restaurant with him frequently and have a worshipful look when he talked. Other Senators commented that they wished they had someone to listen to them that way. No man could long resist that kind of adoration. The ironic part is that after they were married, Peatsy continued to come up to the Hill and would come running into the dining room, where she would now find her husband eating with his other young pretty employees.

I guess my very favorite Senator was Mark Hatfield, for no particular reason except that he is just a great guy, even though I did on occasion feud with his wife, Antoinette, as you have already seen.

Once I even gave a birthday party for the Senator, his family, and staff, at my own expense, in one of the dining rooms in the Dirksen Building.

I had gotten to know Hatfield because he was a minority member of the Rules Committee, which oversees the restaurants, and almost everything he said and did seemed to be on the right wavelength for me. Of course, we were nothing alike, since he had thirty-six honorary doctorates, was a confirmed egghead, and was a professor of history and political science.

Since everyone is entitled to a mistake, I even forgave him for nominating Nixon in 1960. When it came to his special interest in the Civil War period, we suddenly saw eye to eye. It was Hatfield who got citizenship restored to Jefferson Davis. He introduced a bill, and it didn't pass. He introduced it again. It took six years for him to achieve his goal, but he never gave up.

Of course, he was then able to kid Southern Senators about how it took a tough Northerner to get the job done for them.

At Hatfield's birthday party, his cake was in the shape of a history book, but Hatfield only took a nibble. He is as his office calls him, "a health nut" about not eating sweets and sugar.

I also once personally gave a party for another of my favorite Senators, who, by coincidence, also didn't touch sweets for health reasons. Gale McGee of Laramie, Wyoming, had diabetes. By sheer good fortune, McGee was born on St. Patrick's Day, so I had a birthday cake made in the shape of a cloverleaf and decorated with shamrocks.

McGee and Mike Monroney were the two Senators who seemed to be most concerned about working people and fought for the interests of employees on Capitol Hill. Hatfield and McGee were my two favorite men on the Hill, and they were good friends with each other as well. I was sorry to see the team broken up when McGee became an ambassador to the Pan-American Union.

Though Senators seldom made arrangements for their own parties, they would still be the stars of the show, once the party began. I would make the host look good by hovering near him and taking orders only from him. If he had made his wife the important one, I would single her out instead.

In every office, someone would be assigned as the Senator's party planner, and on the planning, I would deal only with that person. For Senator Hansen's office (Clifford P. of Wyoming), his private secretary, Patti MacMillan, had the authority. For Robert Byrd of West Virginia, it was Ethel Low, his good right arm. When she retired, he really missed her expertise in party planning. With Herman Talmadge of Georgia, it was his wife, Betty Talmadge, who made all party decisions. After his divorce, I wondered how he would survive socially. He didn't.

Ted Kennedy of Massachusetts had Angelique Lee, who had a great sense of humor—except, alas, with me. She handled everything that made the Senator's life run smoothly and involved the doling out of money. She paid all his personal bills, I was told. His wife, Joan, once wistfully mentioned to me that "Miss Angelique," as she was called around the Hill, even arranged the allowance for household money.

With Margaret Chase Smith of Maine, I knew it was the voice of authority when a male voice called to give me orders—that of General William C. Lewis, Jr., called Bill by his friends. It was just as well that Bill Lewis dealt with the Senator, because whenever I had dealings with her, she somehow almost always ended up getting angry at me. Once she wrote a letter to the Rules Committee, complaining of my handling of a party. But I didn't worry, because she was always complaining.

After she moved her office from the Russell Building to the Dirksen Building, she could no longer complain about odors, but she could complain about everything else—party noise, the sound of music after hours. The climax came one evening when a group held a psychedelic party with flashing lights and loud music for dancing. Though her office was almost a block away, Senator Smith became so outraged, she called Chief James Powell, head of the Capitol Hill police. The next day she wrote a letter to the Rules Committee.

Senator Smith was a teetotaler and would not attend a party where drinks were served. She entertained only at lunches on the Hill—usually in her hideaway on the first floor of the Capitol itself. The guests would usually be a few members of her staff and Senator and Mrs. George Aiken of Vermont. Margaret Smith and Lola Aiken had been close friends even before Lola married the Senator.

Lola had been Aiken's secretary when he was governor of Vermont, before coming to Washington. Senator Aiken and Senator Smith were a close-working team, representing the New England states, and Aiken, fortunately, was a teetotaler like her. Both were very conservative Republicans. And both were parsimonious and proud of it.

Most Senators are so tired of grinning and being excessively friendly to all of their constituents, that when they get to the home territory of their Club, they enjoy being grouchy, glum, or whatever comes naturally. I'm sure that many would not be reelected if they talked to their constituents the way they talk to the hired help. But there were wonderful exceptions.

Senator Spessard Holland of Florida, for example, who always spoke to elevator boys and made everyone feel important. It was a sad day on the Hill when he retired in 1971. I knew Holland's wife, Mary Agnes, very well too. In fact, both were extremely nice to me. So it was with special enthusiasm that I worked to make their fiftieth wedding anniversary party a success.

It was supposed to be a surprise. But since it involved bringing between 1,400 and 1,500 people together, including their many relatives from Florida, I will simply say that the Hollands must have been among the greatest actors on the Hill—to look so surprised.

The Senator and his wife entered a darkened room, and suddenly the lights went on, and it was pandemonium. Over a thousand voices yelling and a staid committee room turned into a sparkling fairyland.

The Florida Citrus Industry was financing this most elegant of parties, and they wanted the best. The flowers alone cost $250, and the total bill ran to around $6,000. And that was back in 1969. Today it would be twice or three times as much.

White and gold were the colors of the evening—from the all-white flower bouquets tied with gold ribbons to the gold linen, to the white cake set high on a pedestal topped with a bride and groom and the number "50" in gold. The cake itself was rimmed with white orchids.

The buffet dinner, too, was one of the nicest I ever served. And I remember that not only did the members of the House, Senate and Supreme Court come, but also the current Vice-President, Agnew, and the Vice-President who hadn't made it to the Presidency, Hubert H. Humphrey.

The guests drank their fill at the open bars, and picked and chose from a vast assortment of foods: spiced shrimp, crab balls, chicken salad, stuffed tomatoes, seafood Newburg, tidbits of beef Burgundy, rice pilaf, suckling pig, sliced turkey, roast beef, miniature quiches Lorraines, deviled eggs, stuffed celery, hot biscuits, and hot corn muffins.

Ted Stevens of Alaska was quite a salmon fisherman. Many a time we poached and decorated a salmon for the Stevens' dinner parties. The fish had to be placed on a board to poach, so it wouldn't fall apart. Then we would decorate it on the board, glazing it with clear gelatin, and lines of pimientos and ripe olives for touches of color. Surrounding the salmon would be a cheerful-looking border of stuffed cherry tomatoes. This dish would usually be served at a buffet.

The Senator often served a variety of fish he had caught in Alaska, having them flown down from his own freezer. We would serve it at the Hill with a sharp sauce made of mayonnaise, dry mustard, pickle relish, and chopped pimiento.

You dip the fish into the sauce with a cocktail fork or toothpick and serve it on a cracker. After a few drinks, some guests would be dipping with their fingers and slurping the sauce, saying, "Boy, that's good."

He would also bring back from Alaska king crabs—the whole crabs. I would steam them for his parties. Frequently, he entertained twenty-five to fifty people in his office in the Dirksen Building. There was no charge for that.

Some annual affairs are celebrated on the Hill. The annual New Orleans shrimp-and-crayfish luncheon, in honor of the Mardi Gras, rates high. The Senators love this one because the queen and all her court are young and good looking.

And Inaugural Day luncheon is still another big event—every four years, we serve the first meal that the new President or reelected President eats after the big swearing-in ceremony on the inaugural stand on the east portico of the Capitol. The first luncheon is a stag meal for the President. The First Lady is taken elsewhere in the Capitol to have her luncheon with her friends. The President is the guest of the leaders of Congress, and a few of his important friends are present—a total of about a hundred people.

It's after this luncheon that the Presidents ride—and Carter walked—to the reviewing stand in front of the White House to watch the inaugural parade, featuring bands and floats from all states.

It's the one day that everything is happy and jovial, even a love fest between Congress and the President. After that, for the next four years, it's all downhill.

That all-important first luncheon that the newly sworn in President eats is always held in Room S 207, the Senate reception room on the second floor of the Capitol, right across from the Senate chamber. The meal signals to the Hill leadership who the insiders and pets of the new administration will be. Of course, the campaign manager is rewarded by being present to take his bows. Some members of the Supreme Court also show up—though all are invited.

There is no tradition which says that a similar party must be given for the First Lady. She may be the guest of several Senators' wives or of a particular Senator and his wife. Or she may simply have luncheon in the Senate dining room with the members of her own family. Eventually, the Secret Service gets the Presidential couple back together again for "the last mile"—the distance between the Capitol and the White House along Pennsylvania Avenue.

April was always the month of terror. It had enough problems to keep me in hot water at all times. There was enough work for me all year round, but in April, I needed wings to speed me on my way. Parties round the clock.

The week of the Cherry Blossom Festival, it was standard for me to have as many as thirty-seven breakfasts going at the same time, at which important Senators were hosts to the budding beauties from their states and their entourages. I was expected to show my concern by personally stopping in to ask, "Is everything all right, Senator?"

Right after that "blessed event" would come what we referred to as the Blossoms and Bosoms Week. This was the DAR arriving in Washington with straw hats and flowers on the hats and on their ample bosoms. They were the most indignant group of women I had to deal with, through the years. There was never a year that I pleased them nor did they ever send me a thank-you note.

However, hope springs eternal, and Senators took turns trying to please them. They always had a Congressional reception on the Senate side. They seemed to flow in like a tide and take over the entire food operation. They were breakfasted, dined, and wined every day. There were cocktail parties and dinner parties galore. It was a dreadful time.

But all of this was only the buildup for the most emotional event of all—the Senate Wives' luncheon for the First Lady, on the last Tuesday of April. The Senators' wives would come to the Capitol dressed fit to kill in little furs and jewels, and change into their humble Red Cross uniforms. The First Lady would show up, and there would be much picture taking.

Once the luncheon was over, the ladies would race to outdo each other in getting back into their silks and finery to continue visiting with the First Lady. I would notice that, if the Vice-President's wife was also there, she would stick to her own little clique and not try to muscle in on the First Lady's show.

Occasionally there would be a Hollywood star as honored guest. Once thirty stars stood in the receiving line at a reception sponsored by Senator Pell. I first remember Liz Taylor from a luncheon sponsored by Charles Percy about 1973. She was very busily promoting her favorite charity—a free hospital for natives in Africa. I chatted with her and told her that the elderly of the United States were my special interest.

She said that people here don't realize how desperate the conditions are for elderly and children in Africa. But she was pleased to hear that I was interested in helping anyone—people could be smug and heartless, she said.

I was amazed when I saw her to find that she had changed from the slim but well-stacked beauty that I had drooled over when I saw her in the movies or the late night show. Here she was, and she was big! Her face was beautiful, and I could almost fall into the blue water of those eyes—tremendous eyes. But she really had let her figure go.

Anyway, she wasn't my date. She was being escorted tenderly by Senator Charles Percy. She would come to his office quite often. He even rode her by Senate subway from the Dirksen Office

Building to the Capitol, where they had lunch in the Senators' private dining room. He always ate there, and it was natural for him to take her there, but I'm sure he enjoyed having all the envious eyes on him.

When Liz finally left, the word around the group was she had been told the voters would never stand for financing a hospital in Africa on public funds, when there was so much medical need in this country.

I'll never forget the time the Hollywood guest of honor was Lassie, the richest dog in the land. We fixed up a very fancy hamburger—fit for a king or a collie. Senator Murphy was host.

Senator James Eastland, a powerhouse on the Hill, who hailed from Doddsville, Mississippi—they used to say he thought he came from *Godsville*—held a party every year to raise money for his pet orphanage in Mississippi. He and Mrs. Eastland would hold a bridge party on a Saturday afternoon, and all the money went to the orphanage. Just before the money raiser, he and his wife would have a little private luncheon for only twelve special friends in his office hideaway, and the Senator would pay for it immediately. He was one of the few members of the Club who did not believe in charge accounts.

Of course, among the most important recurring parties were the swearing-in receptions for new Senators or just old Senators renewing their lease on their Senate seats every six years. These parties gave me a chance to meet new Club members and their wives and get an inkling of what troubles I'd be up against in the coming years. But sometimes there would be a pleasant surprise, and there would be a new Senatorial couple who would give us absolutely no trouble.

From the first minute I met Mrs. J. Glenn Beall, Jr., she struck me as the most attractive woman in the Senate. On the score of beauty, I decided, she even edged out Jackie Kennedy. Nancy Beall had come in with the new Senator-elect after the 1970 elections to discuss with me a swearing-in reception, which they wanted me to stage for January 3, when he would take office. Many others had been to see me for the same reason. But this couple—from Frederick, Maryland—were somehow different.

They were not trying to impress me with their social standing *or* their *poverty* as some of our millionaire Senators did—when trying to cut my price to the bare bones. They wanted not a luncheon but a nice cocktail hors d'oeuvres party. They did not question the price, ordered enough so that they would not run short, and what is more, were unusual hosts.

At most swearing-in parties—and every other kind of party— Senatorial husbands and wives ignored each other to the extent that some guests would have to ask me to point out which female was the Senator's wife. They usually guessed it was some babe the Senator was paying attention to at the party. But a more loving couple than Glenn and Nancy I have yet to see. They stood together as a team, and seemed very aware and happy with each other. This impression was confirmed when other Senators commented to me on the fact that Beall was lucky to have a wife who paid attention to him. It's good that Beall did pay such close attention to his wife, because other men seemed ready to cut in the moment Beall's attention wandered—but it never did.

Not only was Nancy beautiful in a tall, slim, well-poised way, but she did not hesitate to wear elegant clothes that most political wives are afraid to wear. I remember her outfit for the swearing-in occasion was very daring compared with what others wore—a printed silk pajama outfit, trimmed in fur. The pants were very full. I was so impressed with her outfit that I commented on it to her.

The early impression of Nancy Beall was confirmed as time went on. They continued to be a close and loving couple—one of the exceptions and much envied by others. Beall quickly acquired a reputation for *not* playing around.

I once wondered aloud how they had met each other. Nancy, it turned out, was also a native Marylander—Nancy Lee Smith of Cumberland, who had gone to finishing school with Jackie Kennedy. And that's about the time she and Beall met—at a formal dance. She had been his blind date.

Another Senator from Maryland was one of the most troublesome legislators when it came to entertaining at his swearing-in. Charles Mathias cried the blues about the projected costs. He figured on having only three hundred guests, and made no provision for more. Fifteen hundred turned up!

His wife, Ann, had put her foot down about drinks. I tried to explain to her that their guests who had worked so hard to get them elected in the 1968 election would be counting on celebrating with a few toasts, and would not have fun without a highball. I even dared comment that, if word got out that there was no liquor, they wouldn't come. She said, "Fine."

I noticed that she did all the talking and the Senator-elect simply went along in dealing with me.

They ordered lemonade, coffee, and tea. The party was early afternoon—so it was still lunchtime. However, all the Mathiases permitted us to serve was finger sandwiches and cookies. It was the least expensive thing we had on our menu. The finger sandwiches were $15 per hundred, and the assorted cookies were 60¢ a dozen. The various beverages were $4 a gallon.

I noticed people came to pay their respects, but left quickly and did their drinking elsewhere by crashing other Senators' parties. In fact, some even sidled up to me and asked where in hell they could find a party with some drinks other than the kid stuff.

I told them it was a state secret, but I believed the liquor was flowing quite freely at Russell Long's party. He had been in the Senate since 1948, when he was elected to fill the unexpired term of John Overton. But he had among the best parties every six years at his successive swearing-ins. Not only did the liquor flow like crazy, but the food was very delectable. And he always ordered far more than needed. Furthermore, Long was too happy and charitable to turn anyone away.

Where was this party? they asked eagerly. I told them that part I could not divulge. I had given them the basic information, and they would have to work out how to find it themselves.

As a matter of fact, Long served Louisiana gulf shrimp, specially flown up and prepared with spice, horseradish, and cocktail sauce. He would have about 150 pounds of shrimp flown up for the happy occasion. It took nine kitchen workers just to hull and devein the damn things. With it, he served steamship round of beef, with sliced turkey breasts and baked ham, deviled eggs, stuffed celery, cocktail-size hard rolls and potato salad. Long didn't serve dessert. But then, who needed it?

I would say that, on swearing-in days, the most popular party would be Long's. A thousand invited guests would come, plus crashers.

Howard Metzenbaum of Cleveland, Ohio, could put a Croesus-rich Texan to shame when it came to entertaining. He came to the Senate as an Ohio industrialist, founder of Metzenbaum, Gaines, Finley and Stern Company. He was also chairman of ComCorp, a group of suburban weeklies in the Cleveland area.

I was much impressed with the new Senator and his wife when they came to me to help plan his swearing-in reception, a cocktail party from 5 to 7 P.M. It would not be too big a party, Shirley Metzenbaum explained, smiling—they were only expecting 1,200 to 1,500 people.

It was soon obvious that the Senator did not care how much the party cost as long as the quality was uniformly excellent, from decorations to liquor to sweets. It was the kind of talk I liked to hear, and what resulted was one of the most beautiful parties I've ever catered, starting with a table decoration of a huge ice mold of the state of Ohio and running through a list of sumptuous foods that brought the total cost to $6,500, booze included.

Suckling pig was only one of the items on the menu. Others were steamship roast of beef with tiny rolls, decorated salmon, spiced shrimp, deviled eggs, stuffed celery, petits fours, and brownies.

Shirley Metzenbaum made a grand entrance at the party, wearing the most gorgeous Russian sable coat I have seen. Few women wear long dresses to Capitol Hill parties because they often come from their offices, but she wore one, and it was a knockout—ruffled from waist down and trimmed with pearls.

One would think that Herman Talmadge, being from a sister Southern state—Georgia—would follow the lead of Louisiana Senator Long. I was surprised at first to learn that this was not the case.

Talmadge made Mathias look extravagant. At his swearing-in,

he would have a cash bar, so everyone could pay for his own drinks. Someone from his office was authorized to be cashier and take the money. He served potato chips and salted nuts. Nothing sweet.

Industry representatives often found an excuse to dine or wine Senators on the Senate's own turf, so there was no excuse for not attending the party, short of death or a late quorum call. Publicity resulted every year when, for example, the Betty Crocker luncheon celebrated awards to a new batch of young homemakers.

Such parties are not cheap, and sometimes what we charged was only part of the total cost. I remember one industry-paid-for party, at which our charge was $18 a head. However, the public relations or lobbying firm that was handling the party as the go-between of the industry and the Senator charged their client $35 a guest and the $17 a head was their profit—around $2,000.

Sometimes it is a member of a Senator's staff who seems to be making money on a party sponsored by the Senator—though I sometimes wondered if the aide pocketed the entire amount or shared it with the Senator, or even turned it over completely.

I recall one party footed by the railroads in which the liquor bill alone was over $1,000. A certain Senatorial aide added 10 percent to the bill.

The traditional Kansas pancake parties, believe it or not, resulted in my meeting Queen Elizabeth of England. The pancake parties were held to coincide with England's famous pancake races, in which housewives and pretty girls make merry and get a little publicity.

And since the British ambassador to the United States couldn't go home for his festival, he would settle for attending our pancake breakfasts. Senators Pearson and Carlson would be joint hosts on the years the breakfasts were held on the Senate side of the Capitol. On alternate years, they would be held on the House of Representatives side.

One year the British ambassador and I got along so well that he invited me to come to England and promised that, when I made my trip, he would arrange for me to meet the Queen. It was one of the highlights of my life when this came about, not just because I was face to face with royalty, but also because I was looking at some of the greatest antique furniture I had ever seen.

The morning I was to go to Buckingham Palace, I showed up in a business suit as the ambassador had instructed. He had also said, "Inasmuch as you have not been trained to bow, don't bother to try. She will understand."

That took a load off my mind, as I waited in an outer room at Buckingham Palace. A male secretary took us in. The Queen was sitting at a desk and came over, and I shook hands with her. I remember commenting on the lovely Louis XIV table which served her as a desk. The high-ceilinged room she was in must have been thirty by fifty feet—a house could have fit in it.

It was certainly a great adventure, but it's always some little thing that sticks most in your mind, and in this case it was meeting the man at the Palace who does nothing but wind the clocks of the approximately three hundred rooms. That adventure was my reward for having catered hundreds of Hill parties.

Sometimes it's not just Senators who attend parties on the Senate side of the Capitol. Some House members are great gate crashers, and if they weren't invited, they took the liberty of coming anyway. Bella Abzug was often a surprise drop-in guest. And Tip O'Neill thought anything on the Hill was open to him—and, come to think of it, it was.

Rogers Morton was another Congressman who showed up, invitation or no. He came early and stayed late. He helped open a party and set the proper mood, and he sometimes stayed to help close it. The staff would wonder how he found out about all these parties, at which everyone else would be a Senator. They decided that he must have heard the clinking of the ice as he passed an open committee door where the party was being put together. He was one of the heavy drinkers on the Hill.

Actually we had two Mortons who were heavy drinkers, though they were there at different times. Rogers Morton was a Congressman from Maryland, who merely dropped in at our parties—and sloshed out, nicely filled with Scotch.

His brother, Thruston Morton, had been a Senator from

Kentucky from 1957 to 1969, as well as chairman of the Republican National Committee from 1959 to 1961.

Thruston, true to his Kentucky heritage, was a heavy drinker of bourbon. However, he held his liquor much better than his brother, made a nice appearance, and was very proper. In contrast, Congressman brother Rogers not only was an uninvited guest at our Senate parties, but with enough of a load, he would storm out of the party, proclaiming, "Everybody here is a son of a bitch."

Norma McClellan, the wife of Senator John McClellan of Arkansas, once gave me a hard time over her great adoration for the singer Glenn Campbell. She would try her damnedest to have the star come to her parties. He did come twice that I recall—once for his birthday. I remember we had a lovely birthday cake for him.

He didn't sing. He looked like a fifteen-year-old farmboy about to do his chores, dressed in blue jeans and a farmerish jacket.

Mrs. McClellan introduced him to me proudly. I was not happy because she had refused to use a private room—which would have required the 20 percent surcharge—and insisted on holding a luncheon for thirty people in the regular dining room.

I had tried to be tactful and had pointed out to Norma McClellan that it would be quite conspicuous to have the star and thirty people in the midst of the Senators who would be eating in a hurry. When this did not move her, I commented that such social gatherings in the dining room were frowned on by other Senators because it took away their tables.

Mrs. McClellan was starting to get angry, as she pointed out that this was the way her husband, the Senator, wanted it.

Since a Senator is never wrong, that's the way it was. But right afterward, I went to the Rules Committee and told them what had happened and how Senators had not been able to be served because of having to wait for thirty people to get out. They finally made a ruling that it would no longer be permitted for tables to be shoved together in the Senators' private dining rooms to accommodate one particular group.

I was grinning from ear to ear the day this notice went around. But damned if, just three days later, one of the Senator's offices didn't tell me to shove a bunch of tables together because they wanted to do the same thing for the Senator. I was happy to tell them they couldn't; new regulations in no way allowed us to put tables together to accommodate parties without an order from the Rules Committee.

They went over my head and called the Rules Committee and immediately got permission. I observed there wasn't even one Senator in the party—all staff. Then I phoned and raised hell. I said, "Why do you tell me one thing and do another?" They said, "Well, forget it. It depends on who it is, and this is Humphrey's office."

The Hill was very excited when the word spread that Senator Huddleston of Kentucky was giving a party for one of Kentucky's favorite sons, Muhammed Ali. About 500 Hill people were going to toast the fighter in the Caucus Room of the Russell Building at a cocktail reception.

Girls lined the halls around the Caucus Room and sneaked in to take a look at the champ. They came out filled with exaggerated shock to report that Ali wore fingernail polish—and not just soft polish, but very shiny stuff.

I remember that Teddy Kennedy was there, and a lot of Congressmen had dropped in. There were no speeches, no receiving line. Ali simply held court. I don't know how many times I heard Ali say, "I'm the greatest!" White and black women alike broke into his magic circle to exclaim about how thrilled they were to meet him. The Senators stood aside with slightly amused smiles. They were not used to taking a back seat to other stars, but were determined to be good sports for the little while their Club was being invaded.

There were three bars, and I was interested to see that Ali appeared to drink with the best of guests, but never showed any signs that it was affecting him. However, he did not go a full fifteen rounds.

13

The Lunch Bunch

I don't want to see another strawberry. When I see a straw-berry, I see Capitol Hill, and I see trouble. Nothing seemed to excite more controversy than the status symbol of a strawberry.

Liz Stranigan of Senator Gale McGee's office (he is now Am-bassador to the Organization of American States) was eternally calling me to order strawberries for the Senator in the dead of winter. It seemed to me that anytime they were hard to get and were too costly, she would call and say the Senator is on his way to the dining room, and he wants strawberries without cream or powdered sugar.

It took two baskets to make a double portion, which Senator McGee got. In dead of winter it would cost up to $3.60 for two cartons for one double order, for which we could charge only $1.10. We had to rush to the Fruit Basket, a fruit store in downtown Washington, to buy them—this involved a chauffeur and station wagon. Meanwhile, important errands hung suspended pending heralded arrival of strawberries. By the time the Senator finished his main course, the strawberries were in the kitchen.

Liz did not want to hear that we did not have strawberries. There went the deficit!

The same thing with Senator Capehart and his damn shrimp.

All we did is fix the shrimp he brought in. We would have to make a special sauce, for which he paid nothing. He would not even come in, which would have meant leaving a tip. He had the shrimp sent to his office and ate it there. Cost to the restaurant: a couple dollars' service. Plus labor, cost of tomatoes and horseradish and all the fixing. Payment to us: zero. There went the deficit.

Just because a Senator is wealthy enough to buy and sell a dozen average men and is getting a little extra under the table doesn't mean he wants to let go of any of it. In fact some of the wealthiest seemed to make a game of seeing how little they could get away with paying for lunch at the Senate restaurants. I recall one penny-pinching Senator who used to fill up on free graham crackers and order just one cup of coffee for ten cents. Actually, he would get a cup and a half served in a silver carafe. No tip, naturally.

And the bargain hunters didn't wait for lunch. Some start with brunch. I remember, soon after I went to the Hill in 1959, that one of the waitresses told me I was wanted by a Senator in the Vandenberg room. This was not a restaurant room but was used for fancy parties, but sure enough, I found a Senator there—Wayne Morse—fussing and fuming.

"I want to know where my newspaper is and my food?" the Senator demanded.

"I'm sorry, sir," I said. "I'm new to the restaurants here. I'm Lou Hurst, the purchasing agent."

"I'm Senator Wayne Morse from Oregon, and the waitresses know what I get." One was hurrying in now with a newspaper. I told her to take care of the Senator, and I went to the kitchen. "What's this about Wayne Morse getting special service in a banquet room?" I asked. "He's in there acting as if he owns the place."

"Well, he's in the Club," said Assistant Chef James, who had been there for some twenty years. "I'll take care of it."

"No, no," I said. "I want to know what's going on—what's special."

James reluctantly confided. "Well, he has to have three freshly baked hot biscuits, a cup of coffee, and a glass of buttermilk."

"But there already are biscuits upstairs in the pantry in the warmer," I protested.

"Not fresh enough for him," said James, shrugging. "He gets charged thirty cents for his meal."

"That's not much of a meal," I said.

"Oh," said James, "I forgot to mention he also gets ham and eggs and home fries. But we don't charge him for that, because he brings his own food in from the farm, and we prepare it—though I have been tempted at least to charge him for the onions he wants added to his fried potatoes."

I was flabbergasted and bewildered and no little annoyed. I left the kitchen muttering to myself and was even more shocked when I learned that the Senator had returned the newspaper and had not paid for it.

I said to the cashier, "He returned it so he didn't have to pay for it?"

She said, "Right. But what can I do? He returned it and also the New York paper. He didn't pay for either."

I said, "You mean a Senator can be so cheap he doesn't pay for a newspaper?"

"Lou, your friend from your home state, Senator Stennis, does the same thing, and Robertson of Virginia plays the same trick. You'll get used to it. The only difference between Morse and Robertson is that Robertson brings in grits from corn ground on his farm."

I couldn't believe what I was hearing. I went to the checker in the pantry and said, "Do you mean this is the way this place operates? No wonder there is a yearly deficit."

This was only the beginning of my orientation. I was to learn that there were tricks in money saving to fit every meal and party occasion.

Actually A. Willis Robertson of Virginia, as I learned, had a leg up on *spendthrift* Morse. Robertson paid only 15¢, and that was for his buttermilk. Naturally, no tip.

Senator Talmadge's wife, Betty, frequently kept meats in our freezers. She always led me to believe they were poor people, though I realized she could not be too hard up, owning a ham business and having a curing plant for bacon and ham—Talmadge Ham.

Betty liked quail on toast for breakfast, and often we would prepare this delicacy for as many as fifty guests. She would have quail flown up from Georgia along with steaks and, of course, ham. We would prepare the food for Betty at 75¢ per head—a real bargain.

Talmadge, when he came to the restaurant, was not hard to please if he was not with his wife. Everyone liked serving him, except when he was drinking, in which case, he forgot to tip and spread curses around instead of money.

When sober, he tipped a little better than average. Unless his wife was with him, he usually ate alone. He was like Senator John McClellan in being a loner, except for one thing. McClellan ate in splendor, insisting on his own reserved chair and his own reserved table. No one dared move that chair from that particular table—in G-211, the Senators' Private Dining Room in the Dirksen Building.

McClellan's chair faced the door and the whole room, so that he could see who was coming in and survey the whole dining room at all times. Some said this was a holdover from the McCarthy hearings, when he had feared for his life because he was attacking McCarthy. Incidentally, Senator Scoop Jackson also faced the whole room from another corner across from McClellan. And a third Senator, who insisted on the safety of his own corner, was William Fulbright, looking very stern. He was not very friendly with anybody. Strict worker. No girls, no fun.

But to return to Talmadge, he didn't care where he sat alone—one place was the same as another.

All the Kennedy brothers ate their lunches in their offices. For very popular public men, they were very private. When John Fitzgerald Kennedy was a Senator, he would call his brother Robert who was chief counsel of the Senate Select Subcommittee on Improper Activities in the Labor or Management Field, to have lunch with him.

The strange thing about the Kennedy brothers is that the two older brothers used to exclude their kid brother, Ted, who was just a University of Virginia law student sticking around his big brothers. I would see Robert and John together—they would even sometimes come into the dining room. But it was said that poor Edward was sort of an outcast—they did not want his advice. It didn't change in 1960, when John was running for President and both brothers were helping him.

It is ironic to look back and see how in those days he was the eager kid outsider. Always on the outside, looking in. Now the whole Kennedy family leans on him.

Ted Kennedy, who took over his brother John's Massachusetts seat, also took over his brother's habit of eating lunch in his office. But he was a hamburger man. He would order a beverage of iced tea. However, what he really liked was a glass of wine from his private stock, kept in his own office.

When John Fitzgerald Kennedy was not yet in the White House, he would order whatever seafood we had. Broiled lobster was a favorite. Robert would frequently have brunch instead of lunch—poached eggs on toast. Also served in solitary splendor in his office.

What the public does not know is that it costs the taxpayer extra money to cater to Senators who want this kind of service. As befits their dignity, Senators as members of this exclusive Club must have a waiter standing by to be of assistance.

The waiter is paid for five hours' work. He cannot wait on several Senators, but must stick with the single Senator who is lunching in his office. The whole procedure of catering and making sure the Club member is kept happy takes about four and a half hours. The waiter sets up the table, serves the food, waits around until the last coffee cup is taken away—in Ted Kennedy's case, change that to iced tea.

When I left the Hill, the waiters were receiving $3.20 an hour. So it costs the taxpayer $16 for each of the extra waiters we had to bring in to spend most of their time waiting around. The only cost to the Senator was the price of the meal. If he ate without even a single guest, this could be as low as $2. Whatever the Senator chose to tip the waiter was up to him.

One Senator was the despair of the waiter who had to serve him, because the Senator did not believe in tipping at all. That was the learned Paul Douglas of Illinois, who never varied from his routine. He would order two shrimp cocktails and steaks, and always eat with his particular girlfriend in the privacy of his office. The steak luncheons would cost $4 apiece. No tip.

We could scarcely be accused of making a profit on these luncheons which cost him $8. The cost of his waiter was $16.

There went the deficit.

I once tried to get the Rules Committee to consider having interns or Senate pages serve luncheons in offices. I gave Senator Jordan the strongest argument I could, pointing out what our earnings had been on a typical day for the four Senators who routinely had lunch in their offices. The cost for the waiters had been $64. The four lunches had cost $12.

I also pointed out that all too often, after we had ordered the extra waiter, the Senator would be invited somewhere away from the building and would not have told us. We would end up paying a waiter who ate lunch, sat around and watched the others work, and left as rested as he had come—with $16 in his pocket.

Senator James Eastland of Mississippi also ate in his office. But he ate alone. Every day he wanted the same thing, a double order of bacon on toast.

Senator James William Fulbright was another Club member who thought all good things were due him automatically. He was very hard to please and didn't believe in tips. He didn't eat in a hideaway, but the waiters in the Senate restaurant kept him for last. Strangely enough, he never caught on. He was not in that big a hurry.

But he did complain about everything else—the food was too cold or too hot. The waiters did not seem to care. No wonder. He didn't tip!

Thruston Morton of Kentucky, one of the most elegant men of the Senate, had a standing order that lunch be served in his office. One waiter was kept exclusively for him. He was very important politically, because he served as chairman of the Republican National Committee for several years, besides performing his Senatorial duties.

The lunches were strictly working lunches, with other political heavies from around the country. The waiter was very happy to serve Thruston, because he was that rare Senator—an excellent tipper, easily pleased.

On the opposite end from Morton's elegant ways was multimillionaire Harry Byrd, Jr., who would behave like one of the lowliest employees at lunchtime. In fact, I knew elevator boys who put on more airs than he.

What do they eat—these men who could have anything? Scoop Jackson never varied: ground-steak patty, frozen peas, and for dessert, apple pie topped with a slice of cheese. Lyndon Johnson, when a Senator, wanted everything fattening—chicken-fried steak, scalloped sweet potatoes, and corn pudding. Nixon was the most waistline conscious as a Senator and Vice-President—small steak on dry toast and tossed salad. Beef stew was his other favorite. And with the stew, a raw apple for dessert.

Breakfast was really Nixon's time to eat hearty, and his favorite breakfast on the Hill was corned beef hash and poached eggs. I was both touched and amused to read that on Nixon's last day in the White House, as his last meal, "the condemned man" ate that favorite breakfast, then walked out of the White House at 9:30, never to return. As President, that is.

Vice-President Rockefeller was one of the easy guys to get along with on food, but even he had his quirks. He liked a double beverage. For lunch he'd have beef on a bun with iced tea. Then he'd follow that up with hot coffee and dessert.

Senator John McClellan of Arkansas not only had a season ticket on "his" chair, but he, too, had his quirks. You could set your watch by him. If we didn't hear otherwise from his office, we knew that we'd better get his food on at three minutes to twelve. He always ate beef on a bun, a glorified hamburger, on which we served him a large slice of raw onion. He would also have a water-packed fruit, such as peaches, pears, or pineapple.

Sometimes the Senator would have cottage cheese with his fruit. Then it was always served to him in a soup bowl, without lettuce, just fruit and cottage cheese. But never did he vary his favorite—beef on a bun with a large slice of onion. He always reeked of onions. He was not alone.

Everyone knows about the famous Senate bean soup, the most popular item on the Senate menu. But few know the well-kept secret of how this bean soup once landed on a columnist's head in the Senate dining room. A pretty girl did it. The Senators were not amused.

What had happened was that the columnist Tris Coffin had made light in his column about a picture a female photographer had snapped of Senator Tom Connally of Texas "with his hand on the globe looking as if he'd discovered it."

The indignant photographer dumped a whole bowl of bean soup over Coffin's head, and he left the restaurant dripping and leaving a trail of beans.

Had she been a Senator or Senator's wife, nothing would have come of it, but since she was not a member of the Club, the impulsive photographer ended up paying $15 in cleaning bills.

The beans taste much better than they wear. You can judge for yourself:

THE SENATE'S FAMOUS BEAN SOUP

Take 2 pounds of small Michigan navy beans, wash, and run through hot water until beans are white again. Put on the fire with 4 quarts of hot water. Then take 1½ pounds of smoked ham hocks, boil slowly approximately 3 hours in covered pot. Braise 1 onion chopped in a little butter, and, when light brown, put in bean soup. Season with salt and pepper, then serve. Do not add salt until ready to serve (8 persons).

As long as I'm giving what is most popular, I may as well give the recipe for the Senators' most popular pie—Senate rum pie:

SENATE RUM PIE

Combine 1½ cups of milk, ½ cup of sugar, and a pinch of salt in a saucepan and bring the mixture to a boil.

Mix 3 tablespoons of cornstarch in ½ cup of milk. Add the cornstarch-milk mixture to 3 eggs and ½ teaspoon vanilla extract. Mix well and combine with the milk and sugar mixture and cook for 2 minutes. Place mixture in a shallow pan to cool.

When custard cream is *cold,* place 5 tablespoons in graham cracker pie shell. Make ¼-inch slices of pound cake. Place the slices of cake on top of the custard cream in the pie shell. Soak the cake with rum syrup, or pure rum to which a little sugar has been added.

Whip 1 cup whipping cream. Blend most of it with rest of custard cream. Heap this mixture on top of the cake. Garnish with reserved whipped cream and shavings of sweet chocolate.

I recall once when Johnson was majority leader, there was an all-night session. At such times I stayed to be of service to the Senators. Toward daybreak Lyndon Johnson and Bob Kerr came to the Senators' dining room, where I had been all night, and I waited to hear their pleasure.

Johnson turned to Kerr and said, "I don't want no damn eggs and bacon this morning. I want a Texas eye-opener."

Kerr said, "You know, I think that would hit the spot."

Johnson winked at me and said, "You call my office and tell them to send up my special brand." In practically no time at all, a Johnson staffer appeared at the door with a bottle in a plain paper bag. It turned out to be Wild Turkey, a sipping bourbon.

The aide said, "Now I'll tell you what the Senator likes. Just put a triple shot over three ice cubes in a plain water glass."

I said, "Well, does Senator Kerr like the same thing?"

The aide said, "Well, he's never turned one away that I know of."

So a waiter fixed two, but they still wanted no food. The bottle went back in the bag and was waiting for them at the hostess' desk, but they had need of the paper bag the second time, which meant six shots apiece for breakfast.

They were finally in good spirits, and eventually they got around to ordering a real Texas breakfast—a twelve-ounce steak, medium rare, with home fries, scrambled eggs, hot biscuits, and a pot of coffee.

The first time I saw Pat and Dick Nixon, it was at a private function—a luncheon where cocktails were served before lunch. I noticed Pat was drinking heavily and having her drinks on the rocks. I was too new to be curious about what she was drinking. I think it came out later in the newspapers that she liked Scotch.

Mamie Eisenhower was very timid and hated to come up to Capitol Hill at all. I observed that, when she arrived at several functions, she already had several drinks under her belt. And they would be serving more at the party. However, I never saw her act intoxicated.

I was dumbfounded, when I went to work in the most exclusive little Club in the world, to learn how many political wives drank excessively.

Senator Allen Ellender was the top cook on the Hill, with his own kitchen in his office. He would cook meals and make fudge and pralines. Ellender, who bragged that he was just a country lawyer and farmer, born in Montegut, Louisiana, hitched his wagon to LBJ's star. He was an LBJ backer, financially and otherwise. This gave Ellender a certain clout around Capitol Hill, and one of the ways this was shown was by the fact that the Rules Committee arranged for Ellender to have his own kitchen.

I would become involved when Ellender was cooking a special meal to entertain Lady Bird Johnson, his very favorite person. She would come from the White House frequently for his cooking—almost always a seafood luncheon.

The Senator would have the shrimp or crabs flown from his home state, but all the supplies—everything to fix it—came from the Senate kitchen. There went the deficit. Even suitable pots and pans would suddenly be called for, and we would have to rush them to the Ellender kitchen.

Once Lady Bird was embarrassed during a party for her and some of her women friends. Her brother-in-law, Sam Houston Johnson, had heard about the party and came barging in, half loaded, to join the festivities. He was eased out with the explanation that it was a party for the girls, and only the chef was permitted to be a male.

Ellender had a way of casually asking us to wrap up a bagful of this and that—cooking oil, corn bread, hot biscuits, butter, various spices, and any number of other items—not expecting to pay for anything. I would let it go on for a while, then suddenly write up a ticket for one "borrowing" just to show we were trying to fight the deficit.

The Senator was frequently mad at me for daring to charge him for food he "borrowed" for his hideaway luncheons.

Leverett Saltonstall had a niece, Sally Saltonstall, who was Senator Ed Brooke's office manager. She got married while working for him. Saltonstall was given a lot of credit for helping Brooke get elected. Sally was a pain in the neck—wanting everything for nothing for Senator Brooke and herself. She would go to lunch with him. She would come over to me and complain or ask for special things.

When food was left over from lunch or a party the Senator gave, she wanted doggie bags and cake boxes for the leftovers for her to take home. He entertained quite a bit in the beginning.

Senator Saltonstall's favorite food was broiled lobster. He could and did eat it religiously with a salad and bread. No baked potato. He was skinny, very skinny. No dessert. He and Senator Pastore ate seafood together every day. Pastore's was filet of sole broiled with lemon butter. We had filet of sole every day because it had quite a following. Saltonstall was so pleased with his lobster, he would not even have a vegetable.

I remember Pastore's AA, C. J. Maisano, was always looking out for his Senator and coming to me to tell her where you could get nice fresh oysters, scallops, and ocean perch. Saltonstall's son, William, was his AA, and he would join them frequently at lunch. This was before nepotism.

One of the cutest things I've seen was Saltonstall sending a box half the size of a big desk with a live lobster for JFK at the White House. And a second one a little smaller for Jacqueline, and one still smaller for Caroline.

As it turned out, after the Secret Service was satisfied, we broiled them in the kitchen and delivered them to the White House in time for their dinner one night. No charge. We were honored to do it. But it cost money in overtime. There went the deficit.

Pastore was a very well-dressed man. I can see it now in my mind's eye, Maisano coming in like a mother hen to get the right table. Pastore liked only one table. He would sit with his back to the wall next to the Jackson table. A third table was always occupied by Margaret Chase Smith. They sat like three monarchs.

The Senators would smile when they saw Saltonstall and Pastore leaving the restaurant together—Mutt and Jeff. Salt was one of the tallest men in the Senate and Pastore the shortest—about five feet tall. He would lean back to look up at his friend if they stood too close together.

Pastore might be short, but he was long on independence. Saltonstall didn't like to walk, and Pastore didn't like to ride the subway, so they would part company. Salt would jackknife his big frame into the underground Toonerville Trolley as we like to call it, and he would pass Pastore chugging along as fast as his short legs could go.

You can't imagine how fussy Senators get about having their state's major products represented on the dining-room menu. You would think the welfare of the nation would collapse without it.

I remember when Senator John Glenn Beall, Jr., of Maryland made a lengthy speech giving the genealogy of the Maryland crab and protesting that those being served as Maryland crab cakes, as the Senate menu claimed, were not from Maryland at all. Personally, I could not see the difference. But after this incident, they were as good as their name.

We tried to have something from each state—Maryland crab, Maine lobster, Idaho and Maine potatoes, Long Island potatoes, New England and Manhattan clam chowder on alternate weeks, Hawaiian Polynesian roast pig actually prepared by us in a pit of coals.

Perhaps you would be amused to see one week of Senate restaurant menus which feature the food of a different state each day. The first is for Monday, August 20, 1979, and it goes through Friday, August 24:

Monday   VERMONT
           Vermont Cheddar Cheese Soup
           Maple State Beef Pudding
           Vermont Boiled Dinner

Green Mountain Lime-Baked Chicken
Squash and Cheese Casserole
Steamed Rice   Fennel and Tomato Salad
Chicken Salad
Rolls
Maple Apples   Fresh Fruit
Coffee   Tea   Milk   Soft Drinks
$4.50

Tuesday   PENNSYLVANIA
Philadelphia Pepper Pot Soup
Ham Apples and Dumplings
Eggplant and Chicken Liver Casserole
Western Pennsylvania Style Perch
Mushrooms with Cream
Fresh Green Peas
Spinach and Bacon Salad
Oatmeal Bran Bread
Rolls
Pennsylvania Chocolate Pie   Fresh Fruit
Coffee   Tea   Milk   Soft Drinks
$4.25

Wednesday   MINNESOTA
Cold Buttermilk Soup
Peppered Tenderloin Casserole
Roast Northern Capon with Wild Rice and Almond Stuffing
Carrots with Celery   Wild and White Rice
Cucumber Salad
Norwegian Dark Bread
Fattigman Scandinavian Cookies   Fresh Fruit
Coffee   Tea   Milk   Soft Drinks
$4.50

Thursday   GEORGIA
Chilled Peach Soup
Deep-Fried Spareribs

Broiled Lemon Butter Chicken
Yellow Squash Soufflé
Sea Island Seafood Salad
Corn Bread

Old Fashioned Georgia Gingerbread   Fresh Fruit
Coffee   Tea   Milk   Soft Drinks
$4.50

Friday   OREGON

Clam Puff Balls
Pacific Fish Chowder
Broiled Salmon Steaks
Portland Stuffed Flank Steak

Green Beans   Rice

Agnes' Oregon Slaw
Zucchini Toss
Stone-Ground Wheat Bread

Pioneer McGinties   Fresh Fruit
Coffee   Tea   Milk   Soft Drinks
$4.50

14

Please Don't Steal the Silver

There were two things on the Hill almost impossible to manage—getting people to pay their bills and guarding the booze. If the booze was left unguarded on the table for one minute, it would disappear. Not just by the bottle but by the case.

I remember once when Senator Howard Baker was entertaining. His AA arranged a dinner and cocktail party and had me supply the booze. I kept the cases locked in my office until time for it to go up to the function room, so that I could go along to guard it or get a bartender to do so.

Either the chef, myself, or bartender would have to walk personally with the rolling truck to the room, and somebody had to stand guard.

But at Senator Baker's affair, a funny thing happened en route to the party room. I had to go to the rest room, but there was a policeman at the door. I thought for sure there was no way booze could disappear with a policeman there.

I rushed the bottles of liquor in, ran to the men's room and back, and in the few minutes I was gone, a whole case of Old Grand Dad disappeared.

The policeman swore he had seen no one. He was guarding the door to the room, so what could I do? Nothing. When Senator

Baker's AA complained about the missing booze, I explained what had happened. He said he didn't want to be billed for it. I had to admit that was reasonable enough, and I said, "I guess I'll have to pay for it out of my pocket."

The AA was upset. "No," he said, "I can't let you do that. Your record is clean."

I kept offering to reimburse the Senator's office, but it ended up with Baker's office paying for the missing booze. He said, "Under no condition will you pay." It was one of the nicest things that ever happened to me by way of learning human nature. He was a rare person.

The party, though billed through Baker's office, was being held by constituents from Tennessee. I could have gone to Diamond and begged him to put it on the deficit or gone to Jordan and thrown myself on his mercy, but I just don't believe in that kind of underhandedness. I would have paid the $143, resigned to the fact that education is expensive.

No one, I'm sure, would ever guess that in just one year—fiscal 1975—we went through some 385 dozen place settings in our Senate restaurant operation, all of which had to be replaced.

It was a good thing some people stole only knives, while others collected forks; that way, at least, we could buy full settings. Also, it was fortunate that in the cafeterias and public dining rooms, frequented by tourists and staffers, we had switched from silver to the less expensive stainless steel.

If anyone cares to know which items are most frequently "collected" in this grand land of ours, it is teaspoons, iced tea spoons, dessert spoons, and the odds-on favorite, demitasse spoons.

With each new Congressional election, loss of items soared because of souvenir hunters and also because new members, living in temporary apartments, seemed to think it was a natural part of the restaurant service to supply things for their home use. Glasses went. China went. Ashtrays, pepper and salt shakers. We bought three hundred dozen shakers one postelection year. Cups, five hundred dozen in such years.

The limit was reached on my patience when one new Senator sent a girl over and dared to ask me for a coffeepot. She said he had everything else he needed but the pot. That was Jesse Helms of North Carolina. One of the ultra-conservatives. I said they sold coffeepots under $20 in most drugstores and dime stores. I didn't care if she told him what I said.

The girl staffer hung on as if she were afraid to go back to the office without it. "But the Senator says he needs it," she wailed.

I said, "Well, the only way I know the Senator is going to have it is if he goes and buys it, because I don't have one."

We even quit lending coffee urns out for parties which staffers gave. The electrician complained that our 4½ gallon coffee urns were left plugged in overnight, and they had to put in new elements. Worse than that, there was danger of setting a fire.

Whenever I had spare help, I sent them to make the complete rounds of the Senate office buildings, starting at the top floor and working their way down, collecting dishes, glassware, and silverware.

They would come back with six bus pans—8 or 10 inches deep, 18 to 20 inches long, and 12 to 15 inches wide—just overloaded. We would try to do it once a month, if we had a chance. If we ran short of tableware in the meantime, we'd just have to send out a round-up.

Once the help reported that Senator Ted Kennedy's office staff refused to let go of two silver coffeepots and two silver teapots. I saw red. I asked, "Did you really try?"

The girl notified me that the secretary informed her that these coffeepots were for the Senator's use, and she planned to keep them as long as she wanted. That was Angelique Lee, said to be the highest paid legislative employee on the Hill. I phoned Miss Angelique myself and asked if there was any way I could indulge on her kindness to return the coffee- and teapots. I would be glad to lend them to her anytime the Senator needed them, I said.

She told me bluntly that she had no intention of returning them. As far as she was concerned, the Senator needed them all the time, and she was going to keep them.

I was furious. But there was nothing I could do. If I continued to object to the Senator's staff keeping restaurant property, she would have reported me to the Rules Committee. And even though I held my tongue, she reported me anyway, declaring that it was none of my business what the Senator had in his office that belonged to the restaurant.

Hugh Alexander, chief counsel of the Rules Committee, came to my office to tell me about the complaint. He told me that I should never have made that call to Kennedy's office. I was mad, and he knew it. He suggested that in the future, if someone refused to send something back, I should just let it go.

I sputtered, "That's how the deficit grows!" That was the trouble with this place, I fumed to myself. There was no backbone around here. I told Alexander that I had no intention of working that way. "And if the situation comes up again, I'll do the same thing."

"It's your hide," he retorted. "That's what keeps you upset all the time." He left, annoyed that I had refused to knuckle under. Then, another complaint came in—this time from Miss Jacobs in Senator Percy's office.

That office had a silver coffeepot belonging to the Senate restaurants. Not only did she refuse to send it back, but she stood guard over it personally. Miss Jacobs was enraged at the thought of letting go of the restaurant's pot for even a moment. She called Hugh Alexander, and shouted, "Do we have to put up with that man down there, keeping watch on everything we do?" She wanted to know why the Rules Committee couldn't control me.

So, again Hugh was telling me to button up. Hugh was an ex-Congressman. He'd been in for two terms—four years—during the '50's. Now he was on the other side, placating legislators.

Dining Room G-211 in the Dirksen Building seated eighty-six. This was the room where our complete service for eighty-six place settings disappeared one weekend, never to be found. These were not stainless steel but expensive silver plate, the best silver plate. The replacement cost for each place setting was $20 to $30 wholesale—two forks, serrated knife, two teaspoons, one iced-tea spoon, soup spoon (four spoons in all). There grew the deficit.

I raised hell at the Architect's Office and with the Rules Committee, saying I could not be responsible. "If they can steal it with the doors locked, what security do we have?" I demanded, and suggested that we change the service to stainless steel.

The Rules Committee took so long thinking about it, that I just took matters into my own hands and changed the service myself. When I left, years later, I still hadn't gotten an answer.

At the time I first came to the Senate restaurants, we used silver gravy boats and coffeepots that held twelve cups and would be placed on the table for the customers to help themselves. There were silver creamers, sugar bowls, individual silver teapots, and silver bread trays. By the time I left, it had all been picked by thieves. We simply switched to stainless steel flatware and used wicker baskets for bread.

A lot of things have turned up missing from the Senate in my years on the Hill. But I'll never forget the Case of the Missing Turkey. It started with a secretary from the office of Senator Karl Mundt of South Dakota rushing into my office as if she had an emergency and saying, "The Senator needs his turkey right away."

I said, "Won't you sit down? Do you have a receipt?"

She said, "No, I don't have the damn receipt. It's his turkey. He doesn't need a receipt."

I explained that we made three copies of receipts showing anything that belonged to a Senator that was being held in our freezers. I explained that the original receipt was taped to the package. A copy was given to the Senator or aide bringing us the item for storage, and the third was kept in our file for a year, after which it was discarded.

I said, "It would be hard to find the package without a receipt. When did the Senator get this turkey?"

"He got it for Christmas," she said. "It was sent to him as a gift. And he needs it."

It was now Thanksgiving time—almost a Christmas away. I wanted to tell her that, even if we could find the turkey, I would not advise eating it. But seeing the angry look on her face, I bit my tongue. Telling her to wait, I went to find the butcher.

"John," I said, "you must have a turkey belonging to Senator Mundt. Can you find it?"

He said, "That woman has been here already. I told her it isn't here. But I'll go with you if you want."

We put on heavy army coats and spent a good half hour in $-10°$ temperature, searching through the walk-in freezer.

I went back and told the grim secretary, "I've never known of any food belonging to a Senator to be missing. Is it possible that in your absence, sometime or another, somebody else on his staff called for it?"

This annoyed her further. "Nobody on that staff better touch anything, and this includes the old man himself, without my knowledge."

Such self-assurance was formidable. Moreover, Mundt was a big man in the Club. I couldn't take chances. I said, "Give me until tomorrow morning. I will have both freezers inventoried."

By the next morning everybody had been involved with her turkey. I had gotten the storeroom manager, plus the butcher, plus two chefs—one in the Capitol and one in the Dirksen Building—to stay up half the night.

Overtime! Overtime! There went the deficit.

Still, I had to tell her, "If the Senator had a turkey, it's not there now. I have no explanation to offer. Can you tell me the approximate date last year when the Senator got the turkey?"

She said, "I didn't say it was last year."

"You didn't?"

She said, "No, I didn't. The Senator got it the Christmas before last, and he is planning to use it for Thanksgiving."

I was starting to see red, as I thought of the hours we had spent searching for that damned turkey in the cold. I had told her we only kept records for a year. I hadn't thought it necessary to overkill by explaining we also threw out the old food along with the receipt. I thought of the importance of Senator Mundt, and the Keep-Our-Senators-Happy Rules Committee, and shut up.

I said, "You tell the Senator to determine what he would like us to do since we cannot find his turkey."

I soon got a phone call telling me that the Senator felt I was responsible as the restaurant manager, and therefore should supply another turkey.

Again I saw red, but I said, "All right. I'll have to take this up with the general manager, and one of us will get back to you."

She was still huffy. "We have waited long enough," she said.

"How much longer do we have to wait?"

I said, through clenched teeth, "Hopefully, I will have an answer before you leave today."

I called Joe Diamond and told him, "We have a hell of a problem." I didn't go to my superior with trivialities. I only bothered him when all else failed, and I thought something was going to hit the fan.

I said to him, "I'll even buy the damned turkey to replace it if you want. I just want this woman off my neck."

Diamond laughed and laughed, especially as he heard about my grand search. "Why didn't you give her a turkey out of the freezer? She'd never know the difference after two years."

I said, "This is government property. I can't give it away. And each of these is twenty-five or twenty-six pounds. I think she said hers was about fifteen pounds."

Diamond said, "So what! Give her a damn turkey and forget it. The deficit is so big already—this won't even be noticed."

I called the lady and said, "I have the Senator's turkey. It's not the original one, but I have a turkey for you. And I'd like to know what you want me to do with it."

She sounded not a bit grateful or delighted or even halfway pleased. Without a thank you, she said, "Oh, why don't you send it up to me right now?"

I had to get a porter to drop what he was doing and deliver it in a plain-brown wrapper—a very shy, meek porter named Jimmie Jackson.

When Jimmie came back, he was almost shaking, and looked smaller and more timid than ever. I said, "What's the matter?" I could tell he was bursting to tell me something. He said, "Man, does that woman hate you! She said she bet you needed that turkey for your own Thanksgiving. And that's what happened to it." Then he chuckled and added, "I didn't tell her that you don't eat turkey. I figured it would make her madder."

"Don't worry about it," I said. "You win one, you lose one. I'm just glad she didn't lose a cow. This way it only cost the government fifteen dollars."

As Jimmie started to move away, I called after him, "Did anyone thank you? Did you get a tip?"

Jimmie turned and gave me a dirty look, "You've got to be kidding."

As he went back to his less stressful chores, I reflected on how this whole turkey trot reflected the power of the Senate. Had Mundt been anyone but a member of the Club, it could never have happened.

Senator Margaret Chase Smith had a TV set stolen right out of her office. But she had clout. The building superintendent had to replace it. There was no way to tell who had walked off with it during the night.

For about a year we had a rash of ripoffs. Someone or a gang was going into offices in broad daylight and lifting women's pocketbooks. They seemed to know just which drawers to look into.

A secretary would go for a snack and to the ladies room, and when she came back, the robbery had taken place. Someone must have been watching in the hall. There must have been twenty such robberies.

It also seemed someone was watching the credit union to see who was cashing a check. One secretary had made the mistake of cashing her whole paycheck of over $500. She was going to buy a coat, I believe, and had gone to the rest room. When she returned to the office, her whole purse with ID cards was gone.

I never heard of them solving a single such case.

The Capitol police, I must say in fairness, had their hands tied. I know of one case when an official of the restaurants was caught taking roasts and hams out of the building.

One Senator said we must give him another chance, and he was not even fired. Nor did he lose pay. As I pointed out, things had been walking out of the storerooms for some time. So it was hard to know how much had been taken by this individual. But there was nothing I could do. A Club member had spoken and was ready to defend him.

Once, my assistant called me at home. He was still working, and I had gotten off early—6:00 P.M. He had been checking the doors before leaving and he found in the private dining room, G 219 Dirksen, on the ground floor, a box with two hams and twelve pounds of bacon and two boxes of hotdogs containing six pounds each. And to top it off, it also contained a shell of beef, the most expensive cut. It was obviously ready to be taken home. He had the box in the office and wanted to know what to do. I said to report it to the police and let them handle it.

We never were told whether anyone showed up to take those boxes or whether they had kept a stakeout. If my aide had not been there, we would have been out several hundred dollars. There goes the deficit.

Sometimes it was just little things. I caught the assistant to a high official stealing a damn sandwich. It was a club sandwich costing only 65¢, but he was stuffing it in his pocket. I told him, "You'd better pay for that. We can't run a restaurant giving away freebees." He was taking it from the pantry.

He said, "You've made your profit. My Senator just ate here." I waited for him to pay for the sandwich, but instead he calmly took it out of his pocket and put it back on the shelf under the heat lamp.

So afraid is everyone, not knowing who is who, that the checker had not tried to stop him.

Another cafeteria trick in the Dirksen Building was to come in and hide toast or extra butter under a newspaper, sandwich, or something. The cashier would not say, "Will you please move your newspaper?" but would tell me to see what was on the tray.

There was nothing I could do. The man or woman using this trick could claim it was already paid for or he was going to go through the line a second time and would take care of it then.

Once we had an embarrassing thing happen when First Lady Betty Ford was the guest of honor of the Senate ladies' club. No effort had been spared. The Botanical Garden had arranged a spectacular array of potted tulips and hyacinths and jonquils around the door of the room and up the stairs leading to the room—a big double marble staircase.

If you were going up the steps, you had to be going to that particular room—318, the Caucus Room of the Russell Building, the only one up there. Adding a green backdrop behind the fabulous tulips were rows of potted palms. As a final touch, the ladies had made special tablecloths with tulips on them, all hand hemmed.

Tuesday morning, the morning of the luncheon, there was not a tulip in sight. Every single one had been stolen. In fact everything had been stolen except the potted palms, which were too heavy to carry, and a few azaleas that looked skimpy and woebegone.

Caroline Long just about died. I heard her tell the chief of police, "There's no damn sense in this kind of carrying on, and the police letting people steal right under their noses." Actually, anyone could have done it—but what is more likely, staffers with a yard to landscape or others who would not be challenged walked off carrying the things.

The telephone wires hummed as the ladies threw themselves on the mercy of the Botanical Garden's nurserymen. They had sent every tulip they had, the gardeners said, annoyed, and the ladies had to settle for a few azaleas and whatever else could be trucked in from three miles away, in a hurry. Now the tablecloths no longer bore relationship to the flowers, and the ladies moaned and groaned. I kidded them, saying they should have gotten mixed-flower print, to be ready for anything around the Hill.

Speaking of that reminds me of when Pat Nixon was First Lady and they insisted Diamond and I use our slim funds to buy pink tablecloths, with napkins to match, because Pat liked pink.

We did as ordered—to the tune of $660. Then they used them only twice, a year apart—announcing pink was tacky, and they were tired of it. Now the Senate ladies insisted we switch back to white.

There went the deficit.

But it may be that we saved something by returning to white, because the pink tablecloths had to be hand laundered and rolled instead of folded to keep from creasing. It cost $300 for this special laundry service.

Sometimes there was a little hanky-panky with the checks. Once a man who had held a party under a Senator's sponsorship came back afterward to ask that his bill be straightened out, because he had been overcharged between $250 and $300. What it amounted to was that two additional cases of booze were being charged to his party.

I had a conference with my superior, but Diamond seemed

reluctant to do anything, and the victim was threatening to blow the whistle and go to the Senator who had sponsored the party.

I said, "I don't feel this is right. This man should have an adjustment on his bill."

Diamond said, "You know I can't do that. This will make it look bad for teacher's pet."

Because a particular employee had friends among the mighty and a lot of material handy for blackmail, he could not be touched, it seemed, no matter what he did. It was an unbelievable situation.

Looking back, I can hardly believe that such things happened but I can understand why I decided to retire before the mandatory age.

The bickering went on for three or four months and eventually the man who had paid for the party came back to me and said he had received a memo from Diamond saying that no adjustment would be made.

My blood pressure was rising. I had not known of the memo, and the man had not blown the whistle and gone to the sponsoring Senator, because he just didn't want to make waves. If he had, we all would have been in the soup, at least temporarily. I felt like Don Quixote, trying to tilt with windmills. Wrong had to be righted.

I said, "Will you be doing any entertaining soon?"

He said, "Yes, but I don't believe I'll be using your facilities."

I said, "Look, let me arrange for you to have the use of the Senators' private dining room for your next affair. The windows have flower boxes. It has beautiful draperies, lots of mirrored wall, which the ladies will like, and even carpeting. Tell your Senator you would like to use G-211."

He said, "It sounds like a great room but what's the advantage?"

"The advantage," I said, "is that you won't have to pay the twenty-percent service charge in that room because that's what the Rules Committee says. It's their pet room."

So that's how, in a roundabout way, I was able to refund the better part of a $250-plus ripoff and see that for one day justice was done.

I am certainly glad that I no longer have to think of places where I can hide money. There is a strict rule on the Hill that no campaign money is to be given on government property, or even donations for charity. No money is to change hands between guests or host and guests, unless the sponsoring Senator so decrees.

Only the restaurant catering service was permitted to handle money, and usually the bill simply went to the office of the Senator who had sponsored the event. But on certain occasions a Senator or his office would tell us we were to present the bill to someone who was at the party—a constituent or a member of an organization.

I dreaded occasions when the individual would insist on paying right after the party in cash. Persons other than myself had duplicate keys to cash registers and even to my office. So I would go home with huge sums of money tucked in every inconspicuous place on my person—pinned here and there and some casually wrapped in a handkerchief.

I had learned my lesson one year when I had a locked box, with the staff Christmas fund money, around $200, nicely ready for a Christmas party. I thought it was safe because I kept it locked in a file cabinet. And the file cabinet was in my office which was also kept locked.

But lo and behold, just as we were ready to order all the food for the party, the cash disappeared along with the box it was in. My boss and I had to reach into our own pockets and help finance the party to the extent of $120. A few wholesale dealers who heard of our plight donated a few goodies for the party. Even when money hadn't been stolen, they donated a bit, but this time they extended themselves. Liquor dealer, meat dealer, vegetable man—all chipped in. And we made our own pastries.

There was so much stealing and pilfering around the Hill that fear even extended to private homes of Senators if Senate employees were around.

When Senator Humphrey had a party for his staff on the roof of Harbour Square, the swank complex where he lived, Muriel came up wearing a mink wrap.

One of the restaurant help who was working at the party started to help her off with it, when the Senator said in alarm, "Oh, no, I don't want anyone to touch that fur, not even you," and he snatched it away from the sheepish-looking helper.

Humphrey himself disappeared with it, taking it back to their apartment. He was not laughing or amused. He was dead serious. I shook my head that we had come to this, but I had to admit he was right.

15

My Kitchen Cabinet

What my "kitchen cabinet" did in their own time was their own business, but dumb me insisted on trying to get my crew to give full measure of work during the hours in which Uncle Sam was paying for the pleasure of their company.

One man was found to be taking groups of employees to the races. He made a mint of money on these outings—which took care of his own track losses. I've known of all-night crap and poker games going on while the employees were getting time-and-a-half for overtime. Senators would have really been amazed to see the backstairs Senate gang—restaurant workers, carpenters, engineers, plumbers, rest-room employees. Supposedly, they were on a rush job.

After I left, a numbers racket and horse-betting operation was found to be flourishing on the Hill, but as usual, no arrests were made. The bookie, who was operating out of a House-side cafeteria area, was tipped off as the FBI was closing in.

Chief of the U.S. Capitol Police James Powell told reporters that in twelve years, he had received various complaints of gambling, and had brought in undercover men, without ever getting an arrest. It's too bad they weren't sleuthing around the Senate employees' locker rooms.

Sometimes employees can't get into a locker room to change clothes, because the room is locked while a card game goes on behind the door. The poor employee has to knock until someone peeks out to see who's at the door.

I have burst in on locker-room crap games, and fired as many as twelve at a time. And I didn't care if they threatened they would tell Senator So-and-So, who had gotten them the job. I was not going to let them get away with those kinds of shenanigans. It didn't add to my reputation as a good guy. The blue-collar workers—black and white—warned each other to be leery of me, because I wasn't a good guy. And maybe I wasn't. But I didn't get hired to help people to make a patsy of the American taxpayer.

Every once in a while, I would hear that Rules Committee Chairman Jordan had been called by another Senator, who demanded, "I want you to get rid of that Lou Hurst. He has put a man on the street for a month without pay."

After finding out that the suspended man had been gambling, Jordan would call back the Senator and say, "He was lucky he didn't get fired permanently. He was warned against gambling the first time he was caught. This was his second offense."

The Senator would say, "Well, I didn't know about that."

Jordan would come back to me and complain, "You know Senator So-and-So is hell on wheels. Why do you make life around here so tough?"

I'd answer, "I'm spending government money, and responsible for the work being done. Don't you guys know gambling is illegal—particularly on the Hill and on the payroll?"

He'd say, "Don't you play poker?"

I'd say, "Sure I do. But at home, among my friends and relatives."

"I'm getting tired of covering your ass," he would say. "Just be sure you never make a false move around here, because I've got people standing in line to tear you apart."

I would look at him and laugh. "Let them try," I'd say. We understood each other. Jordan knew I was not afraid of taking the heat. He also knew that I was forever trying to take the heat for my superior, Joseph Diamond.

Diamond would have done anything in the world to avoid being called before the Rules Committee. He had once had a taste of that. So, when he had a call that a committee staffer wanted to see him the next morning, he took me along because he was nervous and wanted support. He had no idea what it was all about, but he knew it was not a compliment. For, when things go well, you never hear anything.

The staffer lambasted Diamond for over an hour and a half. It was painful to observe. Every time I tried to break in with an explanatory word for Diamond—for Diamond seemed to be in a state of shock—I was told to shut up. I had not been the one called in, the staffer reminded me.

The complaint was simply that Diamond was "the worst, the poorest manager to ever come to Capitol Hill." That he knew nothing about restaurants and was letting a pet waiter determine on whim the cost of food for special events.

Certain men could get anything free or at discount. Others were being outrageously overcharged. Republican Edward Brooke of Massachusetts was being clipped while Democrat Lawton Chiles of Florida got preferential treatment. The facts were all there, and they weren't pretty. The staffer accused Diamond, too. of looking the other way as money was pocketed by some of his help, some of his key staff.

I knew that Diamond was personally honest, and only weak and lacking in experience in large-scale restaurant operation. He wasn't knowledgeable enough to plan the details of a large party. For example, he didn't realize that a waiter serving over twelve people all by himself couldn't do a decent job.

Diamond's restaurant background had been extremely limited—the Mayflower doughnut shops and unsuccessfully trying to run a small suburban restaurant for a short time. When I met him, the restaurant had completely cleaned him out. He didn't even own a topcoat. I gave him one of mine.

He lived only a block and a half from me, so I knew some of his financial difficulties. Diamond had barely managed to retain his home—and had to ask for the help of the VA to get a loan to save it. So I knew Diamond really needed this job. He couldn't afford to quit, no matter how humiliated he felt at being chewed out.

Regular government employees must work thirty-six years to obtain 80 percent of their pay at retirement. On Capitol Hill, however, legislative employees, Congressmen, and Senators only have to work thirty-two years to get the 80 percent retirement benefit.

Diamond was so terrified of losing his job that he just stood there petrified, taking it. All the time the staffer berated him, Diamond made no effort to contradict him. From time to time Diamond would make a half-hearted attempt to find out who had made the complaint. "I'm entitled to know who is complaining," he would mumble.

The staff man cut him off curtly with "Shut up. I'm not through yet. When I'm ready for you to talk, I'll tell you." But poor Joe never did find out. The moment never came when Diamond was allowed to talk, or to learn who had made the complaint.

The scene ended when the staffer, his rage spent, stood up, and dismissed Diamond abruptly with "I think we're through now." He had gotten it all out of his system. And Diamond slunk out.

I tried to reassure Joe, to tell him that he would not be fired, that the fellow was just blowing off steam. Diamond was not convinced, he was certain he would be canned. He reminded me how Senator Robert Byrd had called Diamond's predecessor, Robert Sontag, into his office and told him to clean his desk, and get out.

Then to add insult to injury, Robert Byrd had thundered at poor Sontag to "Leave by the back door." He was humiliating him as much as he could, by instructing him to depart by way of the loading platform at the back door of the Dirksen Building.

On his way out, Robert Sontag had come to my office and cried like a baby. This was back in 1965. And where else would he get a job making $15,000, be able to play golf all the time, and wine and dine to his heart's content? Or eat a whole rum pie at one sitting?

"I remember," I said, "but that was different. Byrd said he was firing Sontag because whenever he left word he wanted to see him, Sontag was either at the golf course or having lunch somewhere off the Capitol grounds."

"I'm the one who gave Sontag the message to go to Senator Byrd's office," Diamond told me.

"I know," I retorted. "And I was the last one to see him as he left the building by the back door. I escorted him there."

Senator Robert Byrd of West Virginia zoomed to fame when he became Senate majority leader in 1977, but I remember a younger Byrd, tackling the job of trying to make head or tails of our restaurant operation. His title then was chairman of the Subcommittee on Restaurants, under the Rules Committee.

Byrd had been outraged when Senator Wayne Morse, a maverick Senator from Oregon, who brought his horse with him when he came to Washington, had stood on the floor of the Senate and made a long speech about how the Senate employees, through being poorly paid, were subsidizing the Senate restaurants. Morse was not even a member of the committee. He had nothing to do with restaurants, but had befriended some employees who had filled his ear with the injustice of it all.

Byrd was not going to be made to look foolish. He immediately ordered a complete investigation of the whole restaurant operation—accounting procedures, management, payroll. GAO—Government Accounting Office—was to complete the audit within a year.

As mentioned, Horwath & Horwath, the noted efficiency expert firm, was called in to give a complete evaluation of why the Senate restaurants continued to maintain a deficit year after year. They came, looked around, $100,000-plus worth, and suggested that the restaurants be farmed out to a food organization like ARA—American Restaurant Association or Marriott.

The report that the efficiency experts made was so secret that copies of it had to be signed for. I got one, read it, and was amazed at the unbusinesslike way our restaurants were run. It was worse than even I had realized.

Byrd's subcommittee invited three famous restaurant chains to come in and tell how they would run the restaurants. All of them said it was impossible to run a business the way the Senate restaurants were run, letting the customers run the restaurant and tell them what to do. It didn't help any to explain that the Senate was a very important Club, and you had to let each Club member have his way.

The restaurant chains all said that if they could not control prices and payroll and how the Senator customers were treated, without favoritism and with an even hand, there was only one solution. They would run the restaurants—however crazy and inefficiently the Senators wanted—and simply charge a fixed fee over and above operating costs. That way any deficits growing out of the Senate's quaint way of running restaurants was the Senate's business.

The Senators on the committee were indignant. It was absurd to pay a restaurant chain a large operating fee, and not have a guarantee that they would even make ends meet. On the other hand, nobody was going to tell them what to charge for food, what to pay the help, and what extra services they could and could not have.

Then, one Senator sagely pointed out that the Senate would have to put into the record the fact that they were paying a big fee to some outsider to run their business and this would get into the newspapers. That did it—Byrd's grand plan died aborning.

That little $100,000 exercise occurred in the mid '60s. A few years later, Robert Byrd went on to better committees and better things, and in 1969 Senator James Allen of Alabama took over the subcommittee as a new Senator.

Poor Senator Allen got initiated into the restaurant problems the hard way—all the waiters went on strike. There had been rumors that the employees of the Senate restaurants were forming a union, but the strike took us completely by surprise.

It was 11:30 A.M. Just before lunch! All the waiters and waitresses formed lines of four abreast, and marched—through the cafeteria, through the subway, and out of the Capitol, down the Capitol steps.

Diamond and I were frantic. The Senate mob was coming in for lunch. What could we do? We ran around, grabbed people from everywhere—out of accounting, the storerooms, bakeshop, the kitchen—to serve food and bus the tables. Somehow—with the help of almost every non-Senate employee on Capitol Hill—we got that lunch served. It may not have been as smooth as usual, but nobody went hungry.

The marchers came back, furious. For they thought they had closed the restaurants down. They were really mad to find out that we had managed to serve lunch somehow, without them. They came back and left their uniforms, ready to walk out again. But Senator Allen, who had taken Byrd's place, managed to calm the staff into sitting down and talking.

Allen did a great job. Although he was new to the committee, he handled the situation with the hand of a master. When lunch was over, at 2 P.M., he sat down with the complaining employees, listened to their gripes—about hours, money, sanitary conditions.

He advised them that if they would go back to work, he personally would see that their legitimate demands were settled to their satisfaction. The strike was over—in time to serve dinner to the Senators.

That solved one problem. Another was much more embarrassing.

Along about January 1969, the Senate restaurants learned some embarrassing news through the media in regard to Senator Henry Bellmon of Oklahoma.

For some reason he took a tubercular skin test, and it was found to be positive. And immediately, the moment it hit the press, the discussion on the Senate floor concerned the fact that the Senate had never recognized any of the D.C. sanitation laws. They had no D.C. sanitation inspections or any other. No inspections at all. No health cards were required of waiters, waitresses, and other food handlers.

Senator Bellmon was quite concerned and was admitted to Walter Reed for a complete checkup. The tests showed that he didn't have tuberculosis after all. But still the uproar in the Senate, on the floor, and in the press continued.

So the Rules Committee called in the Congressional physician, who at that time was a naval officer, to examine the entire Senate. A team of sanitation engineers descended on us from Norfolk naval base on a Friday morning. There were about a half dozen naval officers, plus corpsmen, taking swabs and samples of food, floor surface, and equipment. They observed that only half of the steam table worked and the part that worked leaked.

The carry-out service window of the coffee shop in the Russell Building was condemned, because we were serving all types of sandwiches without refrigeration, and the mop sink for the kitchen served as the back counter of the carry out. Sandwiches were being splattered as they were being prepared. It was horrible. They discovered rat infestation, roaches running free.

In the coffee shop in the basement of the Russell Building, the equipment was found to be completely worn out and outdated. There were bits of rust in the cooking equipment. Some windows were without screens, and flies came in from the street, enjoying the Senate food.

The Dirksen Building had been opened in 1957, so it was in good shape, except for general sloppiness and lack of attention to normal sanitation practices like refrigeration. Since the staff knew there would be no inspection, things that should have been refrigerated were carelessly left lying around.

I had been horrified when I first went there, but had been told that the old management would not be there too much longer. If I would just tolerate the conditions for a short time, I would soon be able to control the sanitation. It was tough, especially since I had attended Johns Hopkins School of Hygiene and learned about proper food handling. I could barely believe my eyes when I saw what was going on in the Senate restaurants.

In those days the Dirksen kitchen served as butcher shop. Sections of beef would be brought in and cut into steaks or ground up into hamburgers. All of this was done in the kitchen, where the temperature went from 90 degrees to 120. A butcher shop, I knew, had to be maintained at approximately 45 degrees to keep the bacteria count down. But since there was no separate room available, everything was prepared in the same room in the Dirksen Building.

All vegetable preparations were done in the three kitchens of the Senate, an unsanitary procedure. Raw vegetables and fruits should be uncrated, washed, and prepared before they ever get to the kitchen. In this way, mice, rats, and bugs, such as roaches, can be destroyed before the food enters the area where it is to be cooked.

So, the first day the naval doctors and sanitation engineers came, the carry-out of the Russell Building was closed. Next, arrangements were made for the Public Health Department to give physical examinations to every employee, which not only included TB testing but testing for venereal diseases.

About two weeks later the coffee shop of the Russell Building was condemned and closed—without warning. The officials came and, on the basis of test results, closed the place. It remained closed for approximately three years, and had to be completely gutted and rebuilt from top to bottom, including light fixtures. The grease traps, which didn't work anyway, were torn out. The entire flooring had to be replaced. The original cement floors absorbed grease and germs and were impossible to keep reasonably clean. Instead, easy-to-clean terrazzo flooring was installed.

The Russell Building had been finished in 1904. Diamond and I had a whole crew of people trying to clean the place up the weekend before the Navy arrived. Monday, after all our work, they found the floor still had bacteria in the concrete. It was impossible to get it really clean, for the grease traps were stopped up down under the floor. The smokestack to the roof over the cooking range was dangerous, stopped up with grease and ready to catch on fire. Moreover, the facility offered no rest room for the kitchen help. For that matter customers also had no place to wash their hands and had to go down the hall. The Navy closed down the entire operation and sealed the door.

Now the Senate restaurants have ladies' and men's rest rooms. There is walk-in refrigeration for meats, produce, eggs—different temperatures for the various food items as required. No longer are deliveries made right into the kitchen from outside. Everything goes through a storeroom first.

But unfortunately all these changes did not come about soon enough to help our poor Filipino chef, who under the old setup had been required to do everything—accept deliveries, cook and clean the food, place orders. Before things improved, he died of a heart attack.

When the new place was open, Mr. Diamond got into the act. Having been a doughnut operator in the past, he still had an admiration for fast-food restaurants such as McDonald's and Roy Rogers. He tried to imitate the fast-food chains in the coffee shop—plastic plates, paper cups, and plastic flatware. The coffee shop became known as the Plastic Palace of the Senate. The Senate gang preferred not to eat there, especially Senator Hayden, who had loved the old place.

During the sanitation drive, I walked into the bake shop one morning between five and six o'clock and found the night baker feeding a pet rat.

I asked, "What in the hell are you doing feeding that rat? No wonder the women are screaming when he runs over their feet. I don't blame them."

The baker retorted, "Hold on. Hold on! This isn't an ordinary rat. This is Oscar. He's my friend."

I said, "How, in the hell do you expect me to get rid of rats and roaches with all our fancy extermination, while you're feeding them? How do you know that one is Oscar?"

"I can tell by his ears," he said.

I said, "The hell you can! Don't ever let me catch you feeding him again, or I'll report you to the Rules Committee. And I'm going to spot-check you in the middle of the night."

From time to time, I would receive a frantic call. Come quickly. There's a rat in the cafeteria or in the kitchen. But once the rats did the unforgivable.

They invaded the holy Inner Sanctum dining room of the Senators, right in the Capitol itself. The Senators behaved like a bunch of excited schoolgirls, shrieking for help. By the time I got there, the rat had escaped down the hall and surely to its rat haven. Had it still been there when I arrived, I really don't know what I would have done. Probably challenged it to a duel with a chair.

Dewey Loselle, Jr., an engineer who was brought in as sanitarian of the Capitol, was unaware that some ambitious person had purchased fancy rodent traps and peppered the Hill with them. Jack Anderson got word that these traps had done a fine job and reported it.

The Anderson report fascinated GSA. If these traps were such a success, why not purchase them for all the government offices? Loselle investigated. These traps, he discovered, had practically no effect. What Anderson didn't know was that the great success attributed to the traps was the result of the many pounds of rat poison that Loselle had placed in strategic places.

Rats were everywhere on the Hill—in the Dirksen Building, the Russell Building, the Capitol itself. When they built the East Front of the Capitol, I saw rats the size of toy poodles, rushing out from every nook and cranny. Their homes in the old dungeons under the East Front, once used for storing coal and wood for the fireplaces, had been disturbed by the excavation.

Because of these sewer rats, as they were called, the area had to be sealed off. The rats were nicknamed the Horses of Capitol Hill, so the tourists wouldn't know what we were talking about and panic. They thought we were talking about the Park Service mounted police—and that's what we wanted them to think.

After a mass testing of the Senate restaurant employees was concluded, about a dozen people had positive TB skin tests, but only two needed hospital care.

Several employees were found to be suffering from venereal disease and were referred to the Public Health Service for treatment. If an employee refused treatment, he or she was either fired or given time off, without pay, to get personal treatment. Before coming back to work, the employee was retested and was only allowed to return after a negative test report.

One of our employees, a woman, came back after three years of hospital care. She had a negative test report and was rehired.

Some people thought the cure was worse than the disease, and I was forced to fire a few who refused treatment for venereal disease. Most understood our position. Only one fired employee gave me a hard time. She appealed to a particular Senator's wife, and the wife wanted me fired. I went to see the Senator and told him the nature of the employee's ailment, and that was the last I heard of wanting me fired.

At least that time.

Before Dewey Loselle, the sanitarian, came aboard, we were unable to get workers to wear hairnets. Afros that stood out as wide as a man or woman's shoulders were the fashion. Women were wearing jewelry at work and bits of food would become lodged in it. Earrings would fall into the food—and occasionally remain.

Dewey made a flat rule: "No hairnets, no job. No jewelry on the job."

Being a new broom, Dewey could accomplish what I could not. And although we almost had some knock-down-and-drag-out fights at first, we ended up with a good working relationship.

Most of the arguments we had were because I was trying to follow the Senators' wishes, and Dewey wasn't hampered by such limitations. The Senators would be mad at me, when it was the sanitary engineer who wasn't letting me break a health rule just to please a Senator.

I had three goals—to keep the Senators happy, to keep them healthy, and to cut the deficit.

The first two were easier to achieve than the third. But, finally, I even accomplished a small change that kept us from wasting $500 or $600 every Saturday.

I had been campaigning for the closing of the large cafeterias on weekends. I kept saying, "Why use the cafeteria which requires twenty-seven employees to service on Saturday, when you can open the carry-out in the Dirksen Building using only six or seven people." The cafeteria would cost eight hundred dollars to operate, and we would take in less than three hundred dollars. Finally, they saw it my way.

I'll never forget the consternation in our kitchens over the bizarre shooting of Senator Stennis.

John Stennis of Mississippi became a world figure when he was the victim of a senseless mugging. Just as he reached home one night, he was robbed and shot right on his own doorstep. His pockets had been practically empty, and that had irritated his attackers. After that, everyone on the Hill was warned to carry at least $10 or $15 at all times to avoid angering a potential mugger.

I was stunned when one of the three boys who was arrested turned out to be related to a woman who worked for me in the Senate restaurant. She got the news at work that he was being held for the crime and was hysterical.

She requested a week's leave, which I granted. She left immediately, and there were rumbles all through the restaurant. The shocking crime hit the Senate as few things ever had.

Even after the boy agreed to turn state's evidence, his relative could not understand how he had gone wrong. He had a nice home, she told me, and was not from a broken family.

During Stennis' long hospital stay, all of us in the restaurant took a huge menu and covered it with our names and good wishes and mailed it to the Senator.

Upon his return, his wife called and told me what special foods he needed until his health was completely restored. We got him sirloin tip and double ground it to make it very easy to eat. Broiled hamburger. He had grits with it instead of potatoes. And coffee. We even prepared enough sirloin tip for him to take home. We charged only $1 a pound—the cost of the sirloin but not of the preparation. We loved him, of course, but there went the deficit.

When I said my fond farewell to the Senate, as its top caterer, the total deficit for the Club's food operation for fiscal year 1975—including replacement of linen, glass, flatware, and china—added up to about three quarters of a million dollars, buried under the heading of building appropriations and building operating funds. Up from $623,000 in 1971.

As a souvenir, I took with me a copy of an entry from the Isaac Bassett diary, circa 1875, telling about the first restaurant of the Senate, quite literally a hole in the wall and so called. It was a ten-foot-in-diameter circular room entered through the old Senate Post Office room.

Bassett writes of the fabled men of the Senate, all dead a decade or more but still mourned, who congregated there to grab a bite of food, whisper a secret, strike a deal and bend an elbow—Clay, Webster, Calhoun, Douglas. But what intrigued me most was how the Hole in the Wall solved its deficit problem:

> In the Hole in the Wall, the lunch consisted principally of ham and bread and other simple eatables, but the supply of liquors was quite liberal. The ham and bread was paid for out of the contingent fund of the Senate and was entered in the accounts as horse hire, until it became too expensive, and it had to be given up, as it was patronized too liberally by members of the House of Representatives. After the Sergeant-at-Arms closed it up it was turned over to a man by the name of Robert Carter, an excellent caterer, who carried it on and made considerable money out of it.

Lucky dog! I can only hope his nerves were in better shape when he retired than mine were.

16

You Can Throw a Party Fit for a Senator or a King – or Jacqueline Kennedy

You and I are going to go adventuring. How would you like to throw a party just the way it is done in the Sweetest Little Club in the World?

It may cost a little more than your parties usually do, but it might be fun for your friends to eat the same thing Jackie Kennedy served the Senate ladies when she was the hostess at a luncheon that she planned with me.

Or a fiftieth-wedding anniversary thrown in the Club for Senator Spessard Holland and his wife?

Or a super cocktail party?

You'll see, it's not that hard.

First, here are the rules we followed on Capitol Hill. You can benefit from many of these suggestions. Never use imitation flowers. If you can't afford real flowers, use a centerpiece that doesn't require them. Use living plants and hide the pots they are in artistically.

Use ivy, trailing around a centerpiece of statuary. Use a grouping of smaller figurines on a glass tray. Use a grouping of American flag and state flags. Use a shield—the emblem of the organization you are honoring. Look around, and you will find any number of things that can make colorful and appropriate centerpieces.

Use an ice carving. Now you can even buy a mold to eliminate the carving. On the Hill, we had several molds—until they became old hat. Use imagination. Almost anything goes. The Hill was fairly conservative but at a Mideastern embassy party, attended by Hill types, an ice camel was the highly praised centerpiece.

A Hill party is planned anywhere from a year to at least a week in advance. In order to do a decent job you should have the menu a little more than a week before the party. Sometimes it will take that long for a tradesman to locate what you want—such as a suckling pig.

A month lead time is ideal for planning a party. And invitations should go out two weeks in advance. We got a final head count the day before a party. This is very important, so you don't overprepare. Still, always assume that there will be several more attending than you plan on. On the Hill, we automatically planned one extra serving for every ten guests. If two hundred guests were expected, we always cooked 220 servings.

I think you are prepared now for the next important point. Don't try to serve something you can't afford. The meal must look lavish. So you must never have an exact count of one for each guest. Everyone loves stuffing himself at a party. People will be far happier if they have a lot of spaghetti than with an allotted three oysters or whatever.

Every social-minded housewife and host can benefit by seeing how we threw parties on the Hill, the most exclusive Club I've been associated with. Everything we did was just a little better than it is done elsewhere. For example, if it was a stag bar and buffet for either lunch or dinner we served eight-ounce portions of meat, compared with five or six ounces, which are served in the average restaurant or club.

If we were planning a stag party, we always served a hot main course. Even if it was something like crab, we would serve it hot—crab flake Mornay or crab Imperial. But men usually preferred steak or prime ribs to seafood. The only other thing which seemed to please them was baked ham—served hot, of course.

The vegetables would be green beans almondine, broccoli with Hollandaise, parsleyed potatoes, corn on the cob, each ear broken in half, baby carrots glazed in the oven—with brown sugar, butter, and lemon juice.

The Senators did not like vichyssoise as soup. They liked

potato-leek soup served hot. Or onion soup with mozzarella cheese. Or, of course, their own famed Senate bean soup.

If it was a hen party, we would serve cold food at a luncheon. Winter or summer the ladies liked cold food better than a hot main course. We would serve a prettied up shrimp salad, crab salad, or chicken salad.

At our Senatorial sit-down banquets, we treated guests in the same way they are treated traditionally at White House parties and State Department affairs; wine with the meal. Demitasse at the end of the meal. And with it, we served individual decanters of brandy.

Guests would pour the amount of brandy they wanted into their demitasse cups, and waiters would pour coffee on top.

We did own the demitasse spoons, which were always being carried away as souvenirs. But we didn't own the brandy decanters. We rented hand-blown glass ones, holding five or six ounces, from Ridgewell Caterers. Once Bob Carson, Senator Fong's AA, ordered brandy for an Easter banquet for the Senator. Some guests use only a little of the brandy, but on this occasion, Senators Jordan and Hayden, both good topers, kept everyone at the table far longer than necessary. They kept drinking coffee as long as the brandy lasted.

We were as careful with our formal place settings at parties for our Club members as if we were serving Presidents and kings. The dessert spoon, always above the plate, the fruit knife in the proper place, and even the cocktail fork, carefully placed at the proper angle across the knives on the right of the plate.

The protocol of Washington for the head table is that you always set an uneven number of places—seven, nine, eleven. Nine is the usual. The guest of honor sits in the middle. At our formal Senatorial dinners, the host and hostess sit on either side. Or two Senator hosts, as sometimes happens.

However, the wife of the guest of honor generally does not sit at the head table. She is usually at another table with Senators and their wives. If an exception is made, the wife is seated at her husband's left, and the host is moved over one seat.

Most people are surprised to learn that when the guest of honor is a foreign chief of state, his wife is not invited to attend a Hill luncheon or dinner. They are almost always stag.

They are even called stag if a female Senator attends. For all intents and purposes, she is just one of the boys.

You don't have to be on the Hill to give a Hill-type party.

Every year I hosted a cocktail buffet that became a tradition on the Hill. It was held at my home in Silver Spring—suburban Washington—between Thanksgiving and New Year's, the date varying with the plans of the Senate.

I wasn't the only one who threw a big bash. Key staffers on the Hill who tried to get ahead took advantage of the holiday season. I was just one of many. Key employees of the architect's office gave them. Someone in the sergeant-at-arm's office would give one. The comptroller's office would give one.

My parties naturally centered on the people involved in the food end of the Senate—the Rules Committee, the Appropriations Committee, the architect's office.

About a hundred would be invited, and between eighty and ninety would show up. For those who wonder what such a party costs, let me confess that the last one I gave—in 1974—cost $1,100, which included the liquor—Wild Turkey, Chivas Regal, and other like brands.

It would have cost more—much more—except that I did much of the work myself. For example, I served the dessert, whose recipe I stole from a fancy restaurant in New York: English lemon nut crisp a la Chantilly. At the Senate, we charged $1.25 for each serving of it. It was used only for parties. I'll tell you how we made it after I give you the menu for my last buffet spread.

Braised shell of beef a la Burgundy—made of the same cut New York sirloin steak comes from. Before it is cut, it is a shell of beef that weighs eighteen to twenty pounds.

But to continue the menu, there was spiced shrimp on a tree, sliced breast of turkey, with hot biscuits, baked ham, vegetables that included a marinated tray of baby carrots, pearl onions, and cauliflower buds, asparagus spears and whole rosebud beets. Along with the marinated vegetables was three-bean salad, which is also marinated.

Potato salad made with hard-boiled eggs and macaroni salad—with sliced tomatoes used as garnishes for all salad and vegetable trays.

After the dessert there were liqueurs and champagne. With the dessert, which I am about to share with you, I served tea and coffee.

Since the Club members would get bored now and then with the same old sumptuous fare, they would send me scouting for something to pick up a jaded appetite. I discovered a marvelous lemon dessert and went to a hell of a lot of trouble to get the recipe for my lords and masters.

I pleaded with the owners of the posh restaurant, assuring them that their wonderful recipe would thrill the Senators of the United States. Giving it would be almost a patriotic act. They finally ordered the pastry chef to open up.

So, here it is:

ENGLISH LEMON NUT CRISP A LA CHANTILLY

Prepare a very tart lemon pie filling, made with only true ingredients, such as fresh-squeezed lemon juice, grated lemon peel, fresh cream and eggs, and granulated sugar.

Take a pastry shell, the same as is used for a cream puff, and insert the filling, using a pastry tube or pastry bag.

Now glaze the shell, using a very thick mixture of confectionary sugar, brown sugar, honey, and minced black walnuts. After it sets, top with real whipped cream and a stemmed maraschino cherry.

I don't know how you will take to this dessert. I can only tell you the Senators would have a fit over it, and order it every chance they could for private parties where money was no object. And when I had to tell them that I had run out of the ingredients to make it on a few occasions, they would get real angry and cuss me out.

So much for gratitude.

Naturally, I was very happy when Senator Jordan, chairman of the Rules Committee, came to my open house, as did Chief Counsel Hugh Alexander and his wife. Also staffer Jim McCenna and his wife, representing his boss, Senator John Pastore, of the Appropriations Committee and his wife, Elena.

Architect of the Capitol George White didn't come. But previous architect, George Stewart, came several times. White was very reserved with me because I had made the terrible mistake of barring him from a private party in one of the committee rooms. I had been told that it was very secret and to keep all outsiders out.

White had tried to come into the room to check on the party and its decor, and I had kicked him out, not recognizing him. Instead of telling me who he was, he left and reported me, returning with the host of the party. I apologized up and down, but we never did get on a friendly basis. It didn't help matters that I refused to be a rubber stamp for the architect's office, which pays the salaries of the restaurant employees, and had many run-ins over money matters.

But this is party time. I was always happy to see Dan Geary, the finance officer of the architect's office, come to my parties. He was the man who actually signed my paychecks. Other staffers who showed up at my parties were Bob Brinkworth, comptroller of the Senate, and Tom Scott, chief clerk of the Appropriations Committee.

HILL COCKTAIL PARTIES

For a two-hour cocktail party on the Hill, we would allow thirteen or fourteen hors d'oeuvres and canapés per person, for a mixed crowd. If only females attended, we allowed nine or ten. For a stag party, the count went up to fifteen or sixteen.

A canapé is an open-faced sandwich or cracker. In other words, something spread or sitting on a dry cracker or toast point.

An hors d'oeuvre is a little chunk of meat or cheese without a cracker. It can be seafood or fowl. We served chicken livers wrapped in bacon, tiny hot dogs wrapped in bacon, cheese cubes wrapped in corned beef. We served oysters Casino.

An easy way to remember is that an hors d'oeuvre is anything on a toothpick or skewered in some way. We used frilled toothpicks for our hors d'oeuvres to add color. We had little wooden skewers to serve tenderloin of beef.

Toothpicks had another use. When women had tea sandwiches, we stuck toothpicks in to hold the various layers together and anchor the decoration on top. On tea sandwiches, we used pitted cherries on top of turkey sandwiches. On each ham sandwich, we placed a chunk of fresh pineapple. On roast beef, we used an olive. For sliced chicken or chicken salad, we used tiny wedges or circles of fresh peach.

For tuna or crab-flake salad, we used sweet-pickle chips or tiny whole gherkins.

The most important tip for party giving, right next to the cardinal rule of *be generous,* is don't take shortcuts on decorating food. Not decorating is like making the bed but not putting on the bedspread. An inexpensive finger sandwich, when decorated, becomes a triumph. One of the cheapest fillings is turkey or egg salad. But it can be beautiful with an olive or a pickle chip or tiny peach wedge on top.

Let me give you a few of the recipes we used for hors d'oeuvres. These were the favorites around the Hill.

CHICKEN LIVERS IN BACON

Take the raw chicken livers and wrap a strip of bacon around each. Pin with an hors d'oeuvre toothpick, which is larger than a regular toothpick. Put on a cookie sheet which has been greased with olive oil or other vegetable oil. Broil for 4 to 5 minutes about 6–8 inches from broiler.

PIGS IN BLANKET

We made them two ways.
Wrapped in bacon: Cut a slit lengthwise in the weenie and stuff with a spear of cheddar cheese. Wrap with a slice of bacon and secure with hors d'oeuvre toothpick. Put in oven for 10 to 12 minutes at 375 degrees, cheese side up.
Wrapped in dough: Cut strips of pie dough a little shorter than the tiny hot dog, and sprinkle dough with grated sharp cheese. Roll weenie in dough so that ends stick out. Bake for 10 to 12 minutes at 400 degrees.

MUSTARD SAUCE

This is served on the side. To 1 pint of mustard, stir in 3 tablespoons horseradish.

DEVILED EGGS

Make hard-boiled eggs, 8 to 10 minutes. If boiled too long, they get green around the edges. Add salt to water, to make them peel easily—2 tablespoons to a quart of water. 1 tablespoon of vinegar added to the water also helps by making the shell brittle—trade secrets.

Cut egg lengthwise, take yolk out. Put yolks in mixing bowl. To 1 dozen eggs, add 3 tablespoons mayonnaise and 2 teaspoons dry mustard. Add salt and white pepper, 1 tablespoon tarragon vinegar, mash and stir till smooth. Keep it thick. Stuff the eggs, fill hollows. Garnish with stuffed olives or strip of pimiento, alternating for color. Sprinkle lightly with paprika. Place on bed of parsley or watercress. (More mayo if you like soft filling.)

CRAB BALLS

One pound of crab meat makes about forty hors d'oeuvres, served on cocktail toothpicks.

For each pound of crabmeat, sauté the following vegetables in just enough olive oil or other vegetable oil to keep from sticking or burning—2 ounces each of peas, chopped, frozen or fresh green beans, chopped frozen carrots, chopped celery, chopped green pepper, and chopped onion. Stir constantly till the vegetables are done, and remove from flame.

Next cut 3 slices of soft white bread (with crust off) into ¼-inch cubes—give or take ⅛ inch. Toss these into a mixing bowl and over these pour the sautéed vegetables and the pound of crab meat. At the Senate, we used only the very finest backfin lump crabmeat.

Now, in a separate mixing bowl, beat 2 eggs and 6 tablespoons mayonnaise into a smooth mixture. Add 2 ounces of finely chopped pimiento and pour over the crab meat-bread-and-vegetable mixture.

Finally, stir carefully to keep the crab meat from breaking up too much. Use a No. 24 size scoop to make tiny bite-size balls. Roll them in a mixture of ½ cup flour to 2 cups of cornmeal to which you have added a little salt and white pepper.

Place on greased cookie sheet and bake in a 500-degree, preheated oven for just a few minutes to brown—watching closely.

Insert toothpicks and serve in a chafing dish, accompanied by two sauces—a bowl of horseradish sauce and a bowl of cocktail sauce.

HORSERADISH SAUCE

To 1 pint of mayonnaise, add ½ cup olive oil, 3 tablespoons tarragon vinegar, and 6 ounces horseradish. Blend them together in blender or hand whip, add salt and pepper to taste. On the Hill we used fresh horseradish, but the bottled variety is almost as good. If olive oil is too expensive, use a good corn oil.

COCKTAIL SAUCE

To one 12-ounce can of Hunt's tomato sauce or other good brand, add 6 ounces of Hunt's chili sauce, 6 ounces fresh or bottled horseradish, two tablespoons A1 sauce and ½ tablespoon Lea & Perrins sauce—L & P, we called it. Stir and serve.

If you will look back at Chapter 12, "Party Time in the Sweetest Little Club in the World," you will see that we have been making some of the things served at Senator Holland's fiftieth anniversary party. So now I'll show you how to make the beef burgundy, as we did for that elegant party:

BEEF BURGUNDY

Cube choice grade lean beef into ½-inch cubes. To 5 pounds beef make a marinade of one pint burgundy, a pint of olive oil, and a whole clove of garlic crushed. Marinate it the day before. Drain meat through collander, pour juice into an oven-proof pan. Heat the pan very hot. Take cubes and roll in flour seasoned with salt and pepper. Drop beef cubes into the hot mixture and brown, stirring constantly. Barely cover with water and place in oven. Bake uncovered one hour at 375 degrees, stirring occasionally.

You will have sufficient natural brown sauce. Serve with rice pilaf, the recipe of which is given later in the chapter.

(Buttered noodles can also be used but are harder to handle than rice at a stand-up buffet.)

To make Beef Stroganoff, another Hill party favorite, use same recipe as for Beef Burgundy but before adding water, stir 1 quart of sour cream into the mixture and bring to a simmer, stirring constantly. Then add water to barely cover and 3 size No. 2½ cans of whole white onions.

Place in oven and bake uncovered for 45 minutes to an hour at 350 degrees, stirring occasionally. Serve over steamed rice, pilaf, or buttered noodles. (Button mushrooms can be substituted for, or added to, the whole white onions.)

At the Holland party, there were three chafing dishes at each end of the buffet. In the center dish was the pilaf, and on each side were the Beef Burgundy and the Seafood Newburg (recipe given later in this chapter).

QUICHE LORRAINE

We used a variety of quiches for Holland's fiftieth anniversary. It was a very popular item on the Hill, and we used a sharp cheddar-cheese base.

However, the original quiche Lorraine, which gets its name from the province in France, was an open-faced tart made of bread dough filled with cream sauce and bacon, but no cheese.

The pastry shell is a great improvement over bread dough, and the modern quiches substitute everything from ham to asparagus for the original bacon. On the Hill, we used a cream sauce with very little egg because of the danger of spoilage. Instead we used cheese to give body and flavor to the cream sauce even in making bacon quiches. In fact, we used the same cream sauce with cheese for all the quiches.

You can buy bite-sized pastry shells at a grocery, bakery, or caterer.

To make the cream sauce, for each egg, well beaten, add 8 ounces of finely grated sharp cheddar cheese and ⅔ cup of heavy cream and a dash of salt and pepper. The average housewife had better use a double boiler to bring the mixture to a boil, stirring constantly until it is thick.

Now remove from heat, beat for a few moments to keep it from lumping and fold in the meat, seafood, or vegetable. For the Holland party, we had quiche of four flavors—bacon, chicken, crab, and shrimp, each minced, of course.

Fill shells and garnish with paprika. Place on chafing dish to keep warm. We alternated the flavors so the guests didn't know which they were getting.

The quiches are very popular but a lot of work. One of our Senate chefs would do anything to get out of making them.

STUFFED CELERY

I used assorted cream cheeses—pimiento, plain, bacon, horse-radish, and olive. Stuff the celery with cheese from a pastry bag, decorate tops with strips of pimiento and halves of stuffed olives. Garnish with radish roses on watercress. This makes pretty platters. I also cut celery sticks into 1½-inch pieces. If I do not have celery hearts, I remove all strings from the stalks.

Here's something else that went over big at the Holland party (the basic recipe is very versatile, as you will see):

CHICKEN SALAD

I served this with tiny, hot buttermilk biscuits. Take 1 pound of finely chopped boiled white meat of chicken.

Set the chicken aside while you combine the following in a mixing bowl, making a 50–50 mix of chicken and other ingredients:

8 ounces finely chopped celery; 4 ounces finely chopped sweet pickles; 4 ounces chopped pimientos. Toss the pound of chopped chicken with the pound of mixture in the mixing bowl and add 6 ounces of mayonnaise.

Place the salad in a mound on a silver platter or other tray, perfect the shape by molding with your hands. Then glaze by spreading a thin coating of mayonnaise over the entire surface. Sprinkle paprika on top.

Garnish with peach halves alternating with canned pineapple rings, in a complete ring around the mold. Place a maraschino cherry in the indentation of each peach half and a spiced crab apple in the center of each pineapple ring.

(We didn't do it for the Holland party, but you can make this dish still more colorful by placing a line of pimientos across the top of the chicken salad mound, instead of paprika.)

When Senators' wives asked me how to cut the cost of this party-type salad, saying breast of chicken was expensive, I suggested they use tuna, diced ham, or turkey breast. However, some wives had the opposite complaint, wanting a more expensive "biscuit filler." I suggested crab or shrimp. The recipe is the same for all.

SEAFOOD NEWBURG

This is not a cheap dish. We used equal amounts each of four kinds of seafood—lobster, cut into ½-inch chunks; baby shrimp, peeled and deveined; backfin lump crab, and baby scallops.

Saute 4 pounds of seafood—1 pound of each of the above—in a little butter and add 1 cup sherry, keeping on a low heat until the wine is half gone. Remove from flame.

Now heat 2½ cups of heavy cream in a large double boiler with 2 blades of mace, until the cream is slightly reduced. Then remove the mace. Remove from heat for a moment. Lightly beat 8 egg yolks and add a few spoonfuls of hot cream, beating all the while with a wire whisk. Gradually add the egg mixture to the hot cream in the double boiler, beating with wire whisk.

Now stir in the seafood. Simmer, stirring constantly, until sauce thickens enough to coat a wooden spoon.

Just before removing from heat, add 4 tablespoons butter, 1 teaspoon salt and ½ teaspoon ground white pepper. If a thinner consistency is desired, add a little milk.

At the Holland party, we served the Newburg with Rice Pilaf, but for a sit-down dinner it is nice served over steamed rice. The recipe serves about six to eight guests when it is the main course, but for a party at which many other things will be served, this amount will take care of eighteen to twenty guests.

A nice variation, if you like a still richer flavor, is to add a splash—2 ounces—of cognac at the time you add the wine.

RICE PILAF

Steam 1 pound rice in salted water. If you stir rice, it gets gummy. So, steam with lid on until it gets very dry, and it will be fluffy.

I pour the fluffy rice into a baking dish, adding a mixture of peas, pimiento and onion. To 1 pound of rice, I use 5 ounces very tiny frozen peas, 2 ounces chopped fresh pimiento, and 1 ounce grated fresh onion. Pour 1 cup chicken broth over the top.

As a final touch I sprinkle 3 tablespoons melted margarine over the top, and bake covered with aluminum foil in a preheated 350-degree oven for 20 minutes.

This is how we made the pilaf for the Holland party, but you can use chopped green pepper as a substitute for the peas and pimiento.

You can use these same Newburg and pilaf recipes for crab Newburg, shrimp Newburg, or even meat Newburgs—ham, chicken, or turkey. Any Newburg is excellent for a Hill party because it is equally good as a sit-down entreé or served at a buffet with a stack of small plates.

Most politicians prefer stand-up buffets, so that they can roam around and talk to people and escape some person who is trying to trap them—unless it happens to be a pretty girl. Sometimes, if they have too big an adoring female audience, they try to escape the whole pack.

Hot German potato salad is made by the gallon in the Senate restaurants, for parties as well as regular meals—winter or summer. There are few who don't call for hot or cold potato salad fairly regularly. You might want to serve it their way. So, here's how both are done.

COLD POTATO SALAD

For potato salad, we boil the potatoes in the jackets for added flavor and for vitamins. For every 5 pounds of potatoes we use 2 tablespoons of salt in the water and 1 tablespoon of onion salt.

After the boiled potatoes have cooled to room temperature, we peel the skins, which come off easily. Then we dice the potatoes into ¼-inch cubes.

Now add:

1 cup of finely chopped celery, ½ cup finely chopped onion, and 6 hard-boiled eggs cut up into small pieces. On top of that, we toss in ¼ cup chopped red pimiento and ¼ cup chopped sweet pickle.

Now, in a bowl, I make the dressing using 1 cup mayonnaise, 1 tablespoon dry mustard, ¼ cup olive oil, and 2 tablespoons tarragon vinegar. We stir this mixture to a smooth consistency, adding just a little salt and pepper.

After the dressing has been mixed thoroughly, the mixture is poured over the potatoes. To keep from tearing up the potatoes, we wash our hands, and fold the mayonnaise into the potatoes by hand.

SENATE GERMAN POTATO SALAD

This salad is served hot from a chafing dish. However, it is always served the day after it is made in order to permit the savory flavor of the vinegar to permeate the potatoes.

To make German potato salad the way we did on the Hill, follow the above recipe for regular potato salad, with a few important changes.

No eggs or mayonnaise. Instead, for 5 pounds potatoes, use a mixture of ½ cup tarragon vinegar, and ¼ cup of olive oil. Before adding the dressing, add ¼ pound of crisp-chopped cooked bacon to the potato mixture.

The seasonings which were used with the mayonnaise are also in German salad dressing—mustard, salt, and white pepper.

The next day, after the German potato salad has been in the refrigerator overnight, reheat, place in a chafing dish, and garnish with fresh parsley and a sprinkling of paprika.

We even made gallons and gallons of Senate potato salads for Senators going on picnics or having parties at their homes. Once a year, Senator Claiborne Pell would throw a lawn party for all the young Rhode Islanders who were college students in the Washington area. His Georgetown home would be crowded with young folks happily eating hot dogs and gallons and gallons of both regular and hot potato salads we had made in the Senate kitchen.

Even in the years when Pell himself would be campaigning or attending to business in his home state, his concern for the kids was such that his staff, headed by Ray Nelson, his AA, would take over and hold the party for him for several hundred guests.

I liked Pell for his devotion to education. He had an open door to all college students of his state, and he spent time and thought helping them with their problems. Few on the Hill take time for students away from home. In my twenty-plus years in the Club, he's the only Senator I saw take such time or throw a party strictly for them.

Along with the potato salad, we would also serve gallons and gallons of cole slaw fixed New Orleans style. Now for how to make it:

NEW ORLEANS STYLE COLE SLAW

To 1 head of white cabbage, approximately 3 pounds, use 1½ pound red cabbage, 1 pound fresh carrots, 1 or 2 stalks celery, 2 green peppers, and 1 large onion. Grate everything on a coarse grater. Mix together in a mixing bowl.

I always cut mayonnaise with olive oil, using ½ cup olive oil to 1 pint mayonnaise. Just stir in. This thins it down and adds flavor. Add 2 tablespoons dry mustard, 1 tablespoon salt, and 1 table-spoon white pepper.

Fold it into the cole slaw. Place on a tray and mold with your hands. Finally, coat the surface with a thin layer of mayonnaise to glaze. As a garnish, I used black olives on a bed of escarole around the cole slaw. Each guest would get about four or five black olives.

This slaw was very popular on the Hill.

My favorite luncheon of my many years on the Hill was the wine-filled one I planned with Jackie, when she was First Lady. It was a very private party, not connected with the Senate ladies' club. She just wanted to entertain some of her close friends with a very posh luncheon.

You'll see what I mean when I tell you the menu and how to follow her lead.

The appetizer was Champagne Strawberries. After this came white wine with cheese straws. Then came Crab Flake Mornay Bordeaux—more wine. The vegetable was Onions and Peas in the Basket, a very tricky dish to make. The dessert was Ice Cream Sherbet Parfait.

Now to don our chefs' hats:

CHAMPAGNE STRAWBERRIES

Clean strawberries the day before, cover with champagne and place in refrigerator overnight. The next day, scoop out with some of the strawberries and champagne into a champagne glass, top with whipped cream and a maraschino cherry. Serve with little strips of semisweet shortbread. At the Hill, we had these in our own bakeshop.

The cheese straws we served are the same as those served at fancy bars with drinks. They are very crisp, almost like pie dough, and twisted.

CRAB FLAKE MORNAY BORDEAUX

This Bordeaux-flavored seafood dish was both delicious and pretty with its ring of potatoes around the edge. We used 8-ounce individual silver casseroles for ramekins. Each held more than a 5-ounce serving of crab meat as well as the fluffy potato ring.

Naturally, we used backfin lump crab meat, being careful not to stir or disturb the crab meat too much. The beauty of the dish is in the large pieces of seafood. Crab is very delicate, and breaks up easily.

First I place the crab meat in the casserole, then pour the Mornay Sauce mixture over it.

For 6 servings, I use 2 pounds of crab meat. This means each guest gets 5 generous ounces of crab meat, and there is room in the ramekin for the Mornay Sauce.

MORNAY SAUCE

Melt 2 tablespoons butter and stir in 2 tablespoons flour, keeping smooth. Add 1 cup half-and-half (milk) slowly and stir constantly with a wooden spoon until it thickens. Remove from heat. Add ½ teaspoon salt, ¼ teaspoon pepper.

Now beat 2 eggs and stir in gradually 2 tablespoons of the hot liquid. Then add the egg mixture gradually to the hot sauce. Now pour in 3 ounces of white Bordeaux wine, return to heat, and stir constantly for about 2 minutes.

Before pouring the sauce over the crab meat, which is already in the ramekins, sprinkle a generous portion of freshly grated parmesan cheese over the crab meat. Now cover with the sauce.

I take a pastry bag filled with loosely fluffed, buttered whipped potatoes, and outline the edge of each silver dish with swirls of potatoes. Then I pop the casseroles under the broiler, about 6 inches from the flame. I take them out when the potatoes begin to turn golden brown, sprinkle with paprika, and serve immediately.

(If you like, you can substitute sherry for Bordeaux.)

PEAS IN THE BASKET

This is one of the most unusual dishes I was privileged to serve on the Hill. It is only suitable for sit-down occasions.

You would think the basket would be made of dough, but it isn't. It is made of shoestring potatoes. I use Idaho baking potatoes. The Senate has facilities for making shoestring potatoes, but the average cook would have to buy them ready-made frozen.

I do not recommend that the average housewife try weaving her own baskets. It takes a gourmet chef with years of experience. However, they can be ordered from a caterer. On the Hill we charged $1.50 a basket, when we served them at a fancy meal, but I recently heard that the price had gone up to over $4 apiece.

Expert pastrymen can weave them in their hands without a mold but beginners must learn to weave the baskets by interlocking the strings of potatoes around a form—using a Chinese teacup or small dessert casserole cup.

At any rate, when made, the baskets must be deep-fat fried—two at a time sit comfortably on a ladle which can be lowered into the bubbling deep fat—and they must be kept hot until serving to avoid going limp.

Filling for peas in the basket. Actually you will need not only peas but onions, carrots, and cauliflower buds. I use tiny cooked fresh green peas, combined with a smaller amount of tiny-tot canned onions and tiny-tot canned carrots. Put the hot buttered and seasoned vegetable mixture into the baskets, after they are on the serving plate, so they will not go limp, and serve immediately.

For a topping, place a small buttered, fresh-cooked cauliflower bud on the surface, and garnish with a strip of red pimiento on each bud. The baskets are beautiful and colorful with their green, white, and red.

Jacqueline Kennedy loved intricate recipes, and price was no object. Some Hill ladies liked the vegetables in the basket in cream sauce. It must be stiff enough not to ooze through the basket.

ICE CREAM SHERBET PARFAIT

In a parfait glass, put a layer of black raspberry sherbet, a layer of vanilla ice cream, a layer of lime sherbet. Top with real whipped cream and a stemmed maraschino cherry. It's a heavy but lovely dessert. (Sprinkle any fruit liqueur on top.)

Of the hundreds of formal parties I supervised at the Sweetest Little Club in the World, one of the most elegant parties was that of Anna Chennault, widow of World War II hero General Claire Chennault of Flying Tiger fame.

It's a good example to use to show the vast array of fancy but easy recipes available for buffet-style entertaining.

It was a joy to work with Madam Chennault in planning this party, because she wanted perfection, and money was no problem. The Dragon Lady, as the beautiful Chinese widow was called, left nothing to chance, and appeared at my office accompanied by her secretary, notebook in hand. All plans were carefully recorded. The Chennault party was sponsored by the Vice-President, informally called the 101st Senator, because he was presiding officer of the Senate.

Spiro Agnew had asked for the use of one of the nicest committee rooms in the Dirksen Building—R-1318. About 150 guests were invited to the reception—a fancy name for a cocktail party—from 8 to 10 P.M.

The sight that greeted the guests was truly impressive, with radiant colors in decoration and food—Suckling Pig with bright-red apple in its mouth; Poached, Decorated Salmon; Steamship Round of Beef; Oysters Casino; chafing dishes of Prime Tidbits of Beef Tenderloin on skewers.

There were trays of artistically arranged hors d'oeuvres and relishes: Deviled Eggs, Corned Beef Horns, Stuffed Cherry Tomatoes, marinated cauliflower, pickles, olives. Around each tray of hors d'oeuvres was a border of stuffed cherry tomatoes alternating with deviled eggs.

STUFFED CHERRY TOMATOES

I used three kinds of salad stuffings for the Chennault party—chicken, backfin lump crab meat, and shrimp. The tomato circles taken out of the tops of the cherry tomatoes are not used in the stuffing, but can be saved for a soup pot.

Stuff the tomatoes and sprinkle the tops with paprika. Use the largest sized cherry tomatoes you can find.

CORNED BEEF HORNS

I used corned round of beef, sliced very thin. It's all lean and more expensive than regular corned beef, which is fat brisket.

Cream cheese can be purchased in various flavors—plain, horseradish, bacon, smoked salmon, chives, and pimiento. I used a variety so that everyone could find his or her favorite—employing a trick, as you will see.

The way to make the horn is to take a slice of the corned beef, place a tablespoon of cream cheese in the center, and roll it so that it looks like a horn or bell. Hold it together with a frilled toothpick. As

I place each horn on the serving tray, I add a tidbit to the end of the toothpick that is the key to the guests' identifying the flavor inside. I have seen guests get so fascinated that they spend most of their time and appetite solving this flavor puzzle.

For the plain cream cheese—a stuffed olive.

For the bacon cream cheese—a small pickled onion.

For the horseradish—a pimiento strip.

For the smoked salmon—a cocktail filet of smoked salmon.

For the chive— a ripe olive.

For the pimiento—a bud of cauliflower.

The average male guest will eat two of these horns, but some people go ape over the combination of corned beef and cream cheese.

The Chennault party is also a good one for showing the lineup of liquor usually served at Hill parties.

Wild Turkey, as a sipping whiskey. Old Grand Dad for bourbon with a mix. Chivas Regal for the Scotch, though some prefer Cutty Sark. For martinis, the gin was Beefeaters.

The beer was Michelob. Besides, there were various wines, fresh fruits—oranges, grapefruit, lemons, and limes for drinks like whiskey sours. Tomato juice for bloody Marys, a dish of powdered sugar, a dish of salt for margaritas. Every kind of liqueur. The Club never disappoints, nor do those who are trying to please the Club members. All labels were impeccable.

The vodka was Smirnoff. The Club prided itself on trying to buy American, and in spite of the Russian-sounding name, Smirnoff is as American as apple pie, though they don't use that phrase as an ad slogan.

Since Madam Chennault wanted a note of elegance, live music was provided by a string orchestra, which was almost drowned out by the happy chatter that followed the first few drinks. It was a trio of piano, violin, and French harp. A beautiful, long-haired woman in a white gown presided at the harp.

STEAMSHIP ROUND OF BEEF

For 150 people, I ordered a 75-pound steamship round with a handle on. That means that the whole hip of the beef—with the bone left in it plus the knee joint—is left on to serve as a handle.

This helps the carver to slice with more ease. It is also possible to get a 40-pound steamship round with handle.

Before baking the 40-pounder, insert cloves of garlic about 6 inches apart, all across the surface, pushing them in about 2 inches into slashes cut with a knife. Then, you must rub surface down with a mixture of salt and black pepper in equal proportions. The beef, with the arm at the top, is placed on a heavy metal sheet pan, and covered with heavy-duty aluminum foil down to the surface of the pan.

Place in a preheated 350-degree oven, and roast for approximately four hours and a half. Every half hour pull out the beef onto the oven door, and where the handle is, pour in 4 ounces olive oil mixed with 4 ounces burgundy. You only need to open a small portion of the tinfoil, and you pour the liquid all the way around the bone so that it slides down the side of the beef.

This is done about eight times, using one cupful each time. It is well worth the effort in flavor, color, and aroma. Also the meat will come out very juicy.

Ours was a stand-up party, but we saved the drippings for making mushroom gravy to be served in the restaurant the next day. It is too delicious to waste.

Our 75-pounder was placed on a 3-foot silver platter with a heat lamp above it, because serving would go on for several hours. Just before the guests arrived, the aluminum foil was removed, and the carver started slicing small slices of medium, well-done, and rare. He carved the meat as the guests made their desires known individually.

Several platters of cocktail-size hard rolls sat beside the meat. These are very popular with the Hill crowd.

The tray was heaped with a layer of fresh parsley, on which the beef sat, and around the border sliced tomatoes were placed on the parsley. The tomato slices were kept replenished so that they could be used in the hard rolls with the beef. Shakers of salt and black pepper stood around the beef.

POACHED DECORATED SALMON

I ordered two 30-pound salmons for Madam Chennault's 150 guests. These were steelhead salmon with the heads on. We ordered them cleaned, but you still have to check the insides and the scales, to remove anything that remains.

I washed the fish thoroughly with a vegetable brush. Then I made a paste consisting of 1 cup olive oil, 3 tablespoons each of onion salt, table salt, and white pepper. This is enough for one 20-pound salmon. I rubbed down the fish, inside and out, with this paste. It was then ready to be mounted on a board.

The salmon must be tied to the board with a rope to hold it in place, in two places—behind the fin and the tail. The board should be twelve inches longer than the fish on each end. The fish is placed in a large deep pan of boiling water with the board side up, but submerged.

For home parties, a smaller salmon can be used. A 20-pounder is about 3 feet long.

Boil slowly over medium heat for an hour and a half. You can test the fish using a skewer to poke behind the fin, so the mark will not be obvious.

When the fish is tender and done, remove it from the boiling water, place the board on the table (board side down) and while it is still hot, saturate the fish with dry white wine. Some of the wine will soak right into the skin. Cool.

Now slide the fish, board and all, into the refrigerator and chill overnight. The next day I decorate the salmon.

Remove the ropes gently, and cover the fish with clear unsweetened gelatin just as it is starting to set. Use a brush to apply the gelatin to the fish until it has built up a little thickness. This gives it a nice glaze.

Now place a maraschino cherry in the eye socket. All around the salmon, on the board, spread a mixture of mayonnaise and the remaining gelatin to cover the board and give a neutral background to display the beauty of the fish. In a row, making a border around the board, place slices of citrus fruit, alternating between lemon and lime. As the carver cuts little tidbits of salmon, he places them on guests' plates. On a tray are crackers and toast points.

WHITE WINE SAUCE FOR SALMON

To every 6 ounces of mayonnaise, add 2 ounces of white wine, 3 tablespoons of grated onion, and 3 tablespoons of finely chopped sweet pickles. Blend lightly in a bowl, and sprinkle the top with paprika. This makes enough for 4–5 pounds of salmon.

PRIME TIDBITS OF BEEF TENDERLOIN (SHISH KEBAB)

At least 24 hours before cooking, I marinate the little 1-inch cubes of beef in olive oil and Portuguese burgundy, half-and-half, enough to cover the meat. I add to the liquid a few cloves of fresh garlic wrapped in cheese cloth, so I can retrieve them later, and sprinkle in some salt and pepper. Occasionally, I stir the mixture and turn the meat.

When I'm ready to make the shish kebab, I line up the meat and vegetables—4 cubes of meat to a 7- or 8-inch metal skewer. I use whole canned baby carrots and tiny canned onions. I line them up—meat, carrot, onion—three times, ending up with the fourth cube of meat.

Guests usually use their fingers to take off the pieces of meat. Though most guests will only take one skewer on their plate, it is best to allow two.

I place the shish kebab on cookie sheets and bake in a 400-degree oven for 5 or 6 minutes. This leaves the meat a little pink on the inside and medium brown on the outside.

There was also a tree of spiced shrimp.

SPICED SHRIMP TREE

A shrimp tree is one of the nicest things you can serve at a party, and when the guests had left the Chennault party, there was not a shrimp in sight.

For such an elegant party, I used jumbo shrimp—21 to 25 per pound, as compared with 30 to 35 for average-size shrimp. Even though the guests had many other choices that would get their attention, I allowed 6 or 7 per person.

Now for cooking the shrimp:

For every 5 pounds of shrimp, I use 1 gallon of water and 1 can of Michelob beer, and bring it to a boil, with a spice bag which contains 8 bay leaves, 1 tablespoon of oregano or Italian seasoning, 1 tablespoon thyme, 2 tablespoons celery salt, and 1 teaspoon whole red pepper. Tie the spices in a square of cheesecloth. Add spice bag to water and bring to boil before adding the beer and the shrimp.

After the shrimp, which remain in the shell, have boiled for exactly 3 minutes, remove from the fire, drain off the hot water, and cover with tap water, adding another can of beer and leaving the spice bag in. Let sit for at least 1 hour before hulling and deveining. (You can substitute ½ cup vinegar for beer and 5 tablespoons Old Bay seasoning for spice bag.)

Sprinkle the shrimp with lemon juice, and place in the refrigerator in a closed container, so they do not lose their moisture and flavor.

COCKTAIL SAUCE
for Spiced Shrimp

For best flavor, I make the shrimp sauce the day before. To 1 cup catsup and 1 cup chili sauce, add:

4 teaspoons Tabasco, 3 ounces freshly grated horseradish, 1 tablespoon Worcestershire sauce, 2 tablespoons fresh grated onion, and 2 tablespoons grated fresh celery.

Stir together and chill overnight. This makes enough cocktail sauce for 5 pounds of shrimp.

Building the shrimp tree. It is possible to buy an hors d'oeuvre tree. However, I had designed an especially large tree from the old silver service I found around the Senate restaurant. It would hold 100 pounds of shrimp. It could not be used unless we were serving at least 50 pounds of shrimp. I used 50 pounds for the Chennault party.

I designed it from four silver chafing dishes of graduated sizes, growing smaller to the top tier, which was the sauce container. As I hung the shrimp around the edge of each tier, I inserted a lemon wedge between every two shrimp. On the base, which was a large silver tray, I used a bed of escarole. On the escarole was heaped shrimp skewered with frilled toothpicks of assorted colors. As a border, on the outer edge of the tray, I alternated ripe and stuffed olives. The color combination of pink shrimp, green, red, and black olives, and blue-and-gold frilled toothpicks made this a very colorful attractive tree.

On each shelf or tier of the tree, there was also heaped shrimp with the same toothpick color assortment. The border for these, of course, was the shrimp-and-lemon edging.

The Appropriations Committee room was paneled with walnut, which made a beautiful background for the silver-and-cut glass serving pieces and the spring flowers used at Madam Chennault's party. The bronze torch lights softly glowed against the walls, indirectly lighting the room, and picking up the gold linen and yellow flowers, among the blue, white, and yellow displays.

It was tricky to integrate the colors of gold and silver, but we did it, with the help of the flowers. Since all the service was silver, silver was used for the candelabra and the candles. The tablecloth was gold, and the napkins were white, as were the skirts gleaming below the tablecloths.

What the guests did not know is that I had designed the solid silver flower urn myself out of an old unused fish-platter cover. Actually, there had been fifteen such covers lying around unused, dating back to 1895, the time of the restoration of the Senate Restaurant, and I had converted eight of them to flower and fruit bowls.

I took them to the Senate carpenter shop, and directed the workers to make walnut pedestals in circular shape that would hide the handles. If they had cut off the handles, it would have ruined the value of these covers, because they are antiques. This way, some day, the Senate will be able to use them again if desired for fish or meat. The covers alone are worth $400 apiece. I've seen the platters with the covers sell for $1,100 at auction.

Using the largest of these converted urns, I was able to have a flower display standing three-feet across and two-and-one-half feet high—necessary to overcome the size of the room and the height of the ceiling. All around the pedestal, I used asparagus fern decorated with carnations dyed to match the blue flowers in the centerpiece.

So much for decorations. Now to see a man about a pig.

SUCKLING PIG

The man I always saw for suckling pigs—a favorite hors d'oeuvre on the Hill—was Mr. Bourgh, the owner of the National Hotel Supply Company, Washington's most exclusive meat dealer. We tried to order the suckling pig one month ahead of a party, so it would be the right size and could be properly prepared.

A piglet has to be shaved of hair and washed thoroughly. A host or hostess preparing a suckling pig for a home party could order an 18- or 20-pound piglet and fit it into the average 36-inch home oven—or could take a larger suckling pig to a bakery to have it baked.

On the Hill, we used 30- to 35-pound piglets and baked them in our bakers' ovens. When our suckling pig was an hors d'oeuvre, cut into tidbits as needed and served cold on crackers, we did not stuff the pig. However, if we served suckling pig as a hot, main course, we stuffed it with a spinach forcemeat, which is easy to make.

Spinach Stuffing. For a 30-pound piglet, wash and wilt 1 bushel of spinach in hot salted water. Then combine with 2 cups chopped hard-boiled eggs and 2 pounds minced broiled bacon. Add a little salt and pepper and lightly fill the cavity, sewing it closed. Place on a heavy duty roasting pan.

To prepare the piglet, I rubbed the outside with olive oil—though any good vegetable oil will do—then rubbed salt, pepper, and onion salt into the olive oil, so it would be evenly seasoned.

After the piglet is in the 350-degree oven and begins to bake, I start basting, using equal parts of white wine and olive or vegetable oil. About every 30 minutes, baste it again, until the piglet is done—about 6 hours.

When the piglet has achieved the desired golden-brown color, I cover it with toweling and do the basting over the toweling. This also keeps the skin from cracking open. To be sure that the 350-degree temperature is reached next to the bone, I use two thermometers—one at the shoulder and one in the ham.

The large, bright-red apple, incidentally, must be inserted in the mouth before the pig goes into the oven. Also, insert either ripe olives or maraschino cherries in the eye sockets—also before baking.

After the piglet has cooled, if it is to be used as an hors d'oeuvre, I cover it with a coating of clear, semisweet gelatin, which must be almost ready to set when it is applied, I use a spatula to smooth it. I glaze the apple as well as the pig.

OYSTERS CASINO

Oysters Casino are a still richer cousin of Oysters Rockefeller, because of the addition of bacon. I prefer it to Oysters Rockefeller because of that and because it uses the lemon instead of Pernod.

For Oysters Casino, first take the oysters out of the shells and clean shells thoroughly with a wire brush to get rid of sand.

For every 6 oysters, take 3 slices of bacon and put them in skillet on low heat, until they are transparent. Cut each in half, and put aside. Use the fat in the skillet with a bit of butter to sauté the following ingredients until they start to soften: 1½ tablespoons chopped chives; 1 tablespoon chopped fresh celery; 2 tablespoons chopped green pepper.

Arrange oyster shells on a baking pan, put oyster meat back in, top with the vegetable mix, and cover each with a half strip of bacon.

Sprinkle bacon tops with lemon juice and pop into 375-degree oven, until oysters are hot and bacon is crisp. Must be closely watched.

Fortunately, I did not have to supervise the desserts for the Chennault party. We ordered an assortment of miniature French pastries. Since most of the guests were men, the majority of the pastries were fruited individual tarts, topped with whipped cream and maraschino cherry. The other pastries were eclairs, French horns, cream puffs, and seven-layer pastries made of shortbread which are well liked on the Hill.

Hot coffee and tea were available, as well as brandy and other liqueurs.

Vice-President Agnew attended the party without his wife, Judy. In fact, I don't think there were more than a handful of women. Why more women didn't come, or weren't invited, I don't know. But it made Madam Chennault more popular than ever, and she was radiant that night, in evening dress.

The commandant of the Marine Corps, who had just written a book, was the guest of honor. And there were many military men as well as several members of the Supreme Court. Since Supreme Court justices are very fussy about the parties they attend, this one was considered a great success.

Everything about the tables and food was perfect, and Madam Chennault was very complimentary. In fact, as a result, I got a lovely letter from the Vice-President's office, telling me how well satisfied Madam Chennault had been.

And if you give the same party, I hope you will be well satisfied as well as get a special satisfaction in repeating history.

Index

Abourezk, James, 53
ABSCAM, 36–37
Abzug, Bella, 205
Agnew, Judy, 145, 146, 273
Agnew, Spiro Theodore, 145, 146, 148, 175–76, 196, 265, 273
Aiken, George, 67, 95, 195
Aiken, Lola, 195
Alexander, Hugh, 47, 81–82, 225, 251
Ali, Muhammed, 207
Allen, James, 3, 100, 119, 239
Allen, Maryon, 119
ARA (American Restaurant Association), 238
Anderson, Clinton, 65
Anderson, Jack, 243

Baked apple dumplings, recipe for, 31
Baker, Bobby, 41, 69, 111, 163
Baker, Howard, Jr., 9, 122–23, 222–23
Baker, Howard Henry, Sr., 122
Baker, Irene Bailey, 122
Baker, Joy, 9, 122, 123, 190
Bassett, Isaac, 246
Bayh, Birch, 26, 86–87, 147, 171–72
Bayh, Marvella, 87, 104, 124
Beale, Betty, 158
Beall, John Glenn, Jr., 100, 200–1, 219
Beall, Nancy, 200–1
Bean soup, Senate, recipe for, 214–15
Beef Burgundy, recipe for, 255–56
Begin, Menachem, 157
Bell & Howell, 72
Bellmon, Henry, 83, 131, 240
Bennett, Frances, 74
Bennett, Wallace, 74
Bentsen, Lloyd, 19, 57
Bible, Alan, 66–67, 99
Biden, Joseph R., 72–73
Biden, Naomi, 72
Biden, Neilia, 72
Bilbo, Theodore, 12, 13–15, 16
Blake, Eubie, 158
Blumenthal, Michael, 160
Bolling, Richard, 12
Boren, David, 131

Bourgh, Mr., 271
Brewster, Daniel (Sonny), 57–58
Brezhnev, Leonid, 21, 128
Brinkworth, Bob, 252
Brooke, Edward, 218, 236
Brown, Harold, 160
Brown, Jerry, 181
Brumus, 127
Bryant, Traphes, 96
Brzezinski, Zbigniew, 159, 160, 170
Buckley, James, 65
Burton, Harold, 67
Business Roundtable, 160
Byrd, Harry, Jr., 3, 27–28, 62, 86, 132, 213–14
Byrd, Harry, Sr., 27
Byrd, Robert C., 22, 39, 46, 62–64, 81, 87, 194, 237–38, 239
Byrne, Jane, 178–79

Califano, Joseph, 156
Cameron, Judy, 101–2
Camp Hoover, 149
Campbell, Glenn, 206
Campiolo, Mario, 33
Cannon, Howard, 3
Capehart, Homer, 208–9
Capistrano-by-the-Sea, 179
Caraway, Hattie, 124
Caraway, Lewey, 106, 124, 162
Carlson, Frank, 68–69, 176, 204
Carroll Arms Hotel, 41
Carson, Bob, 249
Carter, Billy, 12, 112, 129–30
Carter, Jimmy, 55, 61, 112, 127, 128, 129, 131–32, 133, 147, 148, 150, 154–59, 160, 165, 169, 170, 171, 172, 179, 184, 197
Carter, Lillian, 112–13
Carter, Rosalynn, 178–79
Carter, Ruth, 112
Case, Clifford P., 91
Castro, Fidel, 161–62
Champagne sauce, recipe for, 115–16
Champagne strawberries, recipe for, 262

Chappaquiddick, 20, 130, 155
Chennault, Anna, 264–65, 266, 267, 270, 271, 273
Chennault, Claire, 264
Chicken livers in bacon, recipe for, 253
Chicken salad, recipe for, 257–58
Chiles, Lawton, 70, 236
Church, Bethine, 178
Church, Frank, 177–78
Churchill, Winston, 185
Cochrane, Bill, 3
Cocktail parties, suggestions for, 252–61
Cocktail sauce, recipe for, 255
Coffin, Tris, 215
Cole slaw, New Orleans style, recipe for, 261
Colmer, William M., 5
Connally, John, 83
Connally, Tom, 215
Cook, Marlow W., 207
Cooper, John Sherman, 87
Corned beef horns, recipe for, 265–66
Cotton, Norris, 12, 99, 130
Council on Foreign Relations, 159
Crab balls, recipe for, 254
Crab flakes Mornay Bordeaux, recipe for, 262–63
Crane, Arlene, 178, 180–81
Crane, Philip, 180–81
Curtis, Carl, 3, 95

Danforth, John, 18
Davis, C. S., 172
Davis, Jefferson, 194
Davis, Shirley, 94
Denver, John, 158
Deviled eggs, recipe for, 253–54
Diamond, Joseph, 2, 25, 26, 44, 47, 50, 82, 91, 121, 175, 223, 228, 231–32, 235–37, 239, 242
Dining facilities, Capitol, 45–48
Dirksen, Everett, 3, 9, 12, 69, 122–23, 190–92
Dirksen, Louella, 9, 190–92
Dirksen Office Building, 43
Dodd, Thomas, 34–36
Dole, Robert, 67, 123, 128–29, 170, 174–75, 176–77
Dominick, Peter, 30
Douglas, Paul, 21, 212
Duke, Joe, 162

Eagleton, Thomas, 127
Eastland, James, 16, 77, 200, 213
Eastland, Mrs. James, 117, 200
Edelstein, Saul, 108
Eisenhower, Dwight D., 10, 154, 161, 166, 171, 173
Eisenhower, Mamie, 10, 216–17
Eizenstat, Stuart, 129
Elizabeth II, Queen of England, 204–5
Ellender, Allen, 35, 104, 217
English lemon nut crisp á la Chantilly, recipe for, 251
Ervin, Sam, 12, 124, 132–33

Fernandez, Benjamin, 185
Filibuster, 39–40
Fishbait (Miller/Leighton), 4
Fleischer, Doris, 147
Fong, Hiram, 92–93
Ford, Betty, 11, 12, 129, 142, 144–45, 189
Ford, Gerald Rudolph, 3, 11, 23, 123, 128, 133, 137, 144, 158, 165, 167–68, 169, 170, 174–75
Fruit Basket (store), 208
Fulbright, William, 117, 128–29, 211, 213

Geary, Dan, 252
German, Marie, 30, 41, 101–2
German potato salad, recipe for, 260
Giles, Carlton, 132–33
Glass, Carter, 40
Golden Age of Chinese Art, The (Scott), 71
Golden Fleece award, 80
Goldwater, Barry, Jr., 125
Goldwater, Barry, Sr., 19, 23, 125, 126, 172–73
Goldwater, Barry, III, 125
Goldwater, Peggy, 172
Goldwater, Susan, 125
Graham, Billy, 166–67
Green, Theodore, 20–21

Haley, Alex, 22
Hallyburton, Billy, 132–33
Hanford, Mary Elizabeth, 174
Hansen, Clifford P., 68, 169, 194
Hansen, Martha Elizabeth, 124
Harlem Globetrotters, 158
Harris, La Donna, 181–82
Harris, Fred, 181–82

Harris, Herb, 32
Harrison, "Pat," 12
Hart, Gary, 83
Hart Senate Office Building, 81
Hartke, Mrs. Vance, 116
Hatfield, Antoinette, 29, 116, 124, 189, 193
Hatfield, Mark, 3, 29, 68, 193–94
Hathaway, William Dodd, 78
Hayakawa, Samuel Ichiye, 19, 70
Hayden, Carl, 7–8, 11, 61, 99, 242, 249
Health problems, 51
Hearst, Catherine, 51
Hearst, Patty, 51
Hearst, Randolph, 51
Heinz, H. John, III, 18
Helms, Jesse, 73, 78, 224
Hirohito, Emperor of Japan, 131–32
Hoke, Louise, 26
Hole in the Wall (restaurant), 246
Holland, Mary Agnes, 196
Holland, Spessard, 196, 247
Hollings, Ernst (Fritz), 9, 95, 103–4, 193
Hollings, Peatsy, 9, 104, 124, 193
Horseradish sauce, recipe for, 255
Horses of Capitol Hill, 243
Horwath & Horwath, 76
How to Go into Politics (Scott), 71
How to Run for Public Office and Win (Scott), 71
Howard, Frances, 120
Hoyt, Ken, 154
Hruska, Roman, 67
Hughes, Harold, 52
Humor, senatorial, 126–34
Humphrey, Hubert (HHH), 3, 68, 69, 99, 108–11, 119, 120–21, 127, 136, 137, 147, 148, 149–52, 183–84, 185, 196, 233
Humphrey, Muriel, 108–9, 119–21, 151, 185, 233
Hurst, Lou
  biographical sketch of, 12–17

Ice cream sherbet parfait, recipe for, 264
Inouye, Daniel Ken, 73–74
Inouye, Margaret, 74

Jackson, Anna Marie, 121

Jackson, Helen, 121–22
Jackson, Henry (Scoop), 34, 46, 121–22, 127, 211, 214
Jackson, Jimmie, 228
Jackson, Peter Hardin, 121
Jacobs, Miss, 225
Jacobsen, Nadine, 21
James (assistant chef), 209–10
Javits, Jacob (Jake, Jack), 9, 43, 104–5, 115
Javits, Marion, 104–5, 115, 116
Jefferson, Thomas, 67
Jennings, Dave, 24
Johns Hopkins School of Hygiene, 16
Johnson, Lady Bird, 29–30, 113, 114, 146, 155, 217, 230
Johnson, Lyndon B. (LBJ), 3, 11, 29, 39, 40, 41, 42, 43, 60–61, 62, 63, 69, 83, 84–85, 99, 113, 128, 136–37, 147, 148, 149, 151, 152, 154–55, 162–65, 169, 185–86, 214, 216, 217
Johnson, Paul, 12
Johnson, R. P., 172
Johnson, Sam Houston, 113–14, 217
Johnston, J. Bennett, 124
Johnston, Olin, 24, 40, 41
Jordan, B. Everett, 2, 3, 8, 29, 44, 68, 77, 82–83, 86, 91, 105–6, 121, 175, 191, 192, 213, 223, 235, 249, 251
Jordan, Mrs. B. Everett, 10

Kansas pancake parties, 204
Kefauver, Estes, 99
Kennedy, Caroline, 218
Kennedy, David, 122
Kennedy, Edward (Ted), 11, 19–20, 21, 26, 55, 58, 72, 97, 99, 122, 127, 128, 129, 155, 156, 171, 172, 179–80, 194, 207, 211–12, 224
Kennedy, Ethel, 10, 54, 127, 172, 180
Kennedy, Jacqueline, 54, 55–56, 96–97, 200, 218, 247, 261–62, 264
Kennedy, Joan, 10, 178, 179, 180, 195
Kennedy, John F., 11, 12, 19, 20, 42, 43, 56, 58, 68, 96, 99, 133–34, 158, 161–62, 165, 172, 211, 212, 218
Kennedy, Robert, 11, 19, 20, 26, 42, 43, 54, 55, 58, 96–97, 122, 149, 211, 212
Kennedy, Robert, Jr., 122

Kerr, Robert, 40, 41, 42, 66, 69, 99, 114, 182, 216
Kimmitt, J. S., 27–28
Kissinger, Henry, 159, 170
Kosher food, 114–15

Lance, Bert, 156
Lassie, 200
Lausche, Frank, 88
Lee, Angelique, 26, 194–95, 224–25
Lennon, Alton, 73
Levin, Carl, 43
Lewis, William C., Jr., 46, 77, 78, 195
Lobbyists, 50–51
Long, Caroline, 12, 29, 124, 188, 231
Long, Huey, 12–13, 114
Long, Russell, 8, 11, 12, 19, 29, 34, 35, 99, 188, 202–3
Longworth Cafeteria, 81
Loselle, Dewey, Jr., 243, 244
Low, Ethel, 81, 194

McCarthy, Joseph, 211
McCenna, Jim, 251
McClellan, John L., 51–52, 59–60, 68, 124, 140, 206, 211, 214
McClellan, Norma, 59, 116, 206
McGee, Gale, 68, 194, 208
McGovern, George, 67, 83, 129, 182–83, 184
McIntyre, Thomas J., 3–4
MacMillan, Patti, 194
Magnuson, Warren, 8, 11, 48–50
Maisano, C. J., 218
Mansfield, Mike, 60–61
Mansfield, Mrs. Mike, 9
Marriott, 76, 238
Marshack, Megan, 144
Mathias, Ann, 202
Mathias, Charles, 201–2, 203
Mathieu, George, 167
Meals on Wheels, 182
Menus, 219–21
Mesta, Perle, 30
Metcalf, Lee, 8, 11, 70
Metzenbaum, Howard, 203
Metzenbaum, Shirley, 203
Miller, Jack Richard, 22–23
Miller, William (Fishbait), 5
Mills, Wilbur, 138
Millsaps College, 15
Minchew, Daniel, 33–34, 82, 94

Mississippi Institute for the Blind, 15
Mondale, Joan, 148–49
Mondale, Walter Frederick (Fritz), 26, 32–33, 87, 121, 128, 144, 147–49, 150, 151, 160
Monroe, Marilyn, 96
Monroney, Mike, 194
Montoya, Joseph, 93, 126
Mornay sauce, recipe for, 263
Morse, Wayne, 209–10, 238
Morton, Rogers, 167, 205
Morton, Thruston, 205–6, 213
Moynihan, Daniel, 133
Mundt, Karl, 226–29
Murphy, George, 74–75, 77
Muskie, Edmund, 12, 26, 46, 169, 171, 177
Mustard sauce, recipe for, 253

National Council for U.S. China Trade, 158
Natinal Democratic Campaign Committee, 24–25
National Hotel Supply Company, 271
National Press Club, 23, 118
Nelson, Carrie Lee, 9
Nelson, Gaylord, 9
Nelson, Ray, 261
Nixon, Pat, 10, 30, 165, 216, 231
Nixon, Richard M., 3, 10, 23, 68–69, 126, 128, 129, 133, 136, 145, 148, 154, 165–68, 169, 170, 172, 175–76, 183, 194, 214, 216
Nunn, Sam, 61, 131

O'Neill, Thomas P., Jr. (Tip), 205
Overton, John, 202
Oysters Casino, recipe for, 272–73

Parties, suggestions for, 247–73
Passman, Otto, 94
Pastore, Elena, 251
Pastore, John, 100, 218–19, 251
Patman, Wright, 160
Pearson, James B., 204
Peas in the basket, recipe for, 263–64
Pell, Claiborne, 3, 19, 43, 199, 260–61
Percy, Charles Harting, 19, 21, 72, 88–90, 154, 199–200, 225
Percy, Jeanne, 72
Percy, Valerie, 72
Pigs in blanket, recipe for, 253

Pike, Otis, 12
Pilferage, 223–26, 229–30, 231–32, 233
Political Action Committees (PACs), 37
Post, Marjorie Merriweather, 124–25
Potato salad, recipe for, 259–60
Powell, James, 195, 234
Powell, Jody, 155, 158
Proxmire, William, 80–81, 174

Quiche Lorraine, recipe for, 256–57
Quorum Club, 41

Ralston Purina, 18
Randolph, Jennings, 68, 87, 99, 175
Randolph Hearst Foundation, 51
Rayburn, Sam, 117, 168
Reagan, Ronald, 67
Recipes, 31, 64, 115–16, 215–16, 251, 253–73
Ribicoff, Abraham, 100, 115
Ribicoff, Marlene, 115
Rice pilaf, recipe for, 259
Ridgewell Caterers, 249
Roast chicken, recipe for, 64
Robertson, A. Willis, 210
Rockefeller, David, 159, 171
Rockefeller, Happy, 142, 171
Rockefeller, Nelson Aldrich (Rocky), 3, 23, 136–44, 167–68, 170–71, 172, 175, 214
Rockefeller Foundation, 159
Rogers, Will, 131
Ronstadt, Linda, 181
Roth, William, Jr., 65–66
Rules Committee, U.S. Senate, 3, 7, 235–37
Rum pie, Senate, recipe for, 215–16
Russell, Richard Brevard, Jr., 61
Russell Senate Office Building, 43

Sadat, Anwar, 157
Salmon, poached decorated, recipe for, 67–68
Saltonstall, Leverett, 218
Saltonstall, Sally, 218
Saltonstall, William, 218
Sanitary conditions, Senate restaurants, 240–44
Schlesinger, James, 160
Schweiker, Richard, 67
Scott, Hugh, 3, 68, 71–72, 80, 100
Scott, Tom, 252
Scott, William, 66

Seafood Newburg, recipe for, 258
Senate Contingency Fund, 24
Shish kebab, recipe for, 269
Shrimp tree, recipe for, 269–70
Shriver, Eunice Kennedy, 9, 23
Shriver, Sargent, 3, 23
Silver Hill, 179
Simpson, Alan, 130
Smathers, George, 12, 41, 58–59, 99
Smith, Clyde Howard, 75
Smith, Margaret Chase, 12, 46, 73, 74–78, 195, 219, 229
Smith, Willis, 73
Snyder, Tom, 130
Sontag, Robert, 237
Spann, Gloria Carter, 112
Sparkman, Ivo, 117–18
Sparkman, John, 117–18
Steamship round of beef, recipe for, 266–67
Stennis, John, 100, 210, 245–46
Stevens, Ted, 197
Stevenson, Adlai E., III, 70–71
Stewart, J. George, 3, 257
Stewart, Sylvia, 64, 155–56
Stimson, Henry, 16
Stone, Lily, 114–15
Stone, Richard Bernard, 19, 114–15
Stranigan, Liz, 208
Strauss, Robert, 129
Stuffed celery, recipe for, 257
Stuffed cherry tomatoes, recipe for, 265
Suckling pig, recipe for, 271–72
Sweeney, Julie Belle, 13, 14

Taft, Robert, Jr., 90–91
Taft, Robert, Sr., 154
Talmadge, Betty, 6, 33, 61–62, 109, 116, 124, 157, 194, 210–11
Talmadge, Herman, 4–6, 11, 12, 19, 33–34, 61, 82–83, 94, 109, 156–57, 193, 194, 203–4, 210–11
Tannenbaum, Henry, 125
Taylor, Elizabeth, *see* Warner, Elizabeth Taylor
Teng Hsiaoping, 158
Thurmond, Strom, 26, 95, 99, 174
Tierney, Gene, 96
Tower, John, 35, 57
Tracy, Jill, 73

Trilateral Commission, 159–60,
169–70, 171
Trudeau, Margaret, 97
Truman, Harry, 65, 133–34
Tsongas, Paul, 43
Tucker, Mary, 73, 77–78
Tunney, John, 26, 70, 99
Twain, Mark, 131
Tydings, Joseph, 93, 124–25
Tyler, Carol, 111

Udall, Morris (Mo), 184

Vance, Cyrus, 160

Warner, Elizabeth Taylor, 7, 19, 64,
199–200
Warner, John, 7, 19, 64
Warrick, Alice, 101

Watergate, 170
Wednesday Club, 90
Weicker, Lowell, 19
Weiland, Fred, III, 185
White, George M., 3, 189, 251–52
Why I Am a Mormon (Bennett), 74
Williams, Harrison (Pete), 3, 36–37,
99–100
Williams, John, 69–70
Willkie, Wendell, 154
Wives, Senate, 28–29, 123–24, 189–93

Yarborough, Ralph, 40–41
Young, Milton, 60
Young, Patricia, 60
Young, Stephen, 121

Zimmerman, Virginia, 14, 15, 16